Lecture Notes in Computer Science

871

Edited by G. Goos, J. Hartmanis and J. van Leeuwen

Advisory Board: W. Brauer   D. Gries   J. Stoer

John Lee Georges G. Grinstein (Eds.)

Database Issues
for Data Visualization

IEEE Visualization '93 Workshop
San Jose, California, USA, October 26, 1993
Proceedings

Springer-Verlag
Berlin Heidelberg
New York London Paris
Tokyo Hong Kong
Barcelona

John P. Lee   Georges G. Grinstein (Eds.)

Database Issues
for Data Visualization

IEEE Visualization '93 Workshop
San Jose, California, USA, October 26, 1993
Proceedings

Springer-Verlag

Berlin Heidelberg New York
London Paris Tokyo
Hong Kong Barcelona
Budapest

Series Editors

Gerhard Goos
Universität Karlsruhe
Postfach 69 80, Vincenz-Priessnitz-Straße 1, D-76131 Karlsruhe, Germany

Juris Hartmanis
Department of Computer Science, Cornell University
4130 Upson Hall, Ithaka, NY 14853, USA

Jan van Leeuwen
Department of Computer Science, Utrecht University
Padualaan 14, 3584 CH Utrecht, The Netherlands

Volume Editors

John P. Lee
Georges G. Grinstein
Institute for Visualization and Perception Research
University of Massachusetts Lowell
1 University Ave., Lowell, MA 01854, USA

CR Subject Classification (1991): H.2, H.5

ISBN 3-540-58519-2 Springer-Verlag Berlin Heidelberg New York

CIP data applied for

© Springer-Verlag Berlin Heidelberg 1994
Printed in Germany

Typesetting: Camera-ready by author
SPIN: 10479138   45/3140-543210 - Printed on acid-free paper

Preface

Data Visualization is a captivating field that transcends traditional computing disciplines by creating visual imagery with scientific data. The production of images having artistic and scientific merit is important for explaining phenomena and motivating further research activity. This sensual and sometimes even seductive means of information display leads many to believe that visualization should reside at the center of a data exploration system. To some extent this is true, but visualization requires *data* to be available for display; it is merely a communications technology. The user needs to experience data in order to conduct research. While visualization seems central because it directly affects our perception, it is just one component of data exploration. *Data-centric* visualization is necessary to allow researchers to interact with data, aided by visualization.

Data-centric visualization places data at the cornerstone of software system development. Data undergoes many transformations from a raw state to a displayed state. These transformations, or fundamental data operations, must be presented at the user interface, and include data storage, selection, and access. Grand challenge problems will require these operations to be supported in addition to visualization. To that end we believe that as visualization systems evolve, they will begin to look more like database management systems (DBMS) with advanced visualization capabilities. The large question is: how will these database tools be incorporated into visualization environments (or vice versa)? Visualization places certain constraints on data management. Issues of capabilities, expressiveness, and performance affect how we determine the right mix of services in the appropriate places within the system.

On October 26, 1993, a workshop on Database Issues for Data Visualization was held during the IEEE Visualization '93 conference in San Jose, California. This was the first workshop of its kind, dealing with issues that focused primarily on the integration of database management systems with data visualization systems. Previous workshops held at various locations focused on data models for visualization, or visualization environments; this workshop had a broader scope. Database management applies to a number of data modeling and access activities within a visualization system such as object modeling, user interface construction, dataflow and program module storage and retrieval, the composition and manipulation of graphical representations, and the integration of knowledge bases and rule-based systems. These proceedings offer a snapshot of current research in this synergistic field, and a portrayal of the problems that must be addressed now and in the future towards the integration of database management systems and data visualization systems.

With these proceedings, the reader is presented with a treatment of a wide range of issues, top to bottom, of the research areas and problems facing the integration of database and visualization systems. We hope to stimulate further research activity in this field, and look forward to the realization of truly integrated systems that accommodate end-user requirements in terms of models, services, displays, and interaction capabilities, We also hope the reader will find the reports and papers as invigorating as the discussion sessions during the workshop.

July 1994, Lowell, Massachusetts

John Peter Lee
Georges G. Grinstein

Table of Contents

Interaction, User Interfaces and Presentation Issues

Workshop Description

A large problem with current data visualization environments is that they offer minimal support for database management and data interrogation methods; the visual presentation of data predominates over all other system functions. With most of the graphical modeling and rendering issues sufficiently addressed by these systems, their focus must shift to the underlying problems of data modeling, data access, and dialog design. This is most important if only to provide the correct data subset for display, a potentially complicated task. The application of database management system (DBMS) technology to data visualization for scientific discovery brings powerful data access methods in addition to the standardization of data models and access interfaces. In light of the huge amounts of data produced by sensors, supercomputer simulations, and telemetry, etc., DBMS assistance is necessitated. Problems exist however, in performance, ease of integration, ease of use, and DBMS expressive power, that must be addressed.

Visualization is an integral component of any scientific discovery system. It is an end product, but it is also a beginning - the images produced offer insight to data which direct further interaction with a data set. The visualization systems popular among many researchers offer only one kind of interaction - interaction with graphical data representations. This is insufficient for any such discovery system. Visualization systems of the future must be able to:

- model a wide variety of data constructs
- support queries over these data constructs
- provide suitable interaction metaphors with data constructs
- visually present data constructs and their interrelationships.

To some degree, these issues are addressed selectively by current DBMS and visualization systems, but not as a collective whole. Visualization systems require database management services, and DBMS must be able to handle image, spatial, and temporal data effectively. More importantly, the complete integrated database-visualization system must adequately utilize the strengths of each component while providing an easy to use interface with suitable interaction metaphors. This workshop is a first attempt at collectively quantifying the issues and developing a plan of attack for these problems.

1 Workshop Goals

The primary goal of the workshop was to provide an open forum for interested researchers to discuss the important issues concerning the integration of database systems and data visualization systems. Since this is a developing research area, it was important to enable communication between like-minded researchers in disparate fields. We are concerned that there is not enough cross-fertilization between disciplines. The secondary goals were to draft a report detailing the research issues and contributing research papers on work in progress.

2 Workshop Format

The papers solicited in the Call For Participation were grouped into three subgroups: Data Models for Scientific Data, Systems Integration Issues, and User Interfaces, Interaction, and Presentation Issues. These became the working subgroups for the remainder of the workshop. The workshop began with introductions and a presentation by the organizers summarizing all accepted position papers and statements. During the work-shop, each subgroup was tasked to describe the key research issues in these areas. This book contains original papers from selected participants as well as the three subgroup reports.

3 Contents Overview

The three workgroup reports summarize the discussion sessions held by the partici-pants. Each has its own distinct flavor and approach to discussing the important re-search topics. A minimum of editing was performed to retain this uniqueness. Needless to say, we have found that there is a great deal of overlap among the three sections. This is expected, and encouraged because the three sections we identified are interde-pendent. The reader should therefore take the three subgroup reports together, as they tend to reinforce each other while introducing distinct concepts.

The three main sections of the book following the reports are arranged in a some-what bottom-up fashion. The section on data models for scientific data takes a fine-grained look at the types of data prevalent in visualization applications. The systems issues section takes a broader perspective and explores the issues related to coupling the two systems, in support of data interaction scenarios. Finally, the interaction, user interface and presentation section deals with the entire database-visualization-human user system, and discusses issues related to interface design, data spaces, data interac-tion, and output representations. Each section is now described in more detail.

The data models section deals with bottom-up data taxonomy strategies based on intrinsic structural data characteristics, as well as top-down, application domain-driven requirements for data types and organizations found in visualization systems. The modeling of scientific data has received a great deal of attention in the recent past, and now visualization objects must also be accommodated by this model. A universal theme emerging is that there are many domain-specific data models evolving, though not one all-encompassing model. Data models are required for many visualization system components: the abstract objects in the domain, logical representations, knowledge bases, and the like. All these subjects are covered in the submissions for this section.

The systems issues section takes a broader view and looks at the coupling issues in the integration of database and visualization systems. From high-level system re-quirements, application topics include the range of data objects to be supported (not only the experiment data), the applicability of particular DBMS (relational, semantic, object-oriented, etc.) to the needs of visualization, aspects of query languages that must be modified to support visualization tasks, concurrency within multi-threaded windowing environments, distributed systems and ancillary services such as finite ele-ment solvers, neural networks, and statistical packages.

The interaction, user interface and presentation section takes an even broader view and presents issues that form the driving functions and evaluations criteria of the human-computer system. One must have an intuitive interface into the data, the ser-vices provided by the database and visualization systems, as well as the appropriate interaction metaphor to accomplish a task. This section's submissions include novel in-terfaces to databases, which are based on supporting the data interaction activities of the application, methods for treating the display of retrieved instances, and interaction metaphors with the displayed data, to gain insight into its structure. Techniques for query specification, types of data retrievals, and evaluation of results are also included in this section.

4 The Editors

John Peter Lee is a doctoral candidate at the University of Massachusetts Lowell and is engaged in research on interaction issues involved with the integration of database management systems and data visualization systems. He is a recipient of a NASA Graduate Student Researchers Award for this research activity. He received his BSEE from Fairleigh Dickinson University in 1986, his MFA in Computer Art from School of Visual Arts in 1991, and his MS in Computer Science from the University of Massachusetts Lowell in 1993. He is also employed in the Human Factors, Displays, and Visualization Department of the MITRE Corporation, where he is involved with virtual environment prototyping. He is a member of ACM, SIGGRAPH, and IEEE. He served as Publicity and Student Volunteer co-chair for the Visualization'93 conference, as well as co-organized the Database Issues for Data Visualization Workshop. He is serving as Student Volunteer co-chair for the Visualization'94 conference.

His research interests include visualization environments, multidimensional data presentation, and the computer-human interface.

Georges Grinstein is a full time Professor of Computer Science at University of Massachusetts Lowell, Director of the Graphics Research Laboratory and Director of the Institute for Visualization and Perception Research. He is also a Principal Engineer with the MITRE Corporation. He received his B.S. from the City College of N.Y. in 1967, his M.S. from the Courant Institute of Mathematical Sciences of New York University in 1969 and his Ph.D. in Mathematics from the University of Rochester in 1978. Dr. Grinstein is a member of IEEE's Technical Committee on Computer Graphics and on the editorial board of several journals including Computers and Graphics and the Eurographics Society's Computer Graphics Forum. He was vice-chair of the executive board of IFIP WG 5.10 (Computer Graphics) and was co-chair of the IFIP Conference on Experimental Workstations held in Boston in 1989. He was panels co-chair for Visualization'90 (San Francisco), program co-chair for Visualization'91 (San Diego), conference co-chair for Visualization'92 (Boston) and for Visualization'93 (San Jose), co-chair of the IFIP 1993 Workshop on Cognitive and Psychological Issues in Visualization and co-chair for the Database and Visualization Issues Workshop. He has chaired several committees for the American National Standards Institute (ANSI) and the International Standards Organization (ISO). He is co-chair for the SPIE'95 Visual Data Exploration and Analysis Conference.

His areas of research include graphics, imaging, sonification, virtual environments, user interfaces and interaction, with a very strong interest in the visualization of complex systems.

5 Acknowledgements

We would like to thank all those who participated in the workshop and assisted us by providing timely submissions of extended papers. Special thanks go to Dan Bergeron and Andreas Wierse for leading the subgroup report writing activity.

We would also like to thank Dan Bergeron for assisting with the planning and execution of the workshop, and Haim Levkowitz, John Seig Jr., and Stuart Smith from the University of Massachusetts Lowell for reviewing papers. We would finally like to extend many thanks to Paul Breen and the MITRE Corporation of Bedford, Massachusetts, who provided technical, logistical, and financial support both before and after the workshop.

Workshop Participants

The following people participated in the workshop:

Manish Arya, IBM Almaden Research Center
manish@almaden.ibm.com

R. Daniel Bergeron, University of New Hampshire, Durham
rdb@cs.unh.edu

John Boyle, University of Aberdeen
john@computing-science.aberdeen.ac.uk

William Cody, IBM Almaden Research Center
cody@almaden.ibm.com

Stephen G. Eick, AT&T Bell Laboratories
eick@research.att.com

Nancy Wright Grady, Oak Ridge National Laboratory
gradynw@ornl.gov

Georges G. Grinstein, University of Massachusetts, Lowell
grinstein@cs.uml.edu

William Hibbard, University of Wisconsin-Madison
whibbard@macc.wisc.edu

Matthias Hemmje, German National Center for Computer Science
hemmje@darmstadt.gmd.de

Greg Jirak, XIDAK, Inc.
greg@xidak.com

David T. Kao, University of New Hampshire, Durham
dtk@cs.unh.edu

Daniel A. Keim, University of Munich
daniel@dbs.informatik.uni-muenchen.de

Peter Kochevar, San Diego Supercomputer Center
kochevar@sdsc.edu

John Peter Lee, University of Massachusetts, Lowell
jlee@cs.uml.edu

Kristina D. Miceli, NASA Ames Research Center
kmiceli@nas.nasa.gov

Karen L. Ryan, Cray Research, Inc.
kryan@paulaner.cray.com

Eric A. Sumner, AT&T Bell Laboratories
sumner@research.att.com

Deborah Swanberg, University of California San Diego
deborah@cs.ucsd.edu

Lloyd A. Treinish, IBM T.J. Watson Research Center
lloydt@watson.ibm.com

Venu Vasudevan, Motorola, Inc.
Venu_Vasudevan@email.mot.com

Len Wagner, San Diego Supercomputer Center
wagner@sdsc.edu

Sandra Walther, Rutgers University
walther@caip.rutgers.edu

Andreas Wierse, University of Stuttgart
wierse@rus.uni-stuttgart.de

Mark A. Woyna, Argonne National Laboratory
woyna@athens.eid.anl.gov

Workshop Subgroup Reports

Database Issues for Data Visualization: Developing a Data Model

R. Daniel Bergeron[1], William Cody[2], William Hibbard[3], David T. Kao[1],
Kristina D. Miceli[4], Lloyd A. Treinish[5], Sandra Walther[6]

[1] University of New Hampshire, Durham
[2] IBM Almaden Research Center, San Jose CA
[3] University of Wisconsin, Madison
[4] NASA Ames Research Center, Moffett Field CA
[5] IBM T.J. Watson Research Center, Yorktown Heights NY
[6] Rutgers University, Piscataway NJ

1 Introduction

The complexity of dealing with large amounts of scientific data has long been
a source of concern and activity for visualization researchers. Early efforts at
addressing the problem were devoted to the very practical goal of dealing with
a myriad of *data format* issues. Specifications (and supporting software) such as
NASA's Common Data Format (CDF) [Goug88, Trei87] and its followers (e.g.,
HDF [Habe89, NCSA89]) have been instrumental in bringing some semblance of
order into the chaos of scientific data files. It is clear, however, that we need to go
beyond data format issues and attempt to develop more general formalizations
of data that we can incorporate into a full-fledged *data model*.

1.1 Value of a Data Model

By defining a data model, a general purpose visualization environment can support a variety of analysis and visualization tools that can cross discipline boundaries. The implementation of the analysis and visualization tools depends only
on the data model and not on the particular application domain. This approach
minimizes software implementation, maximizes software reuse, and generally
provides more opportunity for shared learning among users. The precise definition of the data model is influenced by the complexity of data that must be
represented by the data model and the range of applications the environment
intends to support.

   In developing a formal data model we would like to bring together visualization experts and database experts to provide an interdisciplinary approach that
is appropriate for visualization, but consistent with database concepts. We need
to keep in mind that a comprehensive data visualization environment should
also have an *analysis model* and a *visualization model*, both of which must be
integrated with the data model.

1.2   The Goals of a Data Model

A data model can be developed based on a wide range of potential goals for that
model. At one extreme is a very simple, limited-scope data model that is easy to
understand, easy to implement, but perhaps not as powerful as would be needed
by many applications. As we attempt to increase the breadth of applications that
can be supported by the data model, we necessarily increase the complexity of the
data model. Application data comes in a wide range of formats and dimensions
[Sper91]. We could try to support a diversity of formats by developing a single
unified representation or we can allow multiple representations to coexist within
a single data model. The first option is far more elegant, but may lead to a
model that is difficult to use for the simple cases. The second option is more
practical, but may result in *ad hoc* implementations that grow in complexity
and unreliability.

Another important decision underlying the development of a data model is
whether the data model is intended primarily to support the *implementation* of
the visualization facilities, or their use. In other words, is the goal to define an
internal data model or an *external data model*? Ideally, the internal and external
models should be the same. In principle, however, we could define an external
data model that is seen by the user, and a different internal data model that is
used by the components of the system. The system would support explicit and
implicit translations between data represented in the different models. This two
model approach may be convenient for providing a simpler user interface, while
still maintaining a comprehensive internal representation. The object-oriented
paradigm might be useful in this context.

1.3   Application Domain Scope

The scope of targeted application domains has an effect on the data model
beyond simply the range of data formats that are likely to be encompassed.
Variations in the visualization needs of different disciplines affect the data model
in ways that are likely to be very significant in terms of functions supported by
the data model. In other words, the decisions are likely to be *operations-driven*.

1.4   Scientific Databases

Before developing a data model, we need to clarify the kind of data we need
to model. What is scientific data? What are the characteristics that cannot be
adequately or efficiently represented in a traditional database? How should those
characteristics be reflected in the data model?

One important characteristic of scientific data is that it is often very large.
Size alone, however, is not enough. There are plenty of very large traditional
databases that are not scientific databases.

We also need some definition of the complexity of the data. In some sense
the complexity is related to the interrelationships of the data elements – or at
least interrelationships that are not easily expressed as relations in a relational

database. Even a simple two-dimensional array of *floats* contains implicit relationships between the elements of the array that are cumbersome to represent in a relational database. These relationships are particularly important with respect to analysis functions that are applied to the data. One particularly important characteristic of scientific data is that important relationship among the data elements are often not known *in advance*, but must be *discovered* by the scientist after the database has been created.

1.5 Terminology

The complexity of scientific data is reflected by the often inconsistent use of terms used to describe the data. The terms *multidimensional* and *multivariate* are often used to mean different things in different contexts. We choose to define these terms in the context of the mathematical notion of *dependent* and *independent* variables. A multi-valued mathematical function might return k values given n parameters. The n parameters are considered to be the independent variables, and the k computed function values are the dependent variables. We say that this function has a *domain dimensionality* of n, and a *range dimensionality* of k. Much scientific data can be interpreted as a discrete representation of such a multi-valued function; that is, for some explicit set of combinations of values of the independent variables, we have values for the dependent variables. We adopt the convention that the term *multidimensional* refers to the *domain* dimensionality, while the term *multivariate* refers to the *range* dimensionality.

Of course, one goal of scientific investigation is often to discover which of many parameters in the data are truly the independent and which are the dependent variables. Furthermore, in many situations, there is not a simple relationship among the parameters. However, the *representation* of the data at a given time can be based on the assumption of an independent/dependent variable determination. In fact, the process of exploring the data is often based upon transforming a given set of data from one representation to another in which the dependencies among the variables is different.

1.6 Summary

The remainder of this paper discusses the major issues related to the development of data models for scientific visualization which were identified by the data model subgroup at the IEEE Workshop on Database Issues in Visualization held in October 1993 in San Jose, California. The issues include the need to develop a reasonable *taxonomy* to apply to data models, the definition of *metadata* (or ancillary data), the notion of *levels of abstraction* available for defining a data model, the nature and role of *queries* in a data model, and the effects of *data errors* on a data model.

2   Taxonomy of Data Models

A data model is a mechanism to classify data, and thus provide a way to map data to (visualization) operations. Further, it defines and organizes a set of data objects. Data, however, are typically complex. Each set of scientific data, for example, typically contains several independent variables such as time, spatial, or spectral variables, and many parameters, or dependent variables. A data model must provide a functional structure for data with both logical and physical organizations, and a schema relating them.

2.1   Taxonomy Based on Logical Structure

Although it is possible to describe a data model in terms of the physical layout of bits in a computer system, here we assume that data objects are described in terms of their behavior with respect to access operations. However, it is natural to think of the behavior of data access in terms of a logical structure. In fact, there are no practical data models that we are aware of whose behavior cannot be defined in terms of a logical structure. Consider a simple model where data implies a field or parameter of one or more dependent values,

$$[y_1, y_2, ..., y_n] = [f_1(x_1, x_2, ..., x_k), f_2(x_1, x_2, ..., x_k), ..., f_n(x_1, x_2, ..., x_k)]$$

This simple functional model addresses the fundamental dimensionality, rank and parameterization of data [Butl92a, Trei92]. To be effective for the implementation of useful applications, such a data model must be self-describing at several levels. The model must provide 1) a representation of the physical storage structure (i.e., format), 2) a structural representation of the data (e.g., data base schema) and 3) a higher-level logical structure.

Thus, we describe a taxonomy of data models in terms of their logical structure, based on how they address the following issues:

1. The types of primitive data values occurring in data objects.

   A primitive type defines a set of primitive values, which can be classified according to whether the values are ordered, whether arithmetic operations are defined on them, and how they are sampled (e.g., integers versus reals).

2. The ways that primitive values are aggregated into data objects.

   This may include how dimensionality is mapped to a physical domain, such as a mesh describing the base geometry for the mapping of the functions or dependent variables to some (physical) coordinate system. This also includes aggregation of higher-order primitives, such as groups, hierarchies, series, composites, multi-grids, etc.

   We borrow terms from set theory to classify data models as *extensive* or *intensive*. An extensive data model defines a finite list of types of aggregates, such as image, polygon list, vector list, 3-D field, color map, etc. Access and analysis operations on data are generally defined as functions specific to each type. On the other hand, an intensive data model defines rules for constructing an infinite set of types, and defines polymorphic functions that may be applied to broad classes of types. Extensive data models require applications to adapt to their data types, whereas intensive data models adapt to applications by defining appropriate types.

3. Ancillary information about the relation between data and the things that they represent.

For example, given a meteorological temperature, ancillary information includes the fact that it is a temperature, its scale (Fahrenheit, Kelvin, etc.), the location of the temperature and whether it is a point or volume sample, the time of the temperature, an estimate of its accuracy, and how it was produced (e.g. by a simulation, by direct observation, or deduced from a satellite radiance).

We use the term *metadata* to characterize these higher-level attributes of the data. These may include domain- or application- specific information as well as abstractions of the data structures. The term, metadata, is often used in the context of database systems to describe structural or organizational information. Its use for characteristic information in a scientific context dates to early data systems [Chat75, McCa85, Trei85, Hibb86] as well as to self-describing, application-enabling data formats, structures and access software (among the earliest were [Smit86, Trei87] and eventually for visualization [Trei89, Hibb92, Kao94]).

2.2 Implementation Taxonomy

In recent years, these issues have been recognized by a few groups in the support of a number of scientific applications. As a result, several data models have been defined, some within very domain-specific contexts while others are more general. Their implementations can be characterized in the following manner:

- *Unified*, which utilizes a single, generalized data model
- *Diffuse*, which utilizes multiple data models
- *Focused*, which utilizes a single, domain-specific data model

A *unified* implementation includes an Applications Programming Interface (API) and/or language bindings, which defines operations to be done with data. Such an interface may be "object-oriented", where such operations imply methods that are associated with a class of objects. However, the notion of an abstract data type is sufficient for such an implementation. Hence, the API hides the details of the physical form(s) of storage for data. In general, such implementations permit easy incorporation of new data and applications and offer the potential to develop highly optimized performance for generic applications. The primary limitation of this approach relates to the data model itself. Such implementations are usually hard to extend for new classes of data not considered in the original data model definition.

A *diffuse* implementation includes multiple APIs which define underlying data structures. Each of these structures and hence, APIs, are associated with a single physical form of storage. Usually, separate implementations of specific applications are required for each interface, which may be integrated in some fashion by a higher-level application. Such implementations permit easy incorporation of new data because a new application, interface and structure is added. Hence, it becomes difficult to operate with more than one of the types of data simultaneously. As a result, these implementations are usually difficult to optimize or extend for generalized applications.

A *focused* implementation usually does not include an API for the data model. Any interface to data in such a system defines the underlying physical data format. Therefore, it becomes easy to optimize the performance for very specialized applications and quite difficult to extend to other data and applications.

3 Metadata or Ancillary Data

The use of metadata is essential in the development of concise data models for scientific visualization. Metadata captures syntactic and semantic information about data, their structure, attributes, origin, and processing history. It gives the scientist additional high-level information that is necessary for accurate data analysis.

Metadata is most easily described as data about data. It can take on many forms, from describing the structure of the data, to codifying knowledge about the data. Basically, anything that establishes a context for the primary data (data computed or gathered by scientists) can be considered metadata.

Different terms exist for variants of metadata, each of which serve a special purpose. *Structural metadata*, or data characteristics, describe the type and structure of data, primarily for use by the access mechanism for purposes of storage and retrieval. This information is typically defined by developers and is essentially the schema of the database. This can include information about data type primitives (e.g., float, integer), and structural information such as dimensionality, rank, positions, and connections.

Ancillary information, sometimes called data attributes, describes the relation between data and the things that they represent. This information must be supplied by the scientist and can include information such as the names, units, and ranges of data fields, spatial locations of data, calibration and instrumentation information, error statistics, and missing data indicators.

Documentation metadata helps the scientist to identify facts about the data and its processing history. This type of metadata is usually textual and can include lab notes and text concerning the simulation or observation, a processing history of the data, as well as scripts for future processing sessions.

Ancillary information and documentation metadata are *semantic* in nature, describing information associated with an individual dataset rather than the *syntactic* information described in structural metadata. *Semantic metadata* is domain and application specific, typically provided by the scientist.

The importance of metadata lies in its ability to help scientists understand the meaning and significance of data. Metadata provides scientists with information they can use to browse and search datasets and select data of interest. In fact, a visualization of a dataset could even be considered metadata, providing scientists with a mechanism for visual browsing. Semantic metadata allows scientists to express information about datasets in familiar and consistent terminology. As a result, scientists can query their datasets in a more natural and intuitive manner.

The scope of information that can be considered metadata is broad, and the definition and implementation of metadata is a difficult issue. Metadata must be clear and concise, with a rich functional specification of the data. Metadata should allow for the expression of data and its components, along with the ability to express relationships between components. Since metadata information can take on so many forms, its implementation must be flexible and allow for the addition of new data sources. Many issues remain with regard to the relationship of metadata to data models for scientific visualization. These issues include how metadata is acquired and input into the model, how the scientist can query the model based on metadata, and where metadata fits within the data model framework, both conceptually and in terms of physical implementation.

4 Levels of Abstraction for a Data Model

In the broadest sense, a data model is just an abstraction of data. The goal is to find a common (or universal) abstraction for various kinds of scientific data. A standard data model would facilitate application integration and collaboration among scientists. Based on this common abstraction, applications can be developed accordingly, which eventually make the data sets portable among various software platforms and research disciplines.

Visualization researchers have only recently begun to integrate database facilities into their applications. The database community has a well-established tradition of defining and categorizing ideas about *data models*. Different visualization researchers have very different ideas about what constitutes a data model, while many of us also are not fully aware of the concepts of data models that have been established in the database community. By learning about and adopting these database concepts, we should be able to clarify better the needs and potential approaches for developing scientific data models.

In traditional database terminology, data models can be classified into three categories based on the level of data abstraction – *conceptual, implementation,* and *physical.* How do these levels of data abstraction relate to the needs of scientific visualization?

Physical data models are clearly not adequate to use as a basis for developing a scientific data model. They are not high level enough or flexible enough to capture the common characteristics and operations of scientific data. Nonetheless, they have certainly proven extremely useful as a vehicle for some level of standardization and interchange of data. Successful examples of visualization-oriented physical data models include CDF [Goug88], HDF [NCSA89], and netCDF [Rew92].

Recent developments at the level of *implementation data models* show considerable promise for scientific visualization applications. The *object-oriented* data model and the *extended relational* data model both offer facilities that are suitable for today's complex scientific data. Some visualization researchers suggest using extended relational or object-oriented schema as the basis for a scientific data model. For example, [Mice94] advocates the definition of an object-oriented schema that is flexible enough to be the foundation of all (or at least, a wide range of) scientific data sets. Each different kind of data set uses a specialization of the basic schema.

It is also possible to define a scientific data model as a *conceptual data model.* Two such implementation-independent data models have been proposed – one is based on the notion of a *lattice* [Kao94], the other on the notion of *fiber bundles* [Butl89, Habe91, Butl92b]. A data model defined in this way corresponds well to the conceptual data model in database terminology. This approach provides the ultimate flexibility, but it still requires a mapping to an implementation data model and the overall utility of these models is not yet clear.

Since metadata is essential to scientific data analysis and visualization, we recognize the need to develop a data model for *metadata* in addition to the data model for data. Although it is not always clear where the metadata ends and data begins, it is clear that metadata has to be modeled and the interaction between data and metadata has to be studied. There is also a strong consensus that the demands of the metadata data model can be met by existing database systems – relational, extended relational, or object-oriented. It is not clear whether the data model for the data and the data model for the metadata need to be (or even can be) supported by the same database. The ultimate scientific data model may be supported by a hybrid system [Auro93].

Even though a common level of data abstraction may not be adopted by all visualization scientists in the near future, it is certainly fruitful to raise the issue of the data abstraction level and try to base our further discussion on established database terminology.

5   Query Form and Functionality

Two models of *query strategy* arise out of two types of *information situations*: *viz,* 1) the model where data has "known" intrinsic structure imposed on it by its domain or the manner of its collection or generation and 2) the model where data relations cannot be identified prior to their discovery through probes or data mining.

5.1 Query Strategy with "Known" Data Relationships

For data with known relationships, it appears that the structure of queries (e.g., what kinds of queries are to be serviced, how they are to be formulated, and how their servicing is to be implemented) should arise out of the logical structure of the data itself. This approach seeks to exploit the fact that scientific databases are not random collections of unrelated items but represent a domain of information and presuppose users trained in the methods of that domain who have informational purposes when they confront data. In any case, designing user interfaces to scientific databases requires close collaboration with real users. When scientific data does exhibit internal logical relations that underlie the implications to be drawn from the data, that internal relatedness can be used as the organizing principle for data storage. In other words, the predominant query paths can be identified *a priori* and the implementation strategies can incorporate that "metadata" to enhance performance.

An example of this is shown in [Walt94] which is concerned with the efficient interaction and query of single mesh-based datasets. The data management structures are memory-based structures that have been optimized for *a priori* identified predominant query paths. The query paths themselves are not overly complicated in terms of predicates and interrelated logical conditions, though clearly complicated models are applied to the data. In this situation, data interactions are expressed as equations about the properties of the data objects in the database and the behavior of those data objects can be explored and even extended through such queries. This is possible because the foundation of those behaviors is implicit in the data itself.

5.2 Query Strategy with "Unknown" Data Relationships

Many scientific data bases are "accumulated" rather than computed. That is, they contain data gathered from instruments, images, or historical sequences. They may even contain or reference data that is modeled [Arya94]. Such data situations raise questions of optimization across multiple datasets, motivated by scientific data in medical image management systems, molecular design systems and GIS (Geographic Information System). In such systems, there is classical record-oriented data (some data and some meta-data) and then a very special data type, the structural molecular model, the maps in GIS, the imagery in medical systems, and the fields in fluid flow modeling systems.

In medical systems and molecular modeling systems, queries that span many instances of the special datatype are interesting from a database point of view. In molecular systems they are common (e.g. pharmaceutical databases), in medical systems not entirely common, but increasing, especially in research and teaching applications.

For example, consider a query like: *Find patients and their PET studies from a sub-population of patients in which there is a region of the brain having average activation greater than some significant threshold, and greater than the average activation for that same region in that patient's previous three PET studies if they were within the last 2 years.*

Since this query involves many patients, and several studies per patient, there is a potential for considerable I/O and there are several execution strategies from which an optimizer might choose. The optimization problem is more interesting still if the "special" datatypes are managed by servers outboard of the database with special access paths tailored to the datatype. The design of these special access paths and the representations they would be based on is a key issue. So too are the cost models which would enable an optimizer to select among alternative access paths. These issues also arise in general multimedia database queries.

5.3 Query models

The first type of query environment has been an active and important research area for some time. The creation of efficient data representations to enable the detailed visual query and modeling of large scientific datasets will certainly continue to be an important area of research. The second query environment has been more limited by the performance implications of querying on such a scale, i.e. large numbers of large datasets. However, the emergence of distributed query environments in which large data sets exist in separate servers and in which the server is specialized to efficiently handle data sets in special representations with specialized indexes is opening up the possibilities of such scientific query. Work in several scientific (and multimedia) domains (e.g. medicine and geology) is progressing on query protocols for such specialized servers to exchange query requests and answers so that (interactive) query applications can combine the results for presentation to the scientist. Both query models are important for the creation of visual and interactive scientific discovery environments. Consequently, an appropriate scientific data model must be able to accommodate both query environments.

6 Validity and Models of Error in the Data

Scientific data (unlike most business-oriented data) is usually not exactly accurate. Nearly every data item in a scientific database is created by procedures that introduce error into the information. The error can come from inaccuracies (or even failures) in sampling systems, from round-off and truncation areas in computations, and from incompleteness of a model representation. Scientists are generally aware of the inaccuracies in their data and try to take those inaccuracies into account when interpreting the data. It would be desirable to develop a model to represent error in the data and to incorporate that model into the processing and visualization of the data, as appropriate.

The issue of validity also arises when visualization is used to explore the meaning of numerical data by mapping visual effects to data relationships. In such situations, there is a rule-governed transformation of data values to display events and it is critical that the transformation procedures operating on entities as graphic objects (e.g., shaded polygons) be identified and separated from the numerical and domain specific computational procedures (e.g., vertex order). The danger that a visual artifact is regarded as a representation of a domain fact is minimized to the extent that techniques are provided so that domain expert users can evaluate any "judgement calls" made by the transformation procedures.

7 Conclusions

General-purpose visualization systems are proving to be extremely valuable tools for scientific research. The flexibility and power of these systems provide new and exciting opportunities for data exploration to individual scientists. As successful as these systems are, however, they support very little formalism for the representation of the scientist's data. The development of formal data models and their integration into visualization systems could provide an even more powerful environment in which a user's conceptual understanding of the data is better reflected in the conceptual model presented by the visualization system. This paper focuses on the most important issues associated with the development of a comprehensive model for representing scientific data for visualization. The discussion of these issues is intended to serve as guidance for future research in the area.

Acknowledgements

The issues raised in this paper coalesced and were clarified during the stimulating discussions of the Data Model Subgroup of the IEEE Workshop on Database Issues in Visualization. All members of the subgroup contributed substantially to the discussions that lead to the ideas expressed in this paper. The subgroup members included: Sandra Walther, Karen Ryan, Lloyd Treinish, Kristina Miceli, David Kao, Greg Jirak, Bill Hibbard, Bill Cody, and Dan Bergeron.

References

[Arya94] Arya, M., W. Cody, C. Faloutsos, J. Richardson and A. Toga. QBISM: Extending a DBMS to Support 3D Medical Images, *Proceedings IEEE 10th International Conference on Data Engineering*, Houston, Feb. 1994.

[Auro93] Xidak, Inc. *Aurora Dataserver: Technical Overview*, Palo Alto, CA, October 1993.

[Butl89] Butler, D. M. and M. H. Pendley, "A Visualization Model Based on the Mathematics of Fiber Bundles", *Computers in Physics*, 3, n.5, September/October 1989.

[Butl92a] Butler, D. M. and C. Hansen (ed.), "Scientific Visualization Environments: A Report on a Workshop at Visualization '91", *Computer Graphics*, 26, n.3, pp. 213-216, February 1992.

[Butl92b] Butler, D. M. and S. Bryson, "Vector-Bundle Classes Form Powerful Tool for Scientific Visualization", *Computers in Physics*, 6, n. 6, November/December 1992.

[Chat75] Chatters, G. and V. E. Suomi, "The Application of McIDAS", *IEEE Trans. Geosci. Eectron.*, GE- 13, 137-146. 1975.

[Goug88] Gough, M., et al. *CDF Implementer's Guide*, National Space Science Center, NASA Goddard Flight Center, Greenbelt, MD, 1988.

[Habe89] Haber, R., "Scientific Visualization and the RIVERS Project at the National Center for Supercomputing Applications", *IEEE Computer*, Vol. 22, No. 8, August 1989.

[Habe91] Haber, R., B. Lucas and N. Collins, "A Data Model for Scientific Visualization with Provisions for Regular and Irregular Grids", *Proceedings IEEE Visualization '91*, pp. 298-305, October 1991.

[Hibb86] Hibbard, W. and G. Dengel, "The GOES Catalog on McIDAS", *Proceedings of the Second International Conference on Interactive Information and Processing Systems for Meteorology, Oceanography and Hydrology*, American Meteorology Society, pp. 98-100, January 1986.

[Hibb92] Hibbard, W., C. R. Dyer and B. Paul, "Display of Scientific Data Structures for Algorithm Visualization", *Proceedings IEEE Visualization '92*, pp. 139-146, October 1992.

[Hibb94] W. Hibbard, C. Dyer, B. Paul, "The VIS-AD Data Model: Integrating Metadata and Polymorphic Display with a Scientific Programming Language", To be published in *Database Issues for Data Visualization*, Springer-Verlag, LNCS.

[Kao94] D.T. Kao, R.D. Bergeron, T.M. Sparr, "An Extended Schema Model for Scientific Data", To be published in *Database Issues for Data Visualization*, Springer-Verlag, LNCS.

[McCa85] McCarthy, J. L., "Scientific Information = Data + Meta-data", Department of Statistics, Technical Report, Stanford University, March 1985.

[Mice94] K.D. Miceli, "An Object-Oriented Data Model to Support the Design of Effective Graphics for Scientific Visualization", position paper for IEEE WOrkshop on Database Issues for Data Visualization.

[NCSA89] National Center for Supercomputer Applications (NCSA), *NCSA DataScope Reference Manual*, NCSA, University of Illinois, Champaign-Urbana, IL, 1989.

[Rew92] Rew, R. K. and G. P. Davis, "netCDF: An Interface for Scientific Data Access", *IEEE Computer Graphics and Applications*, 10, n.4, pp. 76 82, July 1990.

[Smit86] Smith, A. Q. and C. R. Clauer, "A Versatile Source-Independent System for Digital Data Management", *EOS Transactions American Geophysical Union*, 67, pp. 188-189, 1986.

[Sper91] Speray, D. and S. Kennon, "Volume Probes: Interactive Data Exploration on Arbitrary Grids", *Computer Graphics*, Vol. 24, No. 5, November 1991.

[Trei85] Treinish, L. A. and S. N. Ray, "An Interactive Information System to Support Climate Research", *Proceedings First International Conference on Interactive Information and Processing Systems for Meteorology, Oceanography and Hydrology*, American Meteorology Society, pp. 72-79, January 1985.

[Trei87]   Treinish, L. A. and M. L. Gough, "A Software Package for the Data-independent Storage of Multi-Dimensional Data", *EOS Transactions American Geophysical Union*, 68, pp. 633-635, July 14, 1987.

[Trei89]   Treinish, L. A., "An Interactive, Discipline-Independent Data Visualization System", *Computers in Physics*, 3, n. 4, July/August 1989.

[Trei91]   Treinish, L. A. (ed)., "Data Structures and Access Software for Scientific Visualization: A Report on a Workshop at SIGGRAPH '90", *Computer Graphics*, 25, n. 2, April 1991.

[Trei92]   Treinish, L.A., "Unifying Principles of Data Management for Scientific Visualization", *Proceedings of the British Computer Society Conference on Scientific Visualization and Animation, December 1992 and Animation and Scientific Visualization Tools and Applications* (R. Earnshaw and D. Watson, editors), Academic Press, pp. 141-169, 1993.

[Walt94]   Walther, S., "Inherent Logical Structure of Computational Data: Its Role in Storage and Retrieval Strategies to Support User Queries", To be published in *Database Issues for Data Visualization*, Springer-Verlag, LNCS.

Database Issues for Data Visualization: System Integration Issues

Manish Arya[1], Nancy Grady[2], Georges Grinstein[3], Peter Kochevar[4], Deborah Swanberg[5], Venu Vasudevan[6], Len Wanger[4], Andreas Wierse[7], Mark Woyna[8]

[1] IBM Almaden Research Center
[2] Oak Ridge National Laboratory, Oak Ridge TN
[3] University of Massachusetts Lowell
[4] San Diego Supercomputer Center
[5] University of California San Diego
[6] Motorola, Inc., Tempe AZ
[7] University of Stuttgart
[8] Argonne National Laboratory, Argonne IL

1 Introduction

This subgroup of the IEEE Workshop on Database Issues for Data Visualization focused on database and visualization system integration issues. We feel that both the end-users of visualizations and databases can strongly benefit from the integration of these systems. In this report we will attempt to describe the needs and problems of each software system. This should be of particular interest to users of visualization systems in that it highlights potential new approaches to the management of data. We first provide an overview of the current problems and shortcomings in integration issues. We then formulate "messages" from the visualization to the database community and vice versa.

In general, there are two approaches that address this integration: either provide a database system user with visualization support to visually analyze retrieved data and its organization; or provide a visualization system user with database support in order to handle large data sets in a reasonable manner. The fundamental question is how to perform this integration.

2 The Current State

Data management support in current visualization systems can be described as poor. Neither AVS [AVS92] nor Iris Explorer [Iris91], for example, provide the user much opportunity to deal directly with the underlying data, except in reading data as input from a file. Even the IBM Data Explorer [DX93] does not provide much additional support, although its internal data model is much more oriented towards data management than the other systems.

Alternatively, the visualization capabilities of common database management are nonexistant. This is evidenced by the text-based nature of current database user-interfaces and by the fact that graphical user interfaces for databases is a subject of much current research [Agar90, Cons90, Cruz87, Gyss90, Vasu94].

Most vendor products in the market today support forms-based front-ends as the main mode of interaction with the database backend. The application development and report generation tools that come with DBMS systems typically produce business graphs (e.g. bar and pie charts) and can sometimes display 2D raster graphics (e.g. digitized photographs). However, they lack the flexibility of environments like Data Explorer for visualizing a wider variety of data types, including surface models (e.g. engineering designs), volumetric data (e.g. medical MRI scans), and even tabular data in 3D graphs. Features to provide a visual clue about the information that is stored in the database are missing, as are means to browse visual data (e.g., satellite images).

Several efforts are underway to provide visualization services integrated with a DBMS. For example, the Sequoia 2000 project [Ston93], arguably the most comprehensive of current projects, seeks to address the large-scale, distributed, visualization and data management needs of earth science researchers studying global change problems. The QBISM project [ArCo94] integrates an extensible RDBMS (and recently an OODBMS), spatial query mechanisms, and Data Explorer for the visualization and querying of human brain imagery. The PAGEIN project [WiLa93] emphasizes a high-performance distributed cooperative environment for fluid flow visualization in the aerospace industry. The integration here is so tightly coupled that the visualization uses the database system for its internal data handling. While each of these efforts has started to tackle the integration problems, much work remains.

3 Architecture

There are three types of architectures identified to support this integration:

1. close-coupled - all components reside on one machine, sometimes all written in the same language, and even existing in the same process. The database manages its own visualization.
2. client-server - two different processes connected over a network. The database acts as a server, and visualization acts as the client.
3. distributed asynchronous process communication - database and interface seperated by a manager layer.

Close-coupling is best suited for single-user, frequent-transaction scenarios. Such interfaces have higher performance and better consistency than the client-server type, at the expense of distribution of services, multi-user access, and in some cases visualization quality (lack of required graphics hardware). The client-server architecture allows the distribution of services to the proper hardware (if available), interoperability, and multiple clients using the services at the expense of network bottlenecks and overall speed. These architectures represent two extremes, and it could well be possible that the best architecture for an interface to a database would lie somewhere in between. It is also possible to have the database and interface seperated by a manager layer, where seperate objects in the database are responsible for informing the display layer about changes in the database [Sawy92].

When considering visualization-database coupling, the degree of closeness of the data to the user (data coupling) is also important. Data coupling can be either loose or tight. Loose data coupling implies that queries specify a certain subset of the entire database to be loaded into the client application, then the client works further on the subset, almost in a batch mode of computing. This implies having the necessary data management facilities at the client as well as the server, in terms of storage, indices, and query processing. Tight data coupling requires each activity by the user to result in some retrieval from the database, and little in the way of data management facilities at the client. The DBMS controls all data movement through the entire application. Such a scheme would greatly enable *data steering*, where the presence and activities of the user changes the way in which the data is generated and displayed.

Thus, there are many architectural details that must be addressed at the logical and physical levels to enable the database-visualization integration. The following subsections describe the key architectural integration design parameters expanding on the above in more detail:

- *Modeling* - compatibility with and support from DBMS data models
- *Queries* - capability to query the visualization data models
- *Importing and Exporting* - exchanging DBMS data with different applications
- *Distribution* - support distribution of users in a wide area network
- *Heterogeneity* - support heterogeneity with respect to the visualization system, hardware, and the API.

3.1 Modeling

What data modeling support do DBMSs provide the visualization system? Are the current and common data models in DBMSs suited for visualization? The first question concerns the level at which the data will be modeled. Should it be modeled at the lower level with languages such as C++ (as supported by many object oriented DBMSs), as relational or extended relational, or should it be modeled at a higher level such as "sampled fields" as found in IBMs Data Explorer and Xidak's Aurora Dataserver [Auro93]. Even in object oriented database management systems it is not at all clear how to map the "real world" into a database: there are currently simply no guidelines. The Data Models subgroup report gives more insight into these issues.

3.2 Queries

The query capabilities provided by the system are closely related to the data model. Are images, sampled fields, and other kinds of complex data represented in the database as first-class types? In this way, query predicates can test their values using methods that operate on these types. Or are these data items stored instead in binary large objects (BLOBs) as long strings of uninterpreted bits?

Here the database management system only knows how to perform simple mass loads and stores of the entire data object. In this case the DBMS lacks the ability to run functions on the data, thus constraining interpretation. Imagine a database that holds satellite images of hurricane Hugo as it approaches the US, and consider a query of the form: *give me all images in which the hurricane is near the east coast of the United States.* Were the system to support the additional type weather image and functions that operate on that type, such as *hurricane position (weather image)*, the entire query could then be posed directly to the DBMS. On the other hand, if the system only supports BLOBs and does not permit developers to add new operators or functions, the application code would then have to retrieve the weather data image from a BLOB and process it directly. The first technique supports better encapsulation of the image analysis operations in one central location (the DBMS) and allows for query optimization within the database.

Aside from accommodating query specification, the integrated system must be able to *process and optimize* queries based on the particular data model. This means that spatial and temporal data, prevalent in visualization domains, must be supported by the system. For example, the Aurora Dataserver allows limited sampling on spatially arranged data attributes via spatial processors located outside of the DBMS, and associative querying on the relational attributes at the data points using an extended relational DBMS core. Research on spatial querying [Günt88] and temporal querying [Daya92] abounds in the literature. It is time to incorporate these advances into commercial products.

3.3   Importing and Exporting

Since many scientists want to work together and jointly access their data as a whole, it must be possible to provide flexible input and output mechanisms for shared data in the database. Scientists have grown accustomed to their special data formats and manipulation routines. A successful system must provide them the flexibility to access and use this system as fast and painlessly as possible. This could be achieved by allowing the interoperability of various visualization and database systems, which clearly implies the need for data translation to overcome data "impedance mismatches". But when and where should this translation occur? If the exchange of data between scientists is small, it might suffice to translate only when another scientist wants to access it and leave it in the "most used" format for storage. In the case of a very frequent exchange, the usage of a general storage format seems to be more efficient to avoid performance drawbacks. Another possibility might be the storage of several formats in parallel. The placement of the conversion tools can also be an issue: should it be part of the DBMS, should it be in the visualization, or should external conversion tools be invoked as necessary?

3.4 Distribution

Systems used by many people are normally distributed. The Sequoia project operates over a network of computers that are distributed throughout California. The data that is handled in the Sequoia project is usually distributed, and queries can easily involve two or more computers located at another site. This distribution should be transparent to the user who should simply formulate the query and see the results (as fast as possible). If the user then decides to work with the result of this query, the next problem presents itself: the selected data may be quite large (e.g. a series of satellite images of several regions for a certain interval in time comprising several tens of Gigabytes), whose transfer even on a T3 (digital 45 MB/s) communications line could take up to an hour or longer. In this case it would be advantageous if the data visualizations were distributed, that is only the data that really will be displayed would be transferred instead of simply sending the whole dataset over the network.

Compression clearly would help here, but its utility strongly depends on the given environment; several lower performance computers connected with higher performance networks would not benefit from that compression, since the time needed to compress the data could be longer than the time saved in the network.

3.5 Heterogeneity

Heterogeneity issues are often closely related to distribution issues. Many distributed scenarios also involve heterogeneous systems. Several approaches present themselves. Different visualization and database management systems could be used in parallel (independently from each other). The hardware on which the distributed integrated system runs might be heterogeneous. The programming languages which might be used in the development of portions of the codes can vary (e.g., on supercomputers FORTRAN is often still the most efficient and popular language, while on workstations C and C++ are used more often).

The presence of different computers is advantageous in the placing of tasks on the computers which will execute most effectively the various algorithms. In a database query however this can lead to a problem: does the data come to where the query originated or do we have to migrate the query code to where the data is? This may be different for different data sizes and types and queries and may also depend on the available network bandwidth.

4 Messages from the Visualization to the Database Community

Visualization deals with many different data types: the experiment-specific "raw" data, two- and three-dimensional spatial data, polygon lists, functionally described data (e.g. finite element data on cubic elements), etc. To support these new types, a DBMS must possess the following extensibility features:

1. new storage models for new data structures

2. abstract data types and functions that operate on these types (i.e. methods) that run under the control of the DBMS

3. an ad-hoc query language which supports user-defined abstract types and functions just as easily as it supports built-ins such as integers and addition

4. rapid query processing over these new data models.

Satellite images, for example, are several Megabytes in size. An image database may have thousands of such images. An image DBMS has to support multi-dimensional indexing so that image contents can be queried based on feature vectors. The image abstract data type has to support operators (methods) that allow the filtering of sub-images (e.g. filter part of the image that contains the Los Angeles area). It should be possible to query this sub-image in the same way as the original image. When new operators are added to the image data type, it should be possible to automatically incorporate them into the query language without taking the database off-line.

In addition to the above, the combination of distribution, heterogeneity and client-server operation poses new challenges in systems integration. Heterogeneity leads to the possibility that different objects may reside on different machines. The objects and their methods may be coded in different languages. An object may itself be distributed among multiple machines, and all of its methods may not reside with the data. Client-server architectures introduce the problem of determining whether to transfer programs to data, or vice-versa. Having all these design options without any clear guidelines for choice has complicated the systems integration task tremendously. Many of these problems are not unique to visualization. However, visualization applications are forced to face all of these problems at once because of the performance constraints they need to satisfy.

From a data modeling point of view, the challenges presented by visualization include the need for scientific data models, support for updatable views, and support for maintaining consistency between different views of the same underlying data. Scientific data models already exist, and are being supported by file-based visualization tools. These models tend to be very complex. Most current data models do not provide direct support for scientific objects. Few databases for example support a declarative (what but not how) specification of views, or view consistency.

The database system should also support the association of semantic information with the data to be visualized. For example, as the scientists explore data obtained from an instrument, different values in the data may correspond to different semantic concepts. Or, independent of the value of the data, different parts of the data may have semantic labels. The database should allow the semantic associations to be coupled with the data to facilitate its use.

5 Messages from the Database to the Visualization Community

There is increasing demand in many visualization domains to combine complex visualizations with a fine-granularity of data modeling. Data modeling needs to be fine-grained so that multiple visualization applications can access different regions of a large data structure without replicating the structure in their own idiosyncratic ways. Complex visualizations arise from the use of this data in visually rich domains such as weather monitoring, volume visualization, and fluid flow analysis.

It is imperative that databases make use of visualization tools for complex visualizations. Duplicating the visualization functionality in the DBMS could be expensive and wasteful. The alternative architecture is for the database to interface with a diverse set of visualization tools. This requires the tools to be very open, so that the DBMS can have access not only to an entire presentation but to finer-grained units of the presentation.

Visualization tools need to provide APIs (Application Programming Interfaces) in the DDLs (data description languages) and DMLs (data manipulation languages) supported by the database. For example, several OODBMSs use C++ as the DML. If the visualization tool provided a C++ API, then database applications could present visualizations by invoking the visualization services. To achieve even tighter integration, it would be useful if one could embed database callbacks in the visualization tool. This is essential for supporting "live" data (i.e direct manipulation of visualizations). Using callbacks, DML procedures can be invoked when the user manipulates images or other presentation objects at the user interface. For a visualization tool to interact in this manner with a variety of database back-ends, it needs to support callback procedures written in multiple languages (i.e it should support at least one DML for each candidate database backend).

6 Conclusion

The systems integration questions really extend beyond database and visualization aspects to include external data processing services such as numerical compute engines, statistical packages, neural networks, and the like. In constructing a system, several different design dimensions must be considered, such as ease of use, performance, size of data, coupling of systems, extensibility, heterogeneity, migration paths, distribution, etc., as outlined previously. In addition, in designing systems such as dataflow or object oriented modeled systems, it may be possible to connect two different procedures, or operations over data, but it may not be meaningful to do so.

Efforts aimed at improving the integration of visualization and database systems are currently underway (e.g. Sequoia 2000, Aurora from Xidak, and PAGEIN), differing in scope and design goals. We hope that heightened awareness of the needs of users with data management and visualization problems will further increase interaction between developers of database and visualization systems in the near future, to address the numerous challenges that lie ahead.

References

[Agar90]   Agarwal, R., Gehani, N. and Srinivasan, J., "Ode-View: A Graphical Interface to Ode", *Proceedings of ACM SIGMOD'90*, 1990, pp. 31-43.

[ArCo94]   M. Arya, W. Cody, C. Faloutsos, J. Richardson, and A. Toga, "QBISM: Extending a DBMS to Support 3D Medical Images", *Proceedings of the 10th International IEEE Conference on Data Engineering (to appear)*, Houston, Texas, IEEE Press, 1994. Also available as IBM Technical Report RJ 9480, August 1993.

[Auro93]   Aurora Dataserver Technical Overview, Xidak Inc., Palo Alto, California, October 1993.

[AVS92]   AVS User's Guide, Advanced Visual Systems Inc., Waltham, Massachusettes, May 1992.

[Cons90]   Consens, M. et al., "Visualizing Queries and Querying Visualizations", *ACM SIGMOD Record*, March 1992, pp. 39-46.

[Cruz87]   Cruz, K. F., Mendelson, A. O., and Wood, P. T., "A Graphical Query Language Supporting Recursion", *Proceedings of ACM SIGMOD'87*, pp. 323-330, 1987.

[Daya92]   Dayal, U., G. Wuu, "A Uniform Approach to Processing Temporal Queries", *Proceedings 18th International Conference of Very Large Databases*, Vancouver, BC, August 1992, pp. 407-418.

[DX93]   IBM Visualization Data Explorer User's Guide, IBM Corp., Hawthorne, New York, Publication No. SC38-0496, October 1993.

[Gree91]   Green, M. and Jacob, R. "SIGGRAPH'90 Workshop Report: Software architectures and metaphors for non-WIMP user interfaces", *Computer Graphics*, v25, n3, (July 1991), pp. 229-235.

[Günt88]   Günther, O., "Efficient Structures for Geometric Database Management", *Lecture Notes in Computer Science 337*, Springer Verlag, 1988.

[Gyss90]   Gyssens, M., Paradaens, J. and Van Gucht, D., "A Graph-Oriented Object Model for Database End-User Interfaces", *Proceedings of ACM SIGMOD'90*, 1990, pp. 24-30.

[IDL]   IDL, Research Systems Inc., Boulder, Colorado.

[Iris91]   'Iris Explorer', Technical Report BP-TR-1E-01 (Rev. 7/91), Silicon Graphics Computer Systems, Mountain View, California.

[Kove93]   L. Koved and W.L. Wooten, "GROOP: An Object-oriented Toolkit for Animated 3D Graphics", *OOPSLA'93 Proceedings*, ACM Press, 1993.

[Obje93]   ObjectStore User Guide, Object Design Inc., Burlington Massachusettes, August 1993.

[PVWa]   PV-Wave, Visual Numerics Inc., Houston, Texas.

[Sawy92]   Sawyer, P., A. Colebourne, I. Sommerville, J. Mariani, "Object Oriented Database Systems: A Framework for User Interface Development", *Proceedings of the International Workshop on Interfaces to Databases*, Springer Verlag Workshops in Computing Series, Glasgow Scotland, 1992, 25-38.

[Stra93]   P. Strauss, "IRIS Inventor, A 3D Graphics Toolkit", *OOPSLA'93 Proceedings*, ACM, 1993.

[Ston93]   Stonebraker, M. et al., "The Sequoia 2000 Architecture and Implementation Strategy", *Sequoia 2000 Technical Report 93/23*, University of California, Berkeley.

[Vasu94] Vasudevan, V., "Supporting high-Bandwidth Navigation in Object-Bases", *Proceedings of the 10th International IEEE Conference on Data Engineering (to appear)*, Houston, Texas, IEEE Press1994.

[WiLa93] A. Wierse, U. Lang, R. Ruhle, "Architectures of Distributed Visualization Systems and their Enhancements", *Workshop Papers of the Fourth Eurographics Workshop on Visualization in Scientific Computing*, Abingdon, April 1993.

Database Issues for Data Visualization: Interaction, User Interfaces, and Presentation

John Boyle[1], Stephen G. Eick[2], Matthias Hemmje[3], Daniel A. Keim[4], J.P. Lee[5], Eric Sumner[2]

[1] University of Aberdeen, Scotland
[2] AT&T Bell Labs, Naperville IL
[3] German National Center for Computer Science, Darmstadt
[4] Institute for Computer Science, University of Munich
[5] University of Massachusetts at Lowell

1 Introduction

Over the last decade, great progress has been made in data visualization techniques, as can be seen in recent SIGGRAPH and Visualization Conference Proceedings. Among the problems facing researchers today are systems issues such as appropriate data models and robust data retrieval paradigms which support the foundation of the visualization process: access to data. In the database area, researchers are improving the efficiency in storing and accessing large amounts of data, but despite major advances in database technology such as object-oriented systems [Kim90], deductive systems[Mink88], and database machines[Su88], little has been done to improve the user interface to data. Interaction with most database systems is still via simple relational languages such as SQL, and query results are usually presented in textual form inadequate for large amounts of data. Graphical query language activity is still predominantly confined to the research laboratory (see [Kim86, Ozso93, Vada93] for surveys). A large body of data that could be stored in DBMSs is inherently non-relational (table-based), having characteristics outlined in [Shos84, Shos85, Trei92].

Until recently, there has been little research on combining visualization and database technology. Related work in Geographic Information System (GIS) and image database systems have received much attention in recent years [Arnd90, Egen88, Jung90, Ooi88]. This report provides insight into the problems arising when combining visualization systems and databases pertaining to user interaction, user interfaces, and data presentation methods, and identifies areas needing further research.

It is paramount that the data organization and management support the *interactions* the user must perform with the data, in order to explore and visualize data. The use of a database management system (DBMS) or information retrieval system (IR) to store data and mediate data access is an important consideration, as such a system can offer unique data interaction services, such as efficient querying and consistency in update operations. Testing and empirical evaluation on real-world problems (in terms of both data dimensionality and volume), however, is necessary to ascertain the value of the integration on one hand, and to monitor progress in the field on the other hand. The ability for the user to interact with the integrated system in an efficient manner is very important, as slow response time may nullify any benefits gained from services provided.

2   Research Areas

To advance the state of the art in combining database and visualization systems from the human user perspective, focused research in five primary areas is required. The five research areas for interaction, user interfaces, and data presentation are:

1. A **taxonomy** of the various information spaces, comprised of graphic, cognitive, perceptual, logical and physical elements. Also of taxonomic concern are the types of data sets resident within the system, which have a profound effect on the information spaces and structures created to deal with them.
2. **Visualization methods**, including interaction metaphors and representation issues. Such methods need to support navigation of the various information spaces. The roles of three-dimensional representations and sound need to be researched as to their effectiveness.
3. **Design rules**, including database-to-visualization mappings. They must ensure that the small test cases undertaken scale gracefully to production-sized systems. Interaction and response guidelines also need to be created.
4. **Formal evaluations** of user-initiated tasks. These are critical to the acceptance of approaches undertaken, and involve the measuring of both task performance efficiency, system response time, and user perception time. Evaluations to resolve the differences between domain-specific querying and general querying are also needed.
5. The **architecture** of combined database and visualization systems. The interface between database and visualization systems needs to be identified and the use of software components such as libraries, toolkits and various environments needs to be researched.

3   Research Area Descriptions

3.1   Taxonomies

The utility of a common language and definitions allows researchers from different disciplines to communicate about issues of interest on a similar level. There has been a noted lack of communication between database and visualization researchers. It is evident that in order to discuss aspects of databases, visualization and interaction, some form of taxonomy of terms and concepts must be devised. One can envision an all-encompassing *information space* that consists all of the data types in the system. Within this space reside cognitive, presentation and database components.

Cognitive Space consists of a mental model the user has of the components in the system, the objective of the interaction, and the visual perception. The mental model is continually modified as the user learns and interacts with the system (an excellent reference on the cognitive elements of system design is [Norm86]). Presentation Space contains data, constructs, and routines that permit visualizations. The presentation method must reveal important structures within the database.

The Database Space consists of a *content space* that is an interpretation of the database (interpreted data is termed information), and is decomposed into the following logical subspaces (refer to Figure 1):

- an *interest space* that should be found or uncovered during a data exploration session, consisting of the structures of interest to the user
- a *context space* that has been visited during a data exploration session
- a *result space* that consists of the relevant areas of the context space to the user, the uncovered part of the interest space.

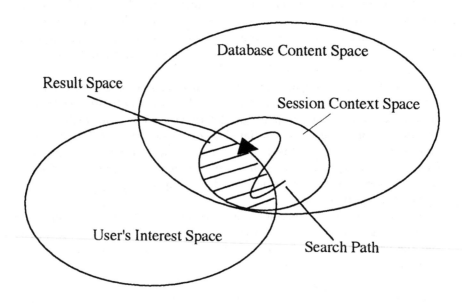

Fig. 1. The database component of an information space

The interest space is navigated in some fashion during an exploration. Explored areas become part of the context space, those specific to the user's interest become part of the result space. Thus, the context space could be larger than the interest space. Ideally, the entire interest space is contained within the result space. For a "bad" query or exploration, the intersection of the context and interest space may be empty.

The types of data under investigation and their relationships must be clearly identified. They include unstructured data (text), semi-structured data (text with numeric data), structured data with a flat structure (tabular or relational), highly structured data (object, hierarchical or semantic nets), as well as specialized structured data (spatial or imagery). On a higher level, database visualization can be thought of as containing four key elements:

- visualization of all of the content space and its organization
- visualization of the query components
- visualization of the result space
- multiple view resolutions (granularity) of visualized results

These elements suggest a framework to develop interfaces. With such a framework, interfaces would need only be customized at the final visualization stage. An important question is what common features should interfaces to databases possess?

3.2 Visualization Methods

Visualization methods are a means of presenting data, and are an active research area. In terms of interaction, formal methods to portray the abstract and concrete objects taxonomized in the previous section are required. Additionally, interaction techniques to manipulate these objects are needed. Visualization techniques must be developed that work for the query-retrieve-display and navigation-through-data scenarios, as well as guidelines for when to apply either method. Some ideas for navigating through the information space are contained in [Fogg84, Lars86, Ston93]. We expect both types will find use exclusively and also in conjuction with each other. Scenarios for visualizations of all of the data in a database at a very high level are needed (a matter of sampling), with the ability for the user to query the visualized structures, and to navigate through the result set. These techniques must support iterative cycles of queries in an incremental fashion (as in [Card93]). It is well-known that users divide a large task into a number of smaller tasks, thus any interface should have the capability to perform incremental querying [Keim92], allow query decomposition, yield approximate results [Chu92, Keim93], and recall previous queries from a history mechanism [Lee92] in a visual fashion.

In a related area, the upper limit on the number of data objects presentable on one display screen will have contributions from both the granularity and codings of the data objects along with the limits due to human perception. Thus, adequate visualization methods are required to present varying resolutions of a data set [Fine92]. The entire result space might be too large to present, so a means of abstracting the visual representation is necessary. The user might only be interested in relevant portions of the output, so subsets of the results only need be displayed [Keim93, Keim94].

Navigation through information spaces is becoming increasingly prevalent, as a result of the availability of faster processing power, the application of Virtual Reality concepts to the data interface [Brys91, Fein90, Mack90, Ware90] and the increased availability of Internet navigators (Gopher, Mosaic, World Wide

Web). As the data set grows larger, these methods *must scale gracefully*. One question is how to present new objects such as database schemas, queries, or the various other information spaces of the previous section. Another is how to portray a schema with thousands of classes, or a large and complex query without resorting to text, or even millions of retrieved objects from the database that satisfy a query [Keim94]. How might queries to the database be constructed taking advantage of the schema or result representation? The ability to portray multiple resolutions (view granularity) of data and seamlessly switch among them will be important [Koch93].

The visualization community has focused on 3-dimensional renderings of data. Does the 3D version offer more expressive power than it's 2D counterpart, or is it used primarily for aesthetic reasons? The ubiquity of realistic, 3D renderings might say more for the technical computer graphics aspects of the visualization method itself than for its ability to accurately present what the end-user requires from a data exploration. Conversely, the interfaces to databases have, over the past decade, been either form-based (Query-By-Example [Zloo77]) or entity-relationship (ER) schema-based [Fogg84, Roca88, Wong82]. If the use of 3D graphics adds expressive power to the interface, as it could for the output representations, then it could significantly enhance the power of the desktop metaphor.

Finally, an often-overlooked presentation domain is that of sound. Research into sonification of data is undertaken at very few research facilities [Smit91]. This activity should be expanded to first quantify sound as a "display" primitive, arrive at useful a taxonomy, and then begin to take advantage of it's useful properties.

3.3   Design Rules

Most published visualization research tends to shy away from the use of "real-world" data sets. The trade-off between system performance in light of the available computing resources and interaction with large data sets often results in the proliferation of small, specialized "test cases" that might not have general applicability in reality. Clearly, there is a need for implementations of interfaces to huge databases, or at least an evaluation of how an implementation would scale up to large data input volumes.

What is the best visualization technique for a particular type of database? This is similar to query optimization. Design rules that govern the application of a particular visualization based on data characteristics has been a subject of recent study [Mack86, Rogo93, Sena91]. This activity should continue, as formal database-to-visualization mappings would lead to the creation of systems that are firmly rooted in scientific methods. For this to occur, we must have a clear categorization of the logical and physical data models to be visualized and the available techniques. There must be a set of rules and guidelines that rationalize why a specific representation or metaphor is used as well as what type of specialization might be required. Having these types of rules and formal models will make visualization more of an engineering activity as opposed to the ad-hoc approaches currently seen. Thus, database systems must be able to store these rules, and whatever domain knowledge and presentation knowledge needed.

As important as display design rules are, they must also extend to the treatment of interaction with data. Interaction is an interface activity involving perception. There should be rules to govern the application of specific interaction techniques, using certain metaphors, depending upon both the underlying data to be accessed and subsequently visualized, and the tasks that satisfy the exploration objectives. To that end, a description of relevant generic and moreso application-specific tasks must be developed for data exploration.

3.4 Evaluations

Evaluations and metrics are often overlooked in visualization research when interaction and perception are concerned. This is primarily due to the subjective nature of dealing with imagery, perception and cognition. Database research does not suffer from this problem as it deals with more concrete constructs and processes. We strongly feel that more evaluations of visualizations and interactions should be undertaken to gauge progress in the domain and impart a more formal foundation for future research. Thus, we must run experiments such as [Albh92, Bell92, Berg94, Doan93, Kepe93] to validate and measure the effectiveness of the techniques we create. Experiments are also needed to achieve better user models [ODay93].

A set of *interaction benchmarks* are required that will allow the evaluation of interfaces to databases. There are two areas for compliance: system activities (actual data retrieval and visualization generation), and human response and interpretation based on the visualization. To implement these, application-specific task-based experiments must be devised. Tasks are high-level descriptions of a sequence of operations to be performed. Tasks will manifest themselves as queries, the specification of data retrieval. There are multiple levels of task types and complexities, and also measures of efficiency that must be developed for these tasks. Also, the decomposition of tasks to actual queries is not necessarily a straightforward process. The completion of a task is not necessarily a binary event; it may very well need to be iterated upon or modified. Important questions are how long will the retrieval and visualization take, and then how long will it take for the user to derive something from the data. Provisions for incremental queries will need to have specialized experiments for evaluating that functionality.

Most implementations use a generic querying technique to produce a domain-specific visualization. A generic interface is presented to access the data (a form or 2D graphical user interface widget), and a domain-specific display is created (as opposed to a standard textual output). What might prove interesting is to explore domain-specific querying techniques (interaction with a visualized data representation in a specific context) producing the domain-specific visualizations. This would be realizable after the taxonomies, visualization methods, and task-based evaluations for a particular domain are determined.

3.5 Architecture

Interaction quality depends greatly on the choice of hardware and software architectures. In combining database and visualization systems, it is important to have an architecture exploiting the benefits of both the database and the visualization system. The Systems subgroup report discusses various tradeoffs. In trying to find an adequate architecture, the proliferation of existing systems needs to be considered. In general, people and organizations are very slow in replacing such legacy systems. Therefore, the architecture should allow the integration of existing database systems with their data model and query language, as well as allow new data models and query languages that are best suited for visualization tasks to be integrated. Additionally, software tools and libraries should provide a common "look and feel", be easy to use, and provide high-performance in display. They must support the style of interaction and the manipulation of the various data objects. The primary goal, again, is to find the architectures that best support user interaction with data.

4 Conclusion

The field of visualization can present to a user in a comprehensible manner the massively large quantities of data produced today. The database management field allows this volume of data to be stored and retrieved in a structured and desired format. A collaboration between these two areas of study will yield a powerful technology that allow users to have easy access to the wealth of information that is becoming available.

This discussion paper has addressed some of the major research issues related to such developments, particularly in the field of human computer interaction. We have targeted the questions arising in five major areas. Most important is an agreed taxonomy, through which researchers can convey their ideas to each other; without such formal notions, communication becomes confused. The idea of a user exploring a content space to discover the areas of interest is an important metaphor. For a user to visualize data in a database, powerful interaction support is needed, so that the desired goal can be satisfied. The abstract data must be seen in such a manner so that its meaning is portrayed effectively, so the user is able to intuitively ask informed questions about its substance. Thus, the visualization lends itself easily to direct querying. The issues associated with the design of database to visualization mappings must be addressed, their impact on representations that should (or shouldn't) be used. Evaluations of an interactive system must be done in such a way as to allow the developers to understand the weaknesses of their systems, and to correct them. Finally the architecture of such complex systems must be considered, as it has profound ramifications upon all aspects of functionality and usability. An architecture must be designed which best reflects the need of the user, with an awareness of the limitations of the underlying hardware.

A number of questions are raised when analyzing the integration of the rich research areas of interaction, visualization and database management systems.

With the "easier" questions of methodology and technique for the respective domains having been addressed, the time has come to focus on the more difficult problems in combining the systems, as outlined in this and the two previous reports. While the need for good visualization and interaction for both database browsing and querying have been recognized for quite some time, very little advancement or standardization has appeared. With powerful visualization techniques becoming available on many platforms, a new era of user interface technology is approaching, and the database visualization domain could well be one of the first technologies to benefit from the evolving ideas.

References

[Albh92] Albherg, C., C. Williamson, B. Schneiderman, "Dynamic Queries for Information Exploration: An Implementation and Evaluation", *Proceedings of CHI'92*, 1992, 619-626.

[Arnd90] Arndt, T., "A Survey of Recent Research in Image Database Management" *Proceedings of the IEEE Workshop on Visual Languages*, 1990, 92-96.

[Bell92] Bell, J.E., L. Rowe, "An Exploratory Study of Ad-Hoc Query Languages to Databases", *Proceedings of International Conference on Data Engineering*, 1992, 606-613.

[Berg94] Bergeron D., Keim D. A., Pickett R., "Test Data Sets for Evaluating Data Visualization Techniques", Proc. Int. Workshop on Perceptual Issues in Visualization, San Jose, CA, 1993.

[Brys91] Bryson, S., C. Levitt, "The Virtual Windtunnel: An Environment for the Exploration of 3D Unsteady Flows", em Proceedings of IEEE Visualization'91, October 1991, 17-24.

[Card93] Cardenas, A., I. Ieong, R. Taira, R. Barker, C. Breant, "The Knowledge-Based Object-Oriented PICQUERY+ Language", *IEEE Transactions on Knowledge and Data Engineering*, August 1993.

[Chu92] Chu, W.W., Q. Chen, "Neighboring and Associative Query Answering", *Journal of Intelligent Information Systems: Integrating Artificial Intelligence and Database Technologies*, v2, 1992, 355-382.

[Doan93] Doan, D.K., N. Paton, A. Kilgour, "Evaluation of Database Query Interface Paradigms for Object-Oriented Databases", *unpublished manuscript*, Heroit-Watt University, Edinburg Scotland, 1993.

[Egen88] Egenhofer, M.J., A. Frank, "Towards a Spatial Query Language, User Interface Considerations", *Proceedings of the 14th Internatinoal Conference on Very Large Databases*, Los Angeles CA, 1988, 60-69.

[Fine92] Fine, J.A., "Abstracts: A Latency-Hiding Technique for High-Capacity Mass-Storage Systems", Sequoia 2000 Technical Report 92/11, University of California at Berkeley, June 1992.

[Fein90] Feinier, S., C. Beshers, "Visualizing n-Dimensional Virtual Worlds with n-vision", *Computer Graphics*, v24, n2n March 1990, 37-38.

[Fogg84] Fogg D., "Lessons from a 'Living in a Database' Graphical User Interface", *Proceedings of ACM-SIGMOD International Conference on Management of Data*, 1984.

[Jung90]   Jungert, E., "Towards a Visual Query Language for an Object Oriented Geographic Information System", *Proceedings of the IEEE Workshop on Visual Languages*, 1990, 132-137.

[Keim92]   Keim D. A., Lum V., "GRADI: A Graphical Database Interface for a Multimedia DBMS", Proc. Int. Workshop on Interfaces to Databases, Glasgow, England, 1992, in: Springer Series 'Workshops in Computing', pp. 95-112.

[Keim93]   Keim D. A., Kriegel H.-P., Seidl T., "Visual Feedback in Querying Large Databases", Proc. Visualization 1993 Conf., San Jose, CA, October 25-29, 1993.

[Keim94]   Keim D. A., Kriegel H.-P., Seidl T., "Supporting Data Mining of Large Databases by Visual Feedback Queries", Proc. Int. Conf. on Data Engineering, Houston, TX, 1994.

[Kepe93]   Keim D. A., Kriegel H.-P., "Possibilities and Limits in Visualizing Large Amounts of Multidimensional Data", Proc. Int. Workshop on Perceptual Issues in Visualization, San Jose, CA, 1993.

[Kim86]   Kim, H.J., "Graphical Interfaces for Database Systems: A Survey", *Proceedings of ACM Mountain Regional Conference*, Santa Fe NM, April 1986.

[Kim90]   Kim, W., "Object-Oriented Database Systems: Definitions and Research Directions", *IEEE Transactions on Knowledge and Data Engineering*, June 1990.

[Koch93]   Kochevar, P., Z. Ahmed, J. Shade, C. Sharpe, "Bridging the Gap Between Visualization and Data Management: A Simple Visualization Management System", *Proceedings of Visualization'93*, San Jose CA, 1993, 94-101.

[Lars86]   Larson, J.A., "A Visual Approach to Browsing in a Database Environment", *IEEE Computer*, v19, n6, June 1986, 62-71.

[Lee92]   Lee, A., "Investigations into History Tools for User Support", PhD Thesis, University of Toronto, Toronto Canada, 1992.

[Mack86]   Mackinlay, J., "Automating the Design of Graphical Presentations of Relational Information", *ACM Transactions on Graphics*, v5, n2, April 1986, 110-141.

[Mack90]   Mackinlay, J., S. Card, G. Robertson, "Rapid Controlled Movement through a Virtual 3D Workspace", *Computer Graphics*, v24, n4, August 1990, 171-176.

[Mink88]   Minkler, J., *Foundations of Deductive Database and Logic Programming*, Morgan Kaufmann, San Mateo, CA, 1988.

[Norm86]   Norman, D., S. Draper eds., *User Centered System Design*, Lawrence Earlbaum Associates, Hillsdale NJ, 1986.

[ODay93]   O'Day, V., R. Jeffries, "Orienteering in an Information Landscape: How Information Seekers Get from Here to There", *Proceedings of InterCHI'93*, Amsterdam, 1993, 438-446.

[Ooi88]   Ooi, B.C., R. Sachs-Davids, K.J. McDonell, "Extending a DBMS for Geographic Applications", *Proceedings of the 5th International Conference on Data Engineering*, Los Angeles CA, 1989, 590-597.

[Ozso93]   Ozsoyoglu, G., H. Wang, "Example-Based Graphical Database Query Languages", *IEEE Computer*, May 1993, 25-38.

[Roca88]   Rogers T. R., Cattell R. G. G., "Entity-Relationship Database User Interfaces", *in Readings on Database Systems, ed. by M. Stonebraker*, 1988.

[Rogo93]   Rogowitz, B., L. Treinish, "An Architecture for Rule-Based Visualization", *Proceedings of IEEE Visualization'93*, October 1993, 236-293.

[Sena91] Senay, H., E. Ignatius, "Compositional Analysis and Synthesis of Scientific Data Visualization Techniques", in *Scientific Visualization of Physical Phenomena (Proceedings of CG International'91)*, N.M. Patrikalas ed., Springer Verlag, 1991, 269-281.

[Shos84] Shoshani, A., F. Olken, H.K.T. Wong, "Characteristics of Scientific Databases", *Proceedings of the 10th International Conference on Very Large Databases*, Singapore, August 1984, 147-160.

[Shos85] Shoshani, A., H.K.T. Wong, "Statistical and Scientific Database Issues", *IEEE Transactions on Software Engineering*, v11, n10, October 1985, 1040-1046.

[Smit91] Smith, S., G.G. Grinstein, R, Pickett, "Global Geometric, Sound, and Color Controls for Iconographic Displays of Scientific Data", *Proceedings of SPIE - Extracting Meaning from Complex Data: Processing, Display, Interaction*, E.J. Farrel ed., 1991.

[Ston93] Stonebraker, M., J. Chen, C. Paxson, A. Su, J. Wu, "Tioga: A Database-Oriented Visualization Tool", *Proceedings of Visualization'93*, San Jose CA, 1993, 86-93.

[Su88]   Su, S., "Database Computers: Principles, Architectures, and Techniques", McGraw-Hill, New York, 1988.

[Trei92] Treinish, L., "Unifying Principles of Data Management for Scientific Visualization" *Proceedings of the British Computer Society Conference on Animation and Scientific Visualization*, Winchester UK, December 1992.

[Vada93] Vadaparty, K., Y.A. Aslandogan, G. Ozsoyoglu, "Towards a Unified Visual Database Access", *Proceedings of ACM SIGMOD'93*, 1993, 357-366.

[Ware90] Ware, C., S. Osbourne, "Exploration and Virtual Camera Control in Virtual 3 Dimensional Environments", *1990 Symposium on Interactive 3D Graphics*, Special Issue of *Computer Graphics*, v24, n2, June 1990, 175-184.

[Wong82] Wong H. K. T., Kuo I., GUIDE: Graphic User Interface for Database Exploration. Proc. Int. Conf. on Very Large Data Bases, Mexico City, 1982.

[Zloo77] Zloof, M.M., "Query-By-Example: A Database Language", *IBM Systems Journal*, v21, n3, 1977, 324-343.

Papers: Data Models

The VIS-AD Data Model: Integrating Metadata and Polymorphic Display with a Scientific Programming Language

William L. Hibbard[1&2], Charles R. Dyer[2] and Brian E. Paul[1]

[1]Space Science and Engineering Center
[2]Computer Sciences Department
University of Wisconsin - Madison
whibbard@macc.wisc.edu

Abstract. The VIS-AD data model integrates metadata about the precision of values, including missing data indicators and the way that arrays sample continuous functions, with the data objects of a scientific programming language. The data objects of this data model form a lattice, ordered by the precision with which they approximate mathematical objects. We define a similar lattice of displays and study visualization processes as functions from data lattices to display lattices. Such functions can be applied to visualize data objects of all data types and are thus polymorphic.

1. Introduction

Computers have become essential tools to scientists. Scientists formulate models of natural phenomena using mathematics, but in order to simulate complex events they must automate their models as computer algorithms. Similarly, scientists analyze their observations of nature in terms of mathematical models, but the volumes of observed data dictate that these analyses be automated as computer algorithms. Unlike hand computations, automated computations are invisible, and their sheer volume makes them difficult to comprehend. Thus scientists need tools to make their computations visible, and this has motivated active development of scientific visualization systems. Explicitly or implicitly, these systems are based on:

1. A data model - how scientific data are defined and organized.
2. A computational model - how computations are expressed and executed.
3. A display model - how data and information are communicated to a the user.
4. A user model - the tasks and capabilities (e.g., perceptual) of users.
5. A hardware model - characteristics of equipment used to store, compute with, and display data.

Robertson et. al. [11] describe the need for a foundation for visualization based on such formal models. The user and hardware models help define the context and requirements for a system design, whereas the data, computational and display models are actually high level components of a system design. Because scientists explore into unknown areas of nature, they need models of data, computation, and display that can adapt to change.

2. Data Model Issues

2.1 Levels of Data Models

A data model defines and organizes a set of data objects. Data models can be defined at various levels of functionality [16]. Data models can describe:

1. The physical layout and implementation of data objects. At the lowest level, a data model may describe the physical layout of bits in data objects. It is widely acknowledged that this level should be hidden from users, and even hidden from systems developers as much as possible. At a slightly higher level, a data model may describe the data objects of a visualization system in terms of the data objects of the programming language(s) used to implement the system.
2. The logical structure of data. This level describes the mathematical and logical properties of primitive data values, how complex data objects are composed from simpler data objects, and relations between data objects.
3. The behavior of data in computational processes. This is a pure object-oriented view of data. The internal structure of data objects is invisible, and all that is specified is the behavior of functions operating on data objects.

While purely behavioral models of scientific data are possible, it is rare to see a behavioral data model that does not refer to the logical structural of data. That is, the behaviors of functions operating on objects are usually explained in terms like "returns a component object" or "follows a reference to another object." In particular, most data models that are described as "object oriented" are object oriented implementations of structural data models. In these cases, the internal structure of objects is hidden in the sense of programming language scope rules, but is not hidden in the user's understanding of object behavior. The idea of defining complex things in terms of simpler things is extremely natural and convenient, so it is not surprising that most data models are essentially structural. Furthermore, structural data models permit automated analysis of data syntax (e.g., for query optimization), but it is difficult to apply similar analyses to purely functional specifications of data.

2.2 Structural Data Models

The physical and implementation levels address issues that should not be visible to scientists using a system, and purely behavioral data models are rare. Thus we focus on the structural level. At this level a data model needs to address the following issues:

1. The types of primitive data values occurring in data objects. A primitive type defines a set of primitive values. It may also define an order relation, basic operations (e.g., addition, negation, string concatenation), and a topology (e.g., the discrete topology of integers, the continuous topology of real numbers) on the set of values.
2. The ways that primitive values are aggregated into data objects. These may be simple tuples of values, they may be functional relations between variables, or they may be complex networks of values.
3. Metadata about the relation between data and the things that they represent. For example, given a meteorological temperature, metadata includes the fact that it is a temperature, its scale (e.g., Fahrenheit, Kelvin), the location of the temperature and whether it is a point or volume sample, the time of the temperature, an estimate of its accuracy, how it was produced (e.g. by a simulation, by direct observation, or deduced from a satellite radiance), and whether the value is missing (e.g., in case of a sensor failure).

A structural data model defines behavior rather than implementation, but does so in terms of an underlying structure. That is, primitive types describe the operations that can be applied to primitive objects, but do so under the assumption that the state of a primitive object is a simple mathematical value. Similarly, aggregate types describe operations that return objects as functions of other objects, but do so in terms of hierarchical and network relations between objects. A purely behavioral model would not place such constraints on operations on objects.

2.3 Extensive Versus Intensive Models for Types of Data Aggregates

The way that a structural data model defines types of data aggregates is an important issue in the context of data visualization. Many visualization systems define data models that are essentially finite enumerations of those aggregate types for which the systems have implemented display functions. For example, a visualization system's data model may include images, 3-D scalar and vector fields, vector and polygon lists, and color maps. On the other hand, scientists writing programs require flexibility in defining aggregate types. Thus programming languages usually define data models in terms a set of techniques that let users define their own (potentially infinite) sets of aggregate types. That is, users are given language features like tuples (i.e., structures in C), arrays and pointers for building their own structures. Visualization systems stress aspects of their data models related to display models, whereas programming languages stress aspects of their data models related to computational models.

In set theory, a set may be defined *extensively* as a list of members, or defined *intensively* by a logical condition for membership. We borrow these terms, saying that an extensive data model is one that defines a finite enumeration of aggregate types, and saying that an intensive data model is one that defines a set of techniques for building a potentially infinite set of aggregate types. Systems designed for particular applications, including many scientific visualization systems, tend to define extensive data models, while programming languages tend to define intensive data models.

Scientists need data models that can support general computational models and can also support general display models for all data objects. Object oriented techniques provide one approach to this need. Each aggregate type in an extensive data model can be defined as a different object class. Inheritance between classes simplifies the task of designing new types of aggregates, and polymorphism allows analysis and display functions to be applied uniformly to many different aggregate types. However, this approach still requires users to explicitly define new object classes and their display functions. An approach based on intensive data models may be easier for scientists to use.

2.4 Models for Metadata

Programming languages and visualization systems differ in their level of support for metadata. While programming languages offer users the flexibility to build their own logic for managing metadata, they have no intrinsic semantics for the relation between data and its metadata. For example, scientists may adopt the convention that -999 represents a missing value, but since the programming languages that they use do not implement any special semantics for this value, their programs must include explicit tests for this value. On the other hand, many scientific visualization systems do intelligently manage the relation between data and its metadata. For example, some systems implement missing data codes, some systems manage information about the spatial locations of data (sometimes called data navigation), and some systems manage information needed to normalize observations to common scales (sometimes called data calibration).

3. Data Lattices

Mathematical models define infinite precision real numbers and functions with infinite domains, whereas computer data objects contain finite amounts of information and must therefore be approximations to the mathematical objects that they represent. For example, a 32-bit floating point number represents real numbers by a set of roughly 2^{32} different values in the range between -10^{38} and $+10^{38}$, plus a few special codes for illegal and out-of-range values. Since most real numbers are not members of this set of 2^{32} values, they can only be approximately represented by floating point numbers. As another example, a satellite image is a finite sampling of a continuous radiance field over the Earth. The image contains a finite number of pixels, and pixels sample radiance values in finite numbers of bits (8-bit values are common). Thus the satellite image can only approximate the continuous radiance field. Satellites and other sensor systems are fallible, so scientists usually define missing data codes to represent values where sensors failed. These missing data codes may be interpreted as approximations that contain no information about the mathematical values that they represent.

We can define an order relation between data objects based on the fact that some are better approximations than others. That is, if x and y are data objects, then we define $x \leq y$ to mean that y is consistent with x, and that y provides more precise information than x does. We illustrate this order relation using closed real intervals as approximations to real numbers. If w is a real number, and if $[a, b]$ is the real interval of numbers between a and b, then $[a, b]$ is an approximation to w if w belongs to the interval $[a, b]$ (i.e., if $a \leq w \leq b$). Given two intervals $[a, b]$ and $[c, d]$, we say that $[a, b] \leq [c, d]$ if $[c, d] \subseteq [a, b]$. This is because the smaller interval provides more precise information about a value than the containing interval does. Letting the symbol $\perp$ represent a missing data code, then $\perp$ provides less precise information about a real value than any interval, so we can say that $\perp <$ $[a, b]$ for any interval $[a, b]$. Figure 1 shows a few closed real intervals and the order relations among those intervals.

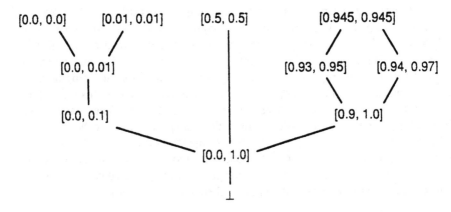

Figure 1. Closed real intervals are used as approximate representations of real numbers, ordered by the inverse of containment (i.e., containing intervals are "less than" contained intervals). We also include a least element $\perp$ that corresponds to a missing data indicator. This figure shows a few intervals, plus the order relations among those intervals. The intervals in the top row are all maximal, since they contain no smaller interval.

We interpret arrays as finite samplings of functions. For example, a function of a real variable may be represented by a set of 2-tuples that are (domain, range) pairs. The set {([1.1, 1.6], [3.1, 3.4]), ([3.6, 4.1], [5.0, 5.2]), ([6.1, 6.4], [6.2, 6.5])} contains three samples of a function. The domain value of a sample lies in the first interval of a pair and the range values lies in the second interval of a pair, as illustrated in Fig. 2. Adding more samples, or increasing the precision of samples, will create a more precise approximation to the function. Figure 3 shows the order relations between a few array data objects.

In general we can order arrays to reflect how precisely they approximate functions. If x and y are two array data objects that are both finite samplings of a function, and if, for each sample of x, there is a collection of samples of y that improve the resolution of the function's domain and range over the sample of x, then $x \leq y$. Intuitively, y contains more information about the function than x does.

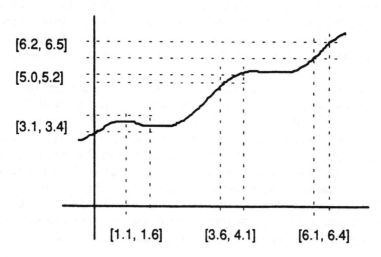

Figure 2. An approximate representation of a real function as a set of pairs of intervals.

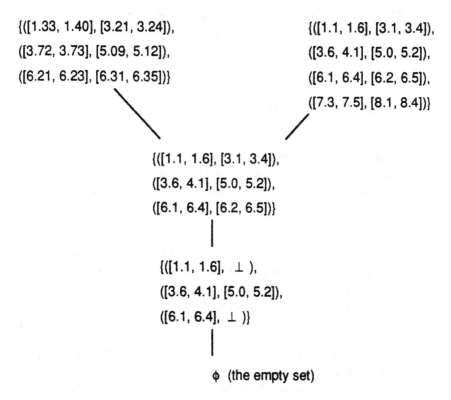

Figure 3. A few finite samplings of functions, and the order relations among them.

3.1 A Scientific Data Model

Now we will define a data model that is appropriate for scientific computations. We describe this data model in terms of the way it defines primitive values, how those values are aggregated into data objects, and metadata that describes the relation between data objects and the mathematical objects that they represent.

The data model defines two kinds of primitive values, appropriate for representing real numbers and integers. We call these two kinds of primitives *continuous scalars* and *discrete scalars*, reflecting the difference in topology between real numbers and integers. A continuous scalar takes the set of closed real intervals as values, ordered by the inverse of containment, as illustrated in Fig. 1. A discrete scalar takes any countable set as values, without any order relation between them (since no integer is more precise than any other). Figure 4 illustrates the order relations between values of a discrete scalar. Note that discrete scalars may represent text strings as well as integers. The value sets of continuous and discrete scalars always include a minimal value $\perp$ corresponding to missing data.

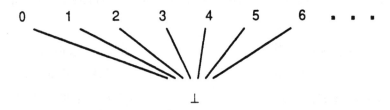

Figure 4. A discrete scalar is a countable (possibly finite) set of incomparable elements, plus a least element $\perp$.

Our data model defines a set T of data types as ways of aggregating primitive values into data objects. Rather than enumerating a list of data types in T, the data model starts with a finite set S of scalar types, representing the primitive variables of a mathematical model, and defines three rules by which data types in T can be defined. These rules are:

1. Any continuous or discrete scalar in S is a data type in T. A scientist using this data model typically defines one scalar type in S for each variable in his or her mathematical model.
2. If $t_1, ..., t_n$ are types in T, then $struct\{t_1;...;t_n\}$ is a *tuple* type in T with *element* types t_i. Data objects of tuple types contain one data object of each of their element types.
3. If w is a scalar type in S and r is a type in T, then $(array\ [w]\ of\ r)$ is an *array* type with *domain* type w and *range* type r. Data objects of array types are finite samplings of functions from the primitive variable represented by their domain type to the set of values represented by their range type. That is,

they are sets of data objects of their range type, indexed by values of their domain type.

Each data type in T defines a set of data objects. Continuous and discrete scalars define sets of values as we have described previously. The set of objects of a tuple type is the cross product of the sets of objects of its element types. The set of objects of an array type is not quite the space of all functions from the value set of its domain type to the set of objects of its range type. Rather, it is the union of such function spaces, taken over all finite subsets of the domain's value set.

A tuple of data objects represent a tuple of mathematical objects, and the precision of the approximation depends on the precision of each element of the tuple. One tuple is more precise than another if each element is more precise. That is, $(x_1, ..., x_n) \leq (y_1, ..., y_n)$ if $x_i \leq y_i$ for each i. Figure 5 illustrates the order relations between a few tuples.

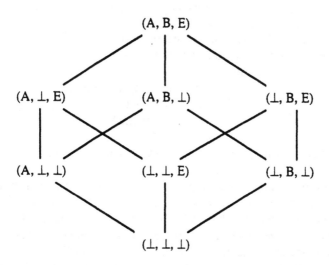

Figure 5. Defining an order relation on a cross product. Members of cross products are tuples. This figure shows a few elements in a cross product of three sets, plus the order relations among those elements. In a cross product, the least element is the tuple of least elements of the factor sets.

An array data object is a finite sampling of a function, and the precision of approximation depends on how precisely the function's domain is sampled and the precision of the array's range values. If an array is indexed by a continuous scalar, the interval values of the index indicate how precisely the function's domain is sampled, as illustrated in Figs. 2 and 3.

By building hierarchies of tuples and arrays, it is possible to define data types in T that represent virtually any mathematical model used in the physical sciences. For example, consider a set of data types appropriate for analyzing meteorological observations. The scalar types used to represent primitive variables for this analysis include:

temperature	- thermometer reading (continuous)
dew_point	- wet bulb thermometer reading (continuous)
pressure	- barometer reading (continuous)
count	- frequency count of values in a histogram (discrete)
station_name	- name of observing station (discrete)
latitude	- latitude of observing station (continuous)
longitude	- longitude of observing station (continuous)
time	- time of observation (continuous)

The complex data types for this analysis include:

```
station_reading = struct{
                        .sta_temp = temperature;
                        .sta_dew = dew_point;
                        .sta_pres = pressure;
                }
station_series = (array [time] of station_reading)
station_set = (array [station_name] of
                struct{
                        .set_series = station_series;
                        .set_lat = latitude;
                        .set_lon = longitude;
                }
temperature_histogram    = (array [temperature] of count)
```

A data object of the *station_reading* type includes one value for each instrument at a weather observing station. A data object of type *station_series* contains a sequence of *station_reading* objects, that finitely sample continuous functions of meteorological fields over *time*. A data object of type *station_set* is an array that associates a time series of readings and *latitude* and *longitude* locations to each of a finite set of *station_names*. A data object of the *temperature_histogram* type contains frequency *counts* of intervals of *temperatures*. In this case, the interval values of the *temperature* represent the bins used for histogram calculation.

The lattice data model defines certain metadata about the relation between data objects and the mathematical objects that they represent, including:

1. Every primitive value in a data object is identified by the name of the primitive mathematical variable.
2. An array data object is a finite sampling of a mathematical function. The set of index values of the array specify how the array samples the function being represented.
3. The interval values of continuous scalars are approximations to real numbers in a mathematical model, and the sizes of intervals provide information about the accuracy of their approximations.

4. Any scalar data object may take the missing value (denoted by ⊥) and this provides information about accuracy (i.e., the fact that the value has no accuracy).

3.2 Interpreting the Data Model as a Lattice

We view a data display process as a function from a set of data objects to a set of display objects. Our data model defines a different set of data objects for each different data type, suggesting that a different display function must be defined for each different data type. However, we can define a lattice U of data objects and natural embeddings of data objects of all data types into U. The lattice U provides us with a unified model for all of our scientific data objects, and enables us to define display functions that are applicable to all data types (i.e., these display functions are polymorphic). Our analysis of the properties of display functions will thus be independent of particular data types.

A *lattice* is an ordered set U in which every pair of elements x and y has a least upper bound $sup\{x, y\}$ [this is z such that $x \leq z, y \leq z$ and $\forall w \in U. (x \leq w$ & $y \leq w \Rightarrow z \leq w)$] and a greatest lower bound $inf\{x, y\}$. A lattice U is *complete* if it contains the least upper bound $sup(A)$ and the greatest lower bound $inf(A)$ for any subset $A \subseteq U$.

We define a data lattice U whose members are sets of tuples. The primitive domains of this data lattice are defined by a finite set S of scalar types, and the tuple space is the cross product of the sets of values of the scalar types in S. Define I_s as the set of values of a scalar $s \in S$ and define $X = \mathbf{X}\{I_s \mid s \in S\}$ as the cross product of these scalar value sets. Members of our data lattice are subsets of X. Figures 1 and 4 illustrate the order relations on the scalar value sets I_s, and Fig. 5 illustrates the order relation on the set X of tuples.

Members of U are subsets of X. However, there is a problem with defining an order relation between subsets of X that is consistent with the order relation on X and is also consistent with set containment. For example, if $a, b \in X$ and $a < b$, we would expect that $\{a\} < \{b\}$. Thus we might define an order relation between subsets of X by:

$$\forall A, B \subseteq X. (A \leq B \Leftrightarrow \forall a \in A. \exists b \in B. a \leq b) \tag{1}$$

However, given $a < b$, (1) implies that $\{b\} \leq \{a, b\}$ and $\{a, b\} \leq \{b\}$ are both true, which contradicts $\{b\} \neq \{a, b\}$. This problem can be resolved by restricting the lattice U to sets of tuples such every tuple is maximal in the set. That is, a set $A \subseteq X$ belongs to the lattice U if $a < b$ is not true for any pair $a, b \in A$. (Actually, the situation is a bit more complex - see [7] for the details.) The members of U are ordered by (1), as illustrated in Fig. 6, and form a complete lattice.

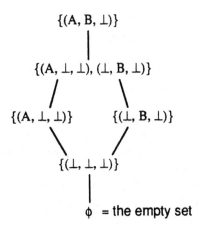

Figure 6. A few members of a data lattice U defined by three scalars, and the order relations between them.

To get an intuition of how data types are embedded in the lattices, consider a data lattice U defined from the three scalars *time*, *temperature* and *pressure*. Objects in the lattice U are sets of tuple of the form (*time*, *temperature*, *pressure*). We can define a tuple data type *struct*{*temperature*; *pressure*}. A data object of this type is a tuple of the form (*temperature*, *pressure*) and can be modeled as a set of tuples (actually, it is a set consisting of one tuple) in U with the form {($\perp$, *temperature*, *pressure*)}. This embeds the tuple data type in the lattice U, and Fig. 7 illustrates this embedding.

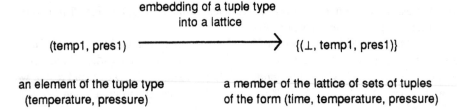

Figure 7. An embedding of a tuple type into a lattice of sets of tuples.

Similarly, we can embed array data types in the data lattice. For example, consider the same lattice U defined from the three scalars *time*, *temperature* and *pressure*, and consider an array data type (*array* [*time*] *of temperature*). A data object of this type consists of a set of pairs of (*time*, *temperature*). This array data object can be embedded in U as a set of tuples of the form (*time*, *temperature*, $\perp$). Figure 8 illustrates this embedding. The basic ideas presented in Figs. 7 and 8 can be combined to embed complex data types, defined as hierarchies of tuples and arrays, in data lattices. The details are explained in [6] and [7].

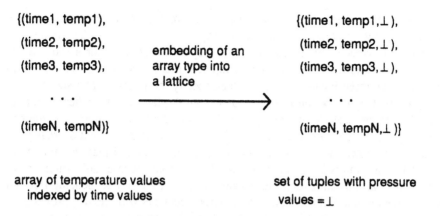

Figure 8. An embedding of an array type (a functional dependency between scalar types) into a lattice of sets of tuples.

If $x \in X$ is the embedding of a data object of a type $t \in T$, and if the scalar s does not occur in the definition of t, then the s values of all the tuples in x will be $\perp$. Also, in order to embed data objects in the data lattice U, we must restrict T to the set of data types t such that no scalar s occurs more than once in the definition of t. We note that, for each type in $t \in T$, the embedding of data objects of type t into U is an order embedding. This means that if a and b are objects of type t then $a \leq b$ if and only if $E_t(a) \leq E_t(b)$, where is E_t is the embedding of objects of type t.

Lattices and other kinds of ordered sets have played an important role in the denotational semantics of programming languages [2, 12, 13, 14, 15], and they can also play an important role in visualization.

3.3 Display Lattices

Our lattice structure can also be used to model displays. This is motivated by analogy with the display model of Bertin [1]. He defined a display as a set of graphical marks, and identified eight primitive variables of a graphical mark: two spatial coordinates of the mark in a graphical plane (he restricted his attention to static 2-D graphics), plus size, value, texture, color, orientation, and shape. Bertin defined diagrams, networks and maps as spatial aggregates of graphical marks. By defining a graphical mark as a tuple of its graphical primitive values, a display can be viewed as a set of tuples.

We define a finite set DS of display scalars that represent graphical primitives and we interpret a tuple of values of the display scalars as a graphical mark. Similar to the data lattice U, we define a display lattice V whose members are sets of tuples of values of display scalars.

We can define a display lattice for static 2-D displays using five continuous display scalars: two for image coordinates plus three for color components (e.g., red, green and blue). In this model, a display is a set of colored rectangles. The interval values of the image coordinate scalars in a tuple specify the size and location of the

49

rectangle on the screen, and the interval values of the color component scalars specify the range of colors used in the rectangle. This model can be extended to dynamic 3-D displays, by adding two more display scalars: one for a third image coordinate and another for indicating a graphical mark's location in an animation sequence. The three image coordinates then specify the locations and sizes of 3-D rectangles that must be projected onto a 2-D display screen (where multiple rectangles are projected to the same screen location, their colors must be combined according to some compositing algorithm). The values of the animation scalar are used to select tuples for display. At any instant during data display, an animation index takes an interval value, and only those tuples whose animation scalar intervals overlap this animation index value are displayed. By sequencing through values of the animation index, the display screen contents will change, providing a dynamic display. Figure 9 illustrates the role of the various display scalars in this display model.

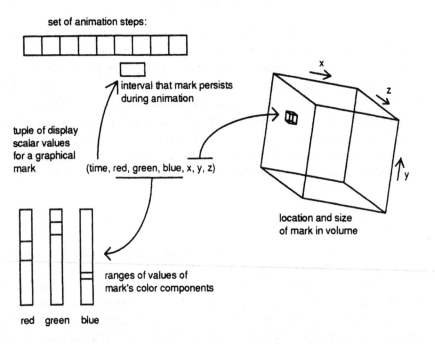

Figure 9. The roles of the display scalars in an animated 3-D display model.

Just like computer data objects, computer displays contain finite amounts of information. Pixels and voxels have limited resolution, colors are specified with limited precision, animation sequences consist of finite numbers of steps, etc. The lattice structure of V orders displays based on their information content.

Display models need not be limited to such primitive values as spatial coordinates, color components and animation indices. For example, consider a display model where a display consists of a set of graphical icons distributed at various locations in a display screen. This display model could be defined using three display scalars: a horizontal screen coordinate, a vertical screen coordinate, and an icon identifier. Then a single value of the icon identifier display scalar would represent the potentially complex shape of a graphical icon. Or, a set of display scalars may form the parameters of a complex graphical shape. For example, 2-D ellipses may be used as graphical marks, parameterized by five display scalars for their center coordinates, orientations, and the lengths of their major and minor axes.

3.4 Data Display as a Mapping From a Data Lattice to a Display Lattice

We model a display process as a function $D:U{\rightarrow}V$ that generates a display in V from any data object in U. Rather than defining such functions constructively, in terms of algorithms for calculating a display $D(u)$ from a data object $u \in U$, we will define conditions on D and study the class of functions satisfying those conditions. For our conditions, we interpret Mackinlay's *expressiveness* conditions [8] in the lattice context. These conditions require that a display encode all the facts about a data object, and only those facts. As we show in [6] and [7], we can interpret these conditions as:

Condition 1. $\forall P \in MON(U \rightarrow \{\bot, 1\})$.
$$\exists Q \in MON(\downarrow D(MAX(X)) \rightarrow \{\bot, 1\}). P = Q \circ D$$
Condition 2. $\forall u \in U. D(u) \in \downarrow D(X)$ and $\forall Q \in MON(\downarrow D(MAX(X)) \rightarrow \{\bot, 1\})$.
$$\exists P \in MON(U \rightarrow \{\bot, 1\}). Q = P \circ D^{-1}$$

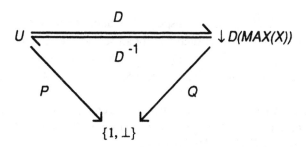

Figure 10. Expressiveness Conditions 1 and 2 interpreted as a commuting diagram. The conditions require that a display function D generate a one-to-one correspondence between the set of monotone functions P and the set of monotone functions Q, going both ways around the diagram.

Here $MON(U \rightarrow \{\bot, 1\})$ is the set of monotone functions from U to the set $\{\bot, 1\}$, $MAX(X)$ is the set of maximal tuples in X and thus the maximal element of U, and $\downarrow D(MAX(X))$ is the set of all displays in V less than the display of $MAX(X)$. A function P is monotone if $x \leq y$ implies $P(x) \leq P(y)$. We interpret facts about data objects as functions in $MON(U \rightarrow \{\bot, 1\})$ and we interpret fact about displays as functions in $MON(V \rightarrow \{\perp, 1\})$ (however, we limit this to displays less than the display of the maximal data object). Condition 1 says that for every P there is a Q that makes the diagram in Fig. 10 commute, and Condition 2 says that for every Q there is a P that makes the diagram commute.

We say that a function $D:U \rightarrow V$ is a *display function* if it satisfies Conditions 1 and 2. In [7] we prove:

Proposition 1. $D:U \rightarrow V$ is a display function if and only if it is a lattice isomorphism from U onto $\downarrow D(MAX(X))$, which is a sub-lattice of V.

The definition of *display function*, and the proof of this proposition, do not refer to the construction of data and display lattices in terms of scalars (although that construction motivates some of the discussion). The set $MAX(X)$ plays a role in the definition of *display function* and in our proofs, but only as the maximal element of the lattice U. Since any complete lattice has a maximal element (i.e., the *sup* of all its elements), this result is true for any pair of complete lattices U and V.

In the special case that the lattice U and V are constructed from scalars and display scalars as described in Sects. 3.2 and 3.3, display functions can be characterized by simple mappings from scalars to display scalars. Specifically, for a scalar $s \in S$, define an embedding $E_s:I_s \rightarrow U$ by $E_s(b) = (\perp,...,b,...,\perp)$ (this notation indicates that all components of the tuple are $\perp$ except b) and define $U_s = E_s(I_s) \subseteq U$. Similarly, for a display scalar $d \in DS$, define an embedding $E_d:I_d \rightarrow V$ by $E_d(b) = (\perp,...,b,...,\perp)$ and define $V_d = E_d(I_d) \subseteq V$. These embedded scalar objects play a special role in the structure of display functions. In [7] we prove:

Proposition 2. If $D:U \rightarrow V$ is a display function, then we can define a mapping $MAP_D:S \rightarrow POWER(DS)$ such that for all scalars $s \in S$ and all for $a \in U_s$, there is $d \in MAP_D(s)$ such that $D(a) \in V_d$. The values of D on all of U are determined by its values on the scalar embeddings U_s (see [7] for the details). Furthermore,
(a)   If s is discrete and $d \in MAP_D(s)$ then d is discrete,
(b)   If s is continuous then $MAP_D(s)$ contains a single continuous display scalar.
(c)   If $s \neq s'$ then $MAP_D(s) \cap MAP_D(s') = \phi$.

This tells us that display functions map scalars, which represent primitive variables like time and temperature, to display scalars, which represent graphical primitives like screen axes and color components. Most displays are already designed in this way, as, for example, a time series of temperatures may be displayed by mapping time to one axis and temperature to another as illustrated in Fig. 11. The remarkable thing is that Prop. 2 tells us that we don't have to take this way of designing displays as an assumption, but that it is a consequence of a more fundamental set of expressiveness conditions. Figure 12 in Sect. 4.4 provides a more detailed example of how a display function is defined by a set of mappings from scalars to display scalars.

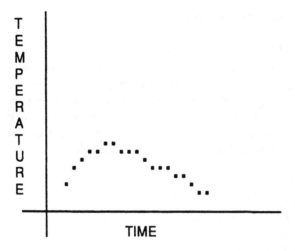

Figure 11. A time series displayed as a graph.

Display functions of the form $D:U{\rightarrow}V$ are polymorphic in that sense that they can be applied to data objects of any type in T. Furthermore, our lattice results show that we can define such functions in terms of a set of mappings from scalars to display scalars. Just as data flow systems define a user interface for controlling how data are displayed based on the abstraction of the rendering pipeline, we can define a user interface for controlling how data are displayed based on the abstraction of scalar mappings.

4. The VIS-AD Data Model

The VIS-AD (VISualization for Algorithm Development) system was designed to help scientists visualize their computations [5]. The system can be understood in terms of its data model, computational model and display model. The VIS-AD computational model is an imperative programming language of the type familiar to scientists (it is similar to C). The system's data model is based on the data lattice defined in Sect. 3.2. The data types and data objects of the lattice are just the types and objects of the VIS-AD programming language. Furthermore, metadata is integrated into this data model and plays a special role in the semantics of the programming language.

The biggest difference between the VIS-AD data model and the data lattice defined in Sect. 3.2 is the way that users define scalar types in S. A VIS-AD program defines scalar types as *real*, *real2d*, *real3d*, *int* or *string*. The *int* and *string* scalars are discrete scalars, and the *real* scalars are continuous scalars. The *real2d* and *real3d* scalars take pairs and triples of real intervals as values, and were included in the VIS-AD system to simplify the definition of spatial data types (e.g., the scalar *latitude_longitude* defined in the next section is a *real2d* scalar used as an index for 2-D image arrays).

53

4.1 Examples of User Defined Data Types

Users of VIS-AD can build types as arbitrary hierarchies of tuples and arrays, which provides the flexibility to adapt to scientific applications. VIS-AD's two- and three-dimensional real scalars make it easier to define types for spatial data like satellite images. The VIS-AD programming language provides a simple syntax for defining data types, as illustrated by the following examples taken from an algorithm for discriminating clouds in time series of multi-channel GOES (Geostationary Operational Environmental Satellite) images.

```
type ir_radiance = real;
type vis_radiance = real;
type latitude_longitude = real2d;
type time = real;
type image_region = int;
type count = int;
type goes_image =
  array [latitude_longitude] of
    structure {
      .im_ir = ir_radiance;
      .im_vis = vis_radiance;
    }
type goes_partition = array [image_region] of goes_image;
type goes_sequence = array [time] of goes_partition;
type histogram = array [ir_radiance] of count;
type histogram_partition =
  array [image_region] of
    structure {
      .hist_loc = latitude_longitude;
      .hist_hist = histogram;
    }
```

In these examples, a *goes_image* data object is an array of pixels indexed by *latitude_longitude* values, where each pixel is a structure containing infrared and visible radiances. A *goes_partition* object divides an image into regions, and includes a *goes_image* object for each value of *image_region*. A *goes_sequence* object is a *time* sequence of *goes_partition* objects. A *histogram* data object provides a frequency *count* of the number of occurrences of each *ir_radiance* value in an *image_region*, and a *histogram_partition* object associates a *histogram* object and a *latitude_longitude* value with each *image_region*.

4.2 Integrating Metadata with Programming Language Semantics

Unlike the situation in other programming languages, VIS-AD's arrays may be indexed by real values, or even by two- or three-dimensional real values.

This is because VIS-AD's array types are defined as finite samplings of functional relations from variables (i.e., from scalar types) to other data types. Thus metadata about the sampling of values is built into the semantics of the VIS-AD programming language. This has important consequences for the way that scientific data are manipulated and displayed. For example, an Earth satellite image is really a finite sampling of a continuous radiance field. If the pixels of an image are stored in an array in an ordinary language, the pixels are indexed in the array by integers, and the Earth locations of pixels must be managed separately. Thus the programming language has no information about the association between pixel values and their locations. However, if this satellite image is stored in a *goes_image* object, then the pixels are indexed with *latitude_longitude* values, and the programming language does have access to the locations of pixels. This enables the system to display a *goes_image* object in an Earth based frame of reference. If images from different sources (each with its own Earth projection) are overlaid in a display, the system can use the information about pixel locations to geographically register these images.

In the VIS-AD data model, all scalar values are managed in terms of finite samplings of infinite value sets. In addition to determining the values of array indices, this also determines the sampling and accuracy of values in arrays and tuples. For example, if a satellite sensor generates radiances as 8-bit quantities, then pixel values are really indices into a set of 256 samples of real radiance values. The scale of these real values may be a standard radiance, in which case the set of 256 values encodes the calibration of the satellite's sensor. Thus VIS-AD's management of sampling information can be used to encode satellite navigation and calibration information. Furthermore, sensor systems are fallible, so it is often the case the no value is defined for some pixels. In the VIS-AD data model, any data object or sub-object may take the special value *missing*, indicating the absence of information. Because missing values are part of the data model, they can be part of programming language semantics and display semantics.

We will use a satellite image example to illustrate how sampling information and missing data indicators are integrated with programming language semantics. In this example, we calculate the difference between images generated by different satellites. Let *goes_east*, *goes_west* and *goes_diff* be data objects of type *goes_image*, and let *loc* be a data object of type *latitude_longitude*. Assume that the *goes_east* and *goes_west* images were generated by GOES satellites at East and West stations over the U.S., so that they have different Earth perspectives. Then the following program calculates the difference between these images:

```
sample(goes_diff) = goes_east;
foreach (loc in goes_east) {
  goes_diff[loc] = goes_east[loc] - goes_west[loc];
}
```

The first line specifies that *goes_diff* will have the same sampling of array index values (i.e., of pixel locations) that *goes_east* has. The *foreach* statement provides a way to iterate over the elements of an array. In this case it iterates *loc* over the pixel locations of the *goes_east* image. The expression *goes_west[loc]* resamples the *goes_west* image at the Earth location in *loc*. If *loc* falls in an area where there are no *goes_west* pixels, then *goes_west[loc]* evaluates to *missing*. VIS-AD's arithmetic operations evaluate to *missing* if any of their operands are *missing*, so if *goes_west[loc]* is *missing* then the difference *goes_diff[loc]* is also set to *missing*.

The VIS-AD programming language provides vector operations, so this little program can also be expressed as:

```
goes_diff = goes_east - goes_west;
```

The resampling of *goes_west* index values, and the evaluation to *missing* where there are no *goes_west* pixels, are implicit in this statement.

Users can access metadata about sampling and missing data explicitly. For example, the statement:

```
foreach (loc in goes_east) { ... }
```

iterates *loc* over the samples of the *goes_east* array. Missing data indicators may be explicitly accessed using these statements:

```
if (goes_east == missing) { ... }
goes_east[loc].im_ir = missing;
```

However, because of the special role of metadata in the semantics of the VIS-AD programming language, users rarely need to do explicit calculations with this metadata.

The integration of sampling information and *missing* data is generic, rather than specific to images. Thus the techniques illustrated in this satellite image example can be applied to any user-defined data types. As our simple programming example shows, this can relieve users of the need to explicitly keep track of missing data, the need to manage the mapping from array index values to physical values, and the need to check bounds on array accesses. The key to these advantages is that metadata is integrated into the data semantics of a programming language.

We can summarize the kinds of metadata that are integrated with the VIS-AD data model. They are:

1. Sampling information; every value in a data object is taken from a finite sampling of primitive values.
2. Missing data indicators; any value or sub-object in a data object may take the special value *missing* which indicates the lack of information.
3. Names for values; every primitive value occurring in a data object has a scalar type, and hence a name (i.e., the name of the scalar type).

Because these kinds of metadata are integrated with the data model, they are part of the computational and display semantics of the VIS-AD system. Note that the VIS-AD programming language semantics do not integrate the accuracy information of interval values. However, this accuracy information could be integrated using interval arithmetic [10].

4.3 Other Types of Metadata

There are a great variety of kinds of metadata that scientists use to interpret their data. While some of these are integrated with the VIS-AD data model, the flexibility to define data types gives users a means to include other kinds of metadata in their data objects. For example, users of satellite images may want to manage the following kinds of information with their images:

1. Sensor identification. Satellites often have redundant sensors for measuring the same radiances, each with slightly different characteristics. Scientists sometimes need to know which sensor was used to generate a particular image.
2. Satellite sub-point. This is the Earth location (i.e., *latitude_longitude*) directly under the satellite, and is useful as a rough guide to image coverage.
3. Pixel scan rate. Images are often scanned over a significant time interval, and the scan rate in pixels per second can help assign precise times to pixel radiances.
4. Various measurements of the sensor systems, like voltages, temperatures and pressures. These are often used to diagnose problems with image quality.

We can create a new image type that includes these kinds of information, as follows:

```
type ir_radiance = real;
type vis_radiance = real;
type latitude_longitude = real2d;
type pixel_rate = real;
type sensor_id = string;
type temperature = real;
type voltage = real;
type annotated_goes_image =
  structure {
    .image_sensor = sensor_id;
    .image_subpoint = latitude_longitude;
    .image_pixel_rate = pixel_rate;
    .image_sensor_temp = temperature;
    .image_sensor_cathode = voltage;
```

```
.image_data =
  array [latitude_longitude] of
    structure {
      .im_ir = ir_radiance;
      .im_vis = vis_radiance;
    }
}
```

While these kinds of metadata are not part of the semantics of the programming language, they are part of data objects and can be accessed by users' programs.

4.4 Data Display in VIS-AD

The VIS-AD display model is similar to the display lattice V described in Sect. 3.3, and is realized as a set of interactive, animated, 3-D voxel volumes. It is defined in terms of a set of display scalars that include:

x, y and z coordinates of graphical marks in a 3-D volume
color values of graphical marks
a set of *contour* values; for each *contour* display scalar iso-surfaces and iso-lines are interpolated through the graphical marks in the 3-D volume
an *animation* value; graphical marks whose *animation* value overlaps an animation index are selected for display
a set of *selector* values, used to model abstract user control over display contents; the user selects a set of values for each *selector* display scalar, and only those graphical marks that overlap that set are displayed

Figure 12 illustrates the way that user's of VIS-AD control how their data types are displayed. An *image_sequence* data object is a time sequence of images with two spectral channels called *ir* (infrared) and *vis* (visible). Image pixels are indexed by pairs of real numbers specifying their Earth locations. Users define mappings from the scalar types of their application to the display scalar types that define the VIS-AD display model. The mappings indicated by arrows in Fig. 12 will cause an *image_sequence* data object to be displayed as an animated sequence of colored terrains, where the *ir* channel will determine the height of the terrain and the *vis* channel will determine its color. Users can interactively change the mappings from scalars to display scalars (e.g., change the mappings in Fig. 12 by mapping *ir* to *color* and mapping *time* to y - this will create a time series of images stacked up along the y axis). They can also interactively control the functions by which scalar values determine display scalar values (e.g., by adjusting color tables for the mapping of *vis* to *color* in Fig. 12). Data objects may be displayed according to multiple sets of mappings simultaneously.

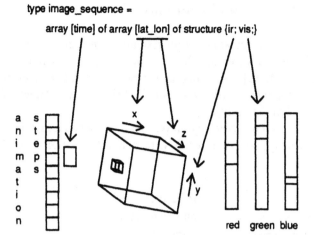

Figure 12. Users of VIS-AD control how data are displayed by defining mappings from the scalar types used to define complex data types to the display scalars used to define the VIS-AD display model.

The interface for controlling displays, consisting of the definitions of scalar mappings, is de-coupled from the VIS-AD programming language. This is important, because it allows users to control the display of their data objects without embedding explicit calls to display functions in their programs.

The VIS-AD system is available by anonymous ftp from iris.ssec.wisc.edu (144.92.108.63) in the pub/visad directory. The README file contains instructions for retrieving and installing the system.

5. Extending Data Lattices to More Complex Data Models

In Sect. 3.4 we described how a function $D:U{\rightarrow}V$ satisfying the expressiveness conditions must be a lattice isomorphism. Although we motivated this result in the context of a specific lattice structure for U and V (i.e., their members are sets of tuples of scalar values), the proof of this result only depends on U and V being complete lattices. Thus it is natural to seek to apply this result to other lattice structures for data and display models. The motive for new lattice structures must be new data models, since display models are themselves motivated by the need to visualize data. The data model defined in Sect. 3 includes tuples and arrays as ways of aggregating data. We will describe the issues involved in extending data lattices to data types defined by recursive domain equations, to abstract data types, and to the object classes of object-oriented programming languages. This discussions of this section are somewhat speculative.

5.1 Recursive Data Types Definitions

The denotational semantics of programming languages provides techniques for defining ordered sets whose members are the values of programming language expressions [4, 13, 14, 15]. An important topic of denotational semantics is the study of *recursive domain equations*, which define *cpos* (defined in the next paragraph) in terms of themselves.

First, we present some definitions used in denotational semantics. A *partially ordered set (poset)* is a set D with a binary relation $\leq$ on D such that, $\forall x, y, z \in D$

$$x \leq x \qquad \qquad \text{"reflexive"}$$
$$x \leq y \,\&\, y \leq x \Rightarrow x = y \qquad \text{"anti-symmetric"}$$
$$x \leq y \,\&\, y \leq z \Rightarrow x \leq z \qquad \text{"transitive"}$$

A subset $M \subseteq D$ is *directed* if, for every finite subset $A \subseteq M$, there is an $x \in M$ such that $\forall y \in A.\ y \leq x$. A *poset* D is *complete* (and called a *cpo*) if every directed subset $M \subseteq D$ has a least upper bound $sup(M)$ and if there is a least element $\perp \in D$ (i.e., $\forall y \in D.\ \perp \leq y$). If D and E are *posets*, a function $f:D \to E$ is *monotone* if $\forall x, y \in D.\ x \leq y \Rightarrow f(x) \leq f(y)$. A function $f:D \to E$ is *continuous* if it is monotone and if $f(inf(M)) = inf(f(M))$ for all directed $M \subseteq D$. If D and E are *cpos*, a pair of continuous functions $f:D \to E$ and $g:E \to D$ are a *retraction pair* if $g \circ f \leq id_D$ and $f \circ g = id_E$. The function g is called an *embedding*, and f is called a *projection*.

We take the following example of a recursive domain equation from [12]. A data type for a binary tree may be defined by:

$$Bintree = (Data + (Data \times Bintree \times Bintree))_{\perp} \qquad (2)$$

Here "+", "$\times$" and "$(.)_{\perp}$" are type construction operators similar to the tuple and array operators we discussed in Sect. 3.1. The "+" operator denotes a type that is a choice between two other types (this is similar to the *union* type constructor in the C language), "$\times$" denotes a type that is a cross product of other types (this is essentially the same as our tuple operator, so that $(Data \times Bintree \times Bintree)$ is a 3-tuple), and the "$\perp$" subscript indicates a type that adds a new least element $\perp$ to the values of another type. Equation (2) defines a data type called *Bintree*, and says that a *Bintree* data object is either $\perp$, a data object of type *Data*, or a 3-tuple consisting of a data object of type *Data* and two data objects of type *Bintree*. Intuitively, a data object of type *Bintree* is either missing, a leaf node with a data value, or a non-leaf node with a data value and two child nodes.

The obvious way to implement binary trees in a common programming language is to define a record or structure for a node of the tree, and to include two pointers to other tree nodes in that record or structure. In general, the self references in recursive type definitions can be implemented as pointers. Thus, recursive domain equations correspond to defining data types with pointers.

5.1.1 The Inverse Limit Construction

The equality in a recursive domain equation is really an isomorphism. As explained quite clearly by Schmidt in [12], these equation may be solved by the *inverse limit construction*. This construction starts with $Bintree_0 = \{\perp\}$, then applies (2) repeatedly to get

$$Bintree_1 = (Data + (Data \times Bintree_0 \times Bintree_0))_\perp$$
$$Bintree_2 = (Data + (Data \times Bintree_1 \times Bintree_1))_\perp$$

etc.

The construction also specifies a retraction pair $(g_i, f_i):Bintree_i \leftrightarrow Bintree_{i+1}$ for all i, such that g_i embeds $Bintree_i$ into $Bintree_{i+1}$ and f_i projects $Bintree_{i+1}$ onto $Bintree_i$. Then $Bintree$ is the set of all infinite tuples of the form $(t_0, t_1, t_2, ...)$ such that $t_i = f_i(t_{i+1})$ for all i. It can be shown that $Bintree$ is isomorphic with $(Data + (Data \times Bintree \times Bintree))_\perp$, and thus "solves" the recursive domain equation.

The order relation on the infinite tuples in $Bintree$ is defined element-wise, just like the order relation on finite tuples defined in Sect. 3.1, and $Bintree$ is a *cpo*. We note that the inverse limit construction can also be applied to solve sets of simultaneous domain equations.

One way of extending our data lattices would be to show how to apply the inverse limit construction to recursive equations involving our tuple and array type constructors. Our tuple constructor is equivalent to the cross product operator "$\times$". While our array constructor is similar to the function space operator "$\rightarrow$" used in denotational semantics, it is not the same. $(A \rightarrow B)$ defines the set of all functions from A to B, while our array constructor (*array* $[A]$ *of* B) defines the set of functions from finite subsets of A to B. Thus we would need to show how to apply the inverse limit construction to equations involving the constructor (*array* $[A]$ *of* B). The *cpos* defined by the inverse limit construction are generally not lattices, but can always be embedded in complete lattices. Specifically, the Dedekind-MacNeille completion, described in [2], shows that for any partially ordered set A, there is always a complete lattice U such that there is an order embedding of A into U.

Note that the set of *Bintree* objects defined by the inverse limit construction includes infinite trees. This is because this set is complete and infinite trees are limits of infinite sequences of finite trees. The development of denotational semantics was largely motivated by the need to address non-terminating computations (the unsolvability of the halting problem showed that there was no way to separate terminating from non-terminating computations), and non-terminating computations may produce infinite trees as their values. Since our result that display functions are lattice isomorphisms depends on the assumption that data and display lattices are complete, it is likely that any extension of our data lattice to include solutions of recursive domain equations must include infinite data objects.

The inverse limit construction defines the set of data objects of a particular data type that solves a particular recursive domain equation. However, our approach in Sect. 3.2 was to define a large lattice that contained data objects of many different data types. It would be useful to continue this approach, by defining a lattice that includes all data types that can be constructed from our scalar types as tuples, arrays, and solutions of recursive domain equations. This is the subject of Sect. 5.1.2.

5.1.2 Universal Domains

A fundamental result of the theory of ordered sets is the *fixed point theorem*, which says that, for any *cpo* D and any continuous function $f:D \to D$, there is *fix(f)* $\in D$ such that $f(fix(f)) = fix(f)$ (i.e., *fix(f)* is a fixed point of f) and such that *fix(f)* is less than any other fixed point of f.

Scott developed an elegant way to solve recursive domain equations by applying the fixed point theorem [4, 14]. In a sense, the solution of a recursive domain equation is just a fixed point of a function that operates on *cpos*. Scott defined a *universal domain* U and a set R of retracts of U (this may be the set of all retracts on U, the set of projections, the set of finitary projections, the set of closures, or the set of finitary closures - note that these terms are defined in [7]). Then he showed that a set OP of type construction operators (these operators build *cpo's* from other *cpo's*) can be represented by continuous functions over R, in the sense that for $o \in OP$ there is a continuous function f on R that makes the diagram in Fig. 13 commute.

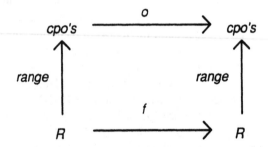

Figure 13. The type construction operator o is represented by function f.

Note that $range(w) = \{w(u) \mid u \in U\}$. For unary $o \in OP$ this is $range(f(w)) = o(range(w))$. Similar expressions hold for multiary operators in OP. Then, for any recursive domain equation $D = O(D)$ where O is composed from operators in OP, there is a continuous function $F:R \to R$ that represents O. By the fixed point theorem, F will have a least fixed point *fix(F)*, and $O(range(fix(F))) =$

range(F(fix(F))) = *range(fix(F))*, so *range(fix(F))* is a *cpo* satisfying the recursive domain equation $D = O(D)$. The solution of any domain equation (or any set of simultaneous domain equations) involving the type construction operators in *OP* will be a *cpo* that is a subset of the universal domain *U*. Thus this approach is similar to the way that the data types of our data model define sets of data objects that are embedded in a single data lattice.

Universal domains and representations have been defined for sets *OP* that include most of the type constructors used in denotational semantics, including "+", "×", "→", and "(.)⊥". In order to apply universal domains to extend our data model to include recursively defined types, we would need to show how our tuple and array type constructors can be represented over some universal domain.

A common example of a universal domain is the set *POWER(N)*, which is just the set of all subsets of the natural numbers **N** (i.e., non-negative integers). *POWER(N)* is a complete lattice. However, it does not include natural embeddings of our scalar data objects. Furthermore, the embeddings of mathematical types into universal domains, as defined by papers in denotational semantics, are not suitable for our display theory. For example, a simple integer and a function from integers to integers are embedded to the same member of *POWER(N)*. A display function applied to the lattice *POWER(N)*, with these embeddings, would produce the same display for the integer and the function from integers to integers. Since the goal of visualization is to communicate information rather than to make it obscure, other embeddings of types into universal domains must be developed. Specifically, an extension of our display theory to recursively defined data types should include a universal domain with natural embeddings of our scalar data types, and should include representations of our tuple and array type constructors that will produce natural embeddings of constructed types.

5.1.3 Display of Recursively Defined Data Types

Since the goal of visualization is to communicate the information content of data to users, an extension of our theory must focus on the data lattice *U*. However, since a display function *D* is a lattice isomorphism of *U* onto a sub-lattice *V*, we should be able to say some things about the structure of *V*. If a subset $A \subseteq U$ is the solution of a recursive domain equation, then $D(A) \subseteq V$ is isomorphic to *A* and must itself be a solution of the recursive domain equation.

For example, if the set *A* is the solution of (2) for *Bintree*, then the set *D(A)* must also solve this equation. The isomorphism provides a definition of the operators "+", "×" and "(.)⊥" in *D(A)* and thus also defines a relation between objects and their "subtree" objects in *D(A)*. The isomorphism does not tell us how to interpret these operators and relations in a graphical display, but it does tell us that such a logical structure exists. Given the complexity of this structure, it seems likely that display objects in *D(A)* will be interpreted using some graphical equivalent of the pointers that we use to implement data objects in *A*.

Two graphical analogs of pointers come to mind immediately:

1. Diagrams. Here icons represent nodes in data objects, and lines between icons represent pointers.
2. Hypertext links. Here the contents of a window represents one or more nodes in a data object, and an icon embedded in that window represents an interactive link to another node or set of nodes. That is, if the user selects the icon (say by a mouse point and click), new window contents appear depicting whatever the icon points at.

In order to extend our display theory to data types defined with recursive domain equations, we need to extend our display lattice V to include these graphical interpretations of pointers. The most interesting problem is to find a way to do this that produces a display lattice complex enough to be isomorphic to a universal domain as described in Sect. 5.1.2.

5.2 Abstract Data Types and Object Classes

Abstract data types and the object classes of object-oriented programming are ways of defining data types that hide the internal structures of data objects from the programs that use those data objects. Definitions of abstract data types and object classes include definitions of *member functions* for basic operations on data objects. Data objects are accessed by applying these member functions, rather than by selecting their primitive sub-objects. In fact, the hidden implementation of data objects may not include sub-objects at all, but may be purely functional. For example, an array data object may be implemented either by explicitly storing elements of the array, or by a function for computing the elements of the array as they are accessed.

5.2.1 Abstract Data Types

In an algebraic setting [17], abstract data types are specified by a signature $\Sigma = (T, F)$ and a set of logical conditions E. T is a set of types and F is a set of member functions among the types in T (that is, the types of the member functions, and the numbers and types of their arguments, are specified). E is a set of first order statements involving quantifiers, equality, the member functions of F, and variables with types in T. It is undecidable whether the statements in E are satisfiable (i.e., no algorithm exists which can tell, for given E, whether any set of data objects and functions satisfy E), so there are no compilers that produce implementations from T, F and E. However, abstract data types are used as the basis of programming methods. System designers use heuristic methods to derive conditions in E by analyzing system requirements, and use these conditions as a guide for implementing the functions in F [9].

Because of the generality of the abstract data type formalism, it can be used to express our lattice theory of display. To see this, define $T_{LAT} = \{U, V\}$, $F_{LAT} = \{inf_U:U\times U\rightarrow U, sup_U:U\times U\rightarrow U, inf_V:V\times V\rightarrow V, sup_V:V\times V\rightarrow V, D:U\rightarrow V\}$ and $E_{LAT} =$

{lattice axioms for U and V, expressiveness conditions on D}. That is, the data types of T_{LAT} are the data and display lattices U and V, the functions in F_{LAT} are the lattice operations on U and V plus the display function D, and the logical conditions in E_{LAT} are the axioms defining U and V as lattices plus the expressiveness conditions. Expressiveness Conditions 1 and 2, as defined in Sect. 3.4, quantify over $MON(U \rightarrow \{\perp, 1\})$ and are thus second order statements whereas E_{LAT} is supposed to consist of first order statements. However, as shown by Prop. 1, Conditions 1 and 2 are equivalent to conditions that can be expressed as first order statements. There are obviously many different sets of lattice U and V satisfying the abstract data type definition in T_{LAT}, F_{LAT} and E_{LAT}.

In Sect. 5.2.3 we will discuss the issues involved with extending our lattice theory to display the data objects of abstract data types.

5.2.2 Object Classes

Like abstract data types, the object classes of object-oriented programming languages define access to data objects in terms of a set of member functions. However, rather than defining logical conditions that the member functions must satisfy, object classes define these functions explicitly as programs. An *object class* in C++ defines members as both data structures and functions, which are divided into private and public parts [3]. The private members are only accessible from member functions defined as part of the class (i.e., they are not accessible from outside the class definition).

In addition to hiding the implementation of object classes, object-oriented languages provide two mechanisms called polymorphism and inheritance that provide a novel style of programming compared to traditional procedural languages. *Polymorphism* means that the same member function name may be defined in the public parts of multiple object classes. Calls to member functions are bound to the appropriate function definitions at run time, determined by the classes of the objects passed as arguments to the functions. *Inheritance* allows an object class to be defined in terms of another. The new class "inherits" the members of the old class, except where those data members are explicitly redefined.

Object-oriented visualization systems define polymorphic display functions. These systems partition their data models into a number of object classes, and their polymorphic display functions may be called to display any data object in their data models. Thus the object oriented approach and our lattice approach both define display functions that can be applied to data objects of any type. However, where the object oriented visualization systems require constructive definitions of display functions as programs, our approach defines data and display lattices and defines display functions as any function satisfying the expressiveness conditions. Thus it is still interesting to investigate how our lattice theory can be extended to the object classes of an object-oriented language.

The private and public members of class definitions include data structures. These may be displayed using the techniques that we developed in Sect. 3, and the techniques for displaying recursively defined data types suggested in

Sect. 5.1. However, this approach does not provide a systematic way to display data objects defined by classes, since class definitions include functions as well as data structures. In the next section we will discuss issues involved in extending our lattice model of display to the member functions of object classes.

5.2.3 Lattice Models for Abstract Data Types and Object Classes

Because of the similarity between abstract data types and object classes, we will discuss them together, using the notation of abstract data types. We let T denote a set of types and let F denote a set of member functions. The types in T may be abstract data types or may be object classes, and the functions in F may be defined by a set E of logical conditions or by a set of programs. The important point is that the functions in F define relations among data objects, and that these relations take the place of a definition of data objects in terms of their internal structure. In fact, we could say that the relations defined by functions in F are a generalization of the relations between objects and their sub-objects that define the internal structures of data objects. In Sect. 3.1 we defined tuple objects in terms of their element sub-objects, and we defined array objects in terms of their domain and range sub-objects. These relations between objects and their sub-objects are special cases of relations between objects expressed by member functions.

Let A be the union of the sets of data objects of all types in T. We could give A the discrete order (i.e., no object is greater than any other object), but this would lead to a very boring theory of data display. In order to define a more interesting order relation on A, we can start with the data lattice that we defined in Sect. 3.2 (here we call it U_0). If T is a set of abstract data types, then we let the objects of U_0 serve as constants in the logical conditions of E. If T is a set of object classes, then we take the continuous and discrete scalar types of U_0 as the primitive values of an object oriented programming language.

If we also assume that the member function in F are monotone, then we can use these functions to derive order relations between objects in A from the order relations between objects in U_0. However, there is no guarantee that there is a order relation on A that is consistent with the assumption that the functions in F are monotone. For example, while it is easy to define monotone arithmetic operators on the scalar types of U_0, there is no reasonable way to define monotone logical and comparison operators on the scalar types of U_0 (we run into inconsistencies assuming either that *false* $\le$ *true* or that *true* and *false* are not ordered). This suggests that a monotonicity assumption is a severe restriction on the member functions in F.

However, in order to define an interesting order condition on A we may assume that member functions are monotone. In this case, we need to verify that the monotone functions of F are consistent with an order relation on A, although this appears to be a difficult problem. If T is a set of object classes, and if member functions are implemented in a programming language that includes logical and comparison operators, then it is generally undecidable whether functions defined among the objects of U_0 are monotone. However, we may be able to design a restricted programming language for member functions that allows us to verify that monotone member functions are consistent with an order relation on A. If T is a set of abstract data types, then the monotonicity requirement must be added to E as a set of logical conditions on the member functions in F (along with conditions that define order relations on the types in T). This may cause a set of satisfiable conditions to become unsatisfiable, and it is generally undecidable whether the addition of monotonicity conditions causes a set E of conditions to become unsatisfiable. Of course, this situation is no worse than without monotonicity assumption, since the question of whether a set of logical conditions is satisfiable is generally undecidable.

Given an ordered set A of data objects (the union of the sets of data objects of each type in T), we can use the Dedekind-MacNeille completion to embed A in a complete lattice U. In order to apply our display theory we would need to construct a display lattice V such that isomorphisms from U onto sub-lattices of V exist, and develop interpretations of display objects in V in terms of a physical display device. Since the display function $D:U{\to}V$ is an isomorphism between the set of data objects and a subset of the set of display objects, and since the relations between data objects expressed by the member functions in F (and subject to the logical conditions in E) are a generalization of the hierarchical relations between objects and sub-objects in the data model defined in Sect. 3.1, it is natural to seek an interpretation of display objects in terms of relations between display objects that generalizes the relation between display objects and graphical marks as described in Sect. 3.3. For example, we may represent data objects by icons in a display, and let users interactively explore the relations between those icons as defined by the functions in F. Finding a systematic way to interpret displays of abstract data types seems like a very open ended and interesting problem.

It is interesting to note that in the case of abstract data types, we can use the generality of the framework to add our display model to an existing set of abstract data types defined by T, F and E. Take T_{LAT}, F_{LAT} and E_{LAT} as defined in 5.2.1, and define

$$T' = T \cup T_{LAT}$$
$$F' = F \cup F_{LAT} \cup \{\text{embeddings of the types in } T \text{ into } U\}$$
$$E' = E \cup E_{LAT} \cup \{\text{monotonicity conditions on the embeddings}$$
$$\text{from } T \text{ into } U\}$$

Of course, there is no algorithm for deciding if the conditions in E' are satisfiable or for constructing the lattice U and V if they are. Furthermore, this tells us nothing about how display objects in V are interpreted in terms of a physical display device.

6. Conclusions

The design of the VIS-AD data model is tightly integrated with a computational model and a display model. The result is a data model whose data objects can be uniformly visualized using polymorphic display functions, and which has the flexibility to adapt to scientists' computations. Several kinds of metadata are integrated with this data model, providing a novel and useful programming language semantics, and also providing the capability to display multiple data objects in common frames of reference.

The VIS-AD data model is based on lattices. These lattices may be applied to models of both data and displays. This provides an interesting context for analyzing visualization processes as functions from data lattices to display lattices. There are also interesting prospects for extending the lattice theory of visualization to more complex data models that involve recursively defined data types, abstract data types, and the object classes of object oriented programming languages.

References

[1]   Bertin, J., 1983; Semiology of Graphics. W. J. Berg, Jr. University of Wisconsin Press.

[2]   Davey, B. A. and H. A. Priestly, 1990; Introduction to Lattices and Order. Cambridge University Press.

[3]   Gorlen, K. E., S. M. Orlow and P. S. Plexico, 1990; Data Abstraction and Object-Oriented Programming in C++. John Wiley & Sons.

[4]   Gunter, C. A. and Scott, D. S., 1990; Semantic domains. In the Handbook of Theoretical Computer Science, Vol. B., J. van Leeuwen ed., The MIT Press/Elsevier, 633-674.

[5]   Hibbard, W., C. Dyer and B. Paul, 1992; Display of scientific data structures for algorithm visualization. Visualization '92, Boston, IEEE, 139-146.

[6]   Hibbard, W., C. Dyer and B. Paul, 1993; A lattice theory of data display. Submitted to IEEE Visualization '94.

[7]   Hibbard, W. L., and C. R. Dyer, 1994; A lattice theory of data display. Tech. Rep. # 1226, Computer Sciences Department, University of Wisconsin-Madison. Also available as compressed postscript files by anonymous ftp from iris.ssec.wisc.edu (144.92.108.63) in the pub/lattice directory.

[8]   Mackinlay, J., 1986; Automating the design of graphical presentations of relational information; ACM Transactions on Graphics, 5(2), 110-141.

[9]   Mitchell, R., 1992; Abstract Data Types and Modula-2: a Worked Example of Design Using Data Abstraction. Prentice Hall.

[10]   Moore, R. E., 1966; Interval Analysis. Prentice Hall.

[11]   Robertson, P. K., R. A. Earnshaw, D. Thalman, M. Grave, J. Gallup and E. M. De Jong, 1994; Research issues in the foundations of visualization. Computer Graphics and Applications 14(2), 73-76.

[12]   Schmidt, D. A., 1986; Denotational Semantics. Wm.C.Brown.

[13]   Scott, D. S., 1971; The lattice of flow diagrams. In Symposium on Semantics of Algorithmic Languages, E. Engler. ed. Springer-Verlag, 311-366.

[14]   Scott, D. S., 1976; Data types as lattices. Siam J. Comput., 5(3), 522-587.

[15]   Scott, D. S., 1982; Lectures on a mathematical theory of computation, in: M. Broy and G. Schmidt, eds., *Theoretical Foundations of Programming*

Methodology, NATO Advanced Study Institutes Series (Reidel, Dordrecht, 1982) 145-292.

[16] Treinish, L. A., 1991; SIGGRAPH '90 workshop report: data structure and access software for scientific visualization. Computer Graphics 25(2), 104-118.

[17] Wirsig, M., 1990; Algebraic specification. In the Handbook of Theoretical Computer Science, Vol. B., J. van Leeuwen ed., The MIT Press/Elsevier, 675-788.

An Extended Schema Model for Scientific Data

David T. Kao, R. Daniel Bergeron, Ted M. Sparr*

Department of Computer Science**, University of New Hampshire, New Hampshire 03824, U.S.A.

Abstract. The absence of a uniform and comprehensive representation for complex scientific data makes the adaptation of database technology to multidisciplinary research projects difficult. In this paper, we clarify the taxonomy of data representations required for scientific database systems. Then, based on our proposed scientific database environment, we present a scientific data abstraction at the conceptual level, a *schema model for scientific data*. This schema model allows us to store and manipulate scientific data in a uniform way independent of the implementation data model. We believe that more information has to be maintained as metadata for scientific data analysis than in statistical and commercial databases. Clearly, metadata constitutes an important part of our schema model. As part of the schema model, we provide an operational definition for metadata. This definition enables us to focus on the complex relationship between data and metadata.

1 Introduction

Interrelationships in scientific data are fundamentally more implicit and difficult to capture than relationships in most other database applications. In other areas, relationships are known (or assumed) in advance and expressed directly as metadata before data are acquired. In contrast, a scientific database system must manage data before its semantic structure is well understood [Spar93]. Some interrelationships among data parameters may be known in advance, but many others are known only qualitatively or not at all. In fact, the objective of Exploratory Data Analysis [Tuke77] is to discover, quantify and further validate them.

Traditionally, such data is handled in an *ad hoc* manner. Virtually every research project ends up employing a unique data representation, which in turn causes highly specialized and nonportable analysis programs to be developed. Clearly, to support the fast-growing area of multidisciplinary research, a flexible

---

* Authors' e-mail addresses: David T. Kao, dtk@cs.unh.edu; R. Daniel Bergeron, rdb@cs.unh.edu; Ted M. Sparr, tms@cs.unh.edu.

** The Scientific Database Research Project at the University of New Hampshire is supported by the National Science Foundation under grant IRI-9117153.

and better integrated environment is needed. This environment should incorporate database support with reusable data analysis functions. This kind of environment is known as a *scientific database system* in the literature.

Over the past several years there have been several notable attempts towards defining a common physical representation for scientific and engineering data: CDF, HDF, NetCDF, to name a few [Camp92]. In order to have an integrated environment to support collaborative research, it is essential to have a scientific database that includes a comprehensive model for representing the syntax and semantics of scientific data.

This problem has to be solved in a top-down fashion. There is little use in defining data representations at lower levels unless the data representations at higher levels are well-defined and understood. In this paper, we present a taxonomy for the data representations at all levels in scientific databases. Then, based on our proposed scientific database system [Spar93], we provide a scientific data representation at the conceptual level; we call it a *schema model for scientific data*. Our ultimate goal is to define a complete schema model for storing various forms of scientific data in such a way that a set of well-defined analysis operations can be applied coherently.

This research goes beyond the work in low-level common data interchange standards such as Common Data Format (CDF) developed at NASA [Goug88, Trei87], Hierarchical Data Format (HDF) developed at NCSA [NCS89], and Network Common Data Form (NetCDF) of the Unidata Program Center [Rew90].

2 Terminology

The term *repository data* refers to data as captured for entry into a database system. Transformation from original raw data to repository data is typically performed by a collecting agency before publication and distribution. Transformations can include digitizing, verification, sampling, summarizing, normalizing, or the attachment of uncertainty or accuracy information.

We assume that all scientific data are subject to further analysis, otherwise there is little reason to retain it. The nature of such subsequent analysis frequently determines what data should be retained and whether a particular representational format is adequate [Fren90].

All scientific data in the database which is not repository data is *derived data*. Derived data results from further analytical transformation of scientific data (both repository and derived), such as the application of analysis techniques. Derivation can also include the addition of semantic structure and relationships. Derived data may simply be a refined form of the original data or it can be in an entirely different form. Examples of derived data include subsets of the original data, graphs, images, statistics, and formulas or rules depicting interparameter relationships.

We use the term *data set* to represent a set of scientific data treated as a unit during analysis. A data set normally represents a collection of individual observations. The term *parameter* refers to a measurement taken as part of a data observation. An *attribute* is the corresponding database property (i.e., the name and value of a characteristic of a database entity representing a data observation).

Given two data sets D and D', we define a binary relation *derived-from* using the notation $\leq_d$ as follows:

$$D' \leq_d D \iff D' \text{ is derived from } D$$

In other words, D' is a *derived* data set of D and D is a *source* data set of D'. It is clear that $\leq_d$ is both transitive and antisymmetric. Further, we make $\leq_d$ reflexive by defining any data set D as its own derived data. With this semantic extension, $\leq_d$ defines a partial ordering and thus a collection of data sets is a partially ordered set with respect to $\leq_d$.

Metadata is data about data. Virtually anything that describes data can be considered as metadata. It includes the information required for identification, access, management, analysis, and validation of the data. Metadata must remain attached to the data or the data becomes unusable [Lund84, Fren90]. As implemented in most relational database systems, the schemas of relations are treated as metadata, while the information stored in relations is treated as data.

In scientific data analysis, more information has to be kept and maintained as metadata. Further, there are times when metadata becomes the object of interest, the object to be analyzed and explored. In those situations, the metadata also has to be treated as data.

3   Taxonomy of Data Representations

Before we examine the taxonomy of data representations in a scientific database, it is worthwhile to look at the taxonomy of data representations in a conventional database system.

A *data model* is a collection of conceptual tools for describing data, relationships, semantics, and constraints [Kort86]. We can categorize data models by the types of concepts they provide to describe the data abstraction. Traditional database architecture partitions data models into three different levels of abstraction: *conceptual, implementation,* and *physical* [Elma89].

Conceptual data models provide concepts that are close to the way users perceive data. They provide a high-level abstraction of the real world entities. The *Entity-Relationship (ER) model* and *enhanced-ER (EER) model* are the two most widely used conceptual data models. A *conceptual schema* is the description of a database at the conceptual level using a particular conceptual data model. For instance, a STUDENT database for managing student information can be defined as a conceptual schema in any conceptual data model. It can be defined as an ER diagram based on the ER model or, for example, as an EER diagram based on the EER model.

Physical data models provide concepts that describe the low level details of how data is stored in the computer. Physical data models are usually invisible to database users. It is the database system designer's job to define the physical data model and how it is implemented. Common physical data models include *B-tree*, B^+-*tree*, B^*-*tree*, *R-tree*, etc.

Between the two extremes is a class of *implementation data models*, which provide concepts at an intermediate level of abstraction still understandable by users but with enough details to define the way data is logically organized within the computer. Common implementation data models include *relational*, *network*, *hierarchical*, and *object-oriented*. An *implementation schema* is the description of a database at the implementation level using a particular implementation data model. For instance, given a conceptual schema (in either the ER or EER model) of the STUDENT database, the implementation schema can be defined as a relational schema in the relational model or an object-oriented schema in the object-oriented model.

It is important to understand the difference and relationship between data models and schemas at conceptual and implementation levels. For instance, the STUDENT database of the University of New Hampshire might share the same conceptual schema with the STUDENT database of Dartmouth College. Although the two STUDENT databases are the same at the conceptual level, chances are that they do not have the same implementation schema, even for two database systems using the same implementation data model. There might be differences between the two at the implementation level which can not be distinguished at the conceptual level.

Clearly, in a scientific database system each database might have its own conceptual schema. However, in order to support multidisciplinary scientific research and fully utilize the analysis functions provided by the scientific database, it is essential to have a uniform functionalities specification for conceptual schemas of various scientific data sets. We call such a specification a *schema model of scientific data*. A schema model is not a conceptual data model in traditional database terminology. In fact it is independent of conceptual data models. It describes the look and feel as well as the capabilities that a conceptual schema supports.

An analogy can be drawn from the relationship between programs and programming languages. We can think of a conceptual data model as a kind of programming language. Then a conceptual schema is just a program written in some particular programming language. In this case, a schema model is just a program specification. It specifies the function a program has to perform as well as the way it interacts with users. In object-oriented terminology, the schema model is just a class definition while each conceptual schema is an instantiation of the schema model.

With such a schema model, different kinds of scientific data sets can be stored and manipulated in the scientific database in a coherent way. The focus of this paper is to define a schema model which is suitable for data storage and analysis in the scientific database system described in the next section.

4 Scientific Database Systems

Most existing database systems are targeted toward commercial data processing. They lack appropriate built-in analysis operators for analyzing the kinds of data encountered in scientific applications [Gent84]. The common approach used now is to have the database system export data for use by external analysis utilities. Once the analysis is done, the database system can import the derived data from those utilities. However, since there is no standard data format, the data conversion process can be very time-consuming and error-prone. More importantly, in this paradigm it is almost impossible to collect and utilize the metadata generated during the analysis process, because the database system lacks the capability to understand the relationship between source and derived data.

Extant statistical database systems also do not provide a solution. While they provide analytical capability, they lack the rich metadata necessary [Dint84]. There is a need for an integrated system which can solve such data management and analysis problems.

Recently *dataflow visualization systems* have become increasingly popular, thanks to their efficiency in software sharing, module reuse, extensibility, and flexibility. Dataflow visualization systems like AVS from AVS [Upso89, AVS92], IRIS Explorer from SGI [IRIS92], and Data Explorer from IBM [Luca92, IBM91, IBM92, Habe91] are used extensively in all aspects of science and engineering. In fact, dataflow visualization systems have capacity well beyond scientific visualization and have the potential to serve as the base for complete, integrated, interactive, and distributed approaches to the computation, manipulation, and analysis of all types of data [Riba92]. Through user-defined modules, it is fairly easy to incorporate existing analysis tools into dataflow visualization systems. This can be done either by modifying the source code of analysis tools and converting them into modules, or by invoking analysis tools from modules.

We envision the tremendous flexibility and power that can be acquired by the combination of scientific database systems with dataflow visualization systems [Spar93, Ston93b]. This paradigm allows seamless, dynamic integration of analysis tools and scientific databases. This system architecture can provide a highly interactive and flexible environment for exploratory data analysis.

5 Schema Model for Scientific Data

In order to make the proposed scientific database environment useful for multidisciplinary scientific data analysis, a comprehensive schema model for scientific data is required. The schema model presented in this paper is one step toward such a comprehensive model.

Our schema model consists of three parts:

1. Data Structure Model
   The data structure model specifies the way scientific data is represented and organized conceptually. It also defines the policy which captures scien-

tific data in digital form. More importantly, it provides the functional data structure to which analysis procedures can be applied. One single schema model can support multiple data structure models.

2. Syntactic Metadata

   Syntactic metadata is the metadata for the scientific database system itself. It is the description of what kinds of data are stored in the database. In other words, it can be considered as the schema of the database system.

3. Semantic Metadata

   Semantic metadata is the metadata associated with data sets instead of the database system. It is both domain specific and application specific.

Conceptually, given any implementation data model, e.g., relational, network, hierarchical, or object-oriented, our schema model can be used as a template to define a conceptual data model which is, in turn, instantiated as a database schema in that particular implementation data model. In practice, conventional implementation data models such as relational, network, and hierarchical are too simple for modeling complex entities [Kim90]. They support only a limited set of atomic data types. The translated database schemas in those conventional data models are hard to implement and inefficient. For instance, analysis functions can only be defined and stored externally.

Currently there are two data models which can potentially serve as the underlying implementation data model for our schema model – the extended relational model and the object-oriented model. The extended relational approach starts with the relational model and a relational query language, and extends them to allow the modeling and manipulation of additional semantic relationships and database facilities. POSTGRES [Ston86, Rhei92, POS92] and its derivative, Montage [Mont94], are the best-known database systems based on the extended relational model. The object-oriented model derives from and extends concepts from object-oriented programming [Elma89, Kim90].

6 Data Structure Model

The data structure model serves as an abstraction of scientific data. It specifies the way scientific data is organized conceptually. Depending on the nature of data sets and analytical procedures, we can have different data structure models as part of our schema model.

Just like those attempts towards defining a common physical representation model (e.g., CDF, HDF, et al.), various work has been done in defining data structure models. Notable recent work includes the *lattice model* by Bergeron and Grinstein [Berg89], the *AVS model* by Gelberg et al. [Gelb90], the *fiber bundle model* by Haber and Collins [Habe91], the *computational grid model* by Speray and Kennon [Sper91], and the *Tioga data model* by Stonebraker et al. [Ston93b].

Each of those models has been implemented in at least one existing visualization tool or scientific database system. The AVS model is actually a set of different data structure models employed in the AVS system. The Tioga data model is implemented in the Tioga system as part of the Sequoia 2000 Project [Ston93a]. The lattice model is the model of choice for the Flexvis system [Beha90, Cald91]. An extended version of the lattice model is also being implemented in the Flexidesc Project (Flow-based EXploratory Interface to Database Environment for Scientific Collaboration) at the University of New Hampshire.

A data structure model is a fundamental part of any schema model for scientific data. However, the definition of our schema model is independent from the actual data structure model to be used. It seems that none of the existing data structure models alone is capable of representing all kinds of scientific data effectively and efficiently. Our schema model allows the coexistence of more than one data structure model in the same database system. By incorporating them into a single schema model, the coexistence of heterogeneous data structure models can be made transparent to database users. There are a lot of interesting research issues in this area, but these are beyond the scope of this paper.

7   Extended Lattice Data Structure Model

In order to elaborate the idea of data structure models, we devote this section to briefly describe one such data structure model — the *extended lattice* data structure model of Flexidesc.

We focus on multidimensional scientific data that is amassed from observations at points in an n-dimensional geometric space. Each observation point typically also includes parameters which identify the location within the geometric space. These two kinds of parameters are called *data parameters* and *location parameters* respectively. For most typical data sets, location parameters consist of time and space coordinates.

The simplest scientific data model for such a data set is a set of tuples which include values for both location and data parameters. Although this model is very flexible, there are no explicit associated relationships among its data entities. Consequently, data in this model is difficult to analyze by existing analysis tools, and difficult to access efficiently by database queries. In order to facilitate the process of analysis, we develop a scientific data structure model for multidimensional scientific data based on the *lattice* model proposed in [Berg89].

Formally, a lattice consists of three components: *data, topology,* and *geometry*. The *data* component is the data values stored in all data tuples. The *topology* defines the connectivity between data elements. The *geometry* component includes the description of the location parameters and a mapping from (topology) × (location parameters) × (data parameters) to geometric space.

In its simplest (and most common) form, the points of a lattice are related to its "neighbors" in a regular rectangular pattern. Such a lattice maps readily to a multidimensional rectangular array, and is called a *rectangular lattice*. Let L_k^n represent an n-dimensional rectangular lattice of points with k data attributes. The *lattice dimension* of L_k^n is defined as n, the *data dimension* of L_k^n is defined as k, and the *norm* of L_k^n is defined as $n + k$. The lattice dimension is actually the dimension of lattice topology. An *n-dimensional lattice* means a lattice with a lattice dimension of n. For instance, L_k^0 is just a set, and L_k^1 is a linear list. Through different geometry mappings, we can have different interpretations of the data being stored in one lattice. The dimension of the geometry need not be the same as the dimension of lattice topology. For example, a 2D lattice can be mapped to a surface in 3D.

There are some pre-assumed structures associated with every non-zero dimensional rectangular lattice; i.e., adjacent elements in the associated array of the lattice are assumed to be related in some way. This pre-assumed structure is described by the indexes of the associated array. By extending the *adjacency* among data tuples in the associated array, we can often capture part of the interrelationships among data points in the sampling space without storing or specifying them explicitly. In other words, not all of the location parameters have to be stored in order to store the geometry. The extended *adjacency* is called the *connectivity* of a lattice and it can be specified by a set of *connectivity methods* defined on the indexes of the associated array. The geometry of the lattice can be reconstructed from array indexes, connectivity methods, and location parameters.

L_k^0 has a 0-dimensional associated array, which has no indexes at all. No connectivity methods can be defined on it. The geometry of the lattice has to be inferred from the location parameters exclusively. It is easy to see that one data set might have more than one lattice representation. The transformation from one lattice representation of a data set to another is said to be *lossless* if the transformation is invertible. A non-lossless transformation is a *lossy* transformation.

Every data set has a trivial 0-dimensional lattice representation. Starting from the 0-dimensional lattice, we can usually transform it to some higher order lattice of the same norm without loss of information by specifying a set of connectivity methods. Some repository data sets with inherent structures have trivial mappings to non-zero dimensional lattices.

The basic lattice design supports a wide range of data representations. In particular, however, multidimensional arrays map directly to rectangular lattices.

8 Definitions of Metadata

The definition of metadata can be best approached from two perspectives, *functional* and *operational* [Lund84]. In a functional approach, the definition of metadata is based on its identified functionalities. One of the major characteristics of functional definitions is that there is always a gray area between metadata and data. Even though the majority of database researchers define metadata based on the functional approach, we think functional definitions are not precise enough for scientific database systems.

In an operational approach, the definition is based on the objects actually used and stored in the database system as metadata. In addition to that, our schema model provides database users with the option to treat any piece of information that describes other data as either data or metadata. Alternatively, an operational metadata definition can be treated as a schema model of meta-data. Unlike the functional approach, the operational approach enables a precise, but context-dependent definition of metadata. Using our schema model, database users can exercise their own judgement dynamically to decide whether the information should be treated as metadata.

We consider the following types of information to be metadata:

1. Management of data
   Metadata of this category contains everything related to the structure of the data, such as data types and attribute definitions.
2. Interrelationships of data
   Three kinds of interrelationships among data are possible:
   (a) interrelationships between attributes
   (b) interrelationships between data points
   (c) interrelationships between data sets
   All this information must be kept in a database system as metadata.
3. Analysis of data
   This category includes any computation or analysis that might be performed on the data, such as interpolation and filtering.
4. Validity of data
   This covers the associated errors and uncertainty of data.

Metadata can be classified into two different categories. One is metadata for the scientific database system; the other describes the relationships among the scientific data itself. The first type of metadata is the description of what kinds of data are stored in the database. In other words, it can be considered as the schema of the database system. The second type of metadata is domain specific and application specific. It might vary from one data set to another. These two kinds of metadata are called *syntactic metadata* and *semantic metadata* respectively.

Among the above four types of information to be treated as metadata, management of data is syntactic, while interrelationships of data, analysis of data, and validity of data are semantic.

8.1 Syntactic Metadata

Syntactic metadata is static and global. It is shared and inherited by all data and by all semantic metadata. It consists of the following two parts:

1. structural definitions of data (i.e., the instantiated schema of the data structure model), and
2. structural definitions of semantic metadata (i.e., the instantiated schema of semantic metadata).

Syntactic metadata is typically specified by scientific database designers instead of scientific database users. Basically, it describes the kinds of services provided and supported by the database system. In the relational data model, syntactic metadata is the collection of schemas for relations. In the object-oriented data model, syntactic metadata contains the class definitions for data structure models as well as various kinds of semantic metadata.

8.2 Semantic Metadata

Semantic metadata is specified by database users rather than by database designers and can vary from one data set to another. We have identified three major classes of semantic metadata: *summaries, errors,* and *derivation histories.* Summaries are the information that can be inferred from data. Errors are usually defined specifically for each data set, though they can be specified and inherited by a collection of data sets. Each data set has its own derivation history, since two distinct data sets can not have the same derivation history.

Summaries Two kinds of summaries can be defined and registered in the scientific database system as semantic metadata. An *analysis summary* is an operation that maps data and metadata to data and metadata. A *characteristic summary* is an operation that maps data and metadata to metadata only. The only difference between analysis and characteristic summaries is its interpretation. An analysis summary can be treated as data which will be further analyzed, while a characteristic summary is always treated as metadata.

The summaries can either be stored explicitly or defined as a function. A function used to define an analysis summary is called an analysis function. A function used to define a characteristic summary is called a characteristic function.

For instance, given the table *invoice* as shown in Fig. 1, we can define a characteristic function *Extended Price* by

$Extended\ Price = Quantity \times Unit\ Price$

Item	Quantity	Unit Price
Colombian	12	4
Mocha	20	2
⋮	⋮	⋮
Kenya AA	7	5

Fig. 1 — A simple relation

From the database point of view, the characteristic function *Extended Price* defines a virtual attribute of the relation *invoice*. In some ways, it functions like a formula cell in a spreadsheet. Further, we can define a compound characteristic function *Total* based on the function *Extended Price*:

$Total = \sum Extended\ Price$

Characteristic functions for a scientific database might be significantly more complicated. For example, statistical or mathematical summary information describes the data in the database and, thus, can be interpreted as metadata.

Analysis functions, on the other hand, can generate new *data structures* into the database (possibly along with associated metadata). Typical analysis functions might transform one data set into another such as by extracting a subset, or applying a filter operation on it, or resampling it.

By providing both analysis and characteristic functions, we give database users the ability to decide whether a piece of derived information should be treated as data or metadata.

Errors The representation and analysis of errors are required to validate scientific data analysis. The need to incorporate accuracy information was recognized in [Spar70, Spar81]. Errors are introduced into the repository data sets through:

1. the data sampling devices
2. the preprocessing procedures

In addition, there might be *missing* data in repository data sets. It is important to represent missing data or to replace them with some assumed or computed values.

Errors for a derived data set come from two sources:

1. errors inherited from the source data sets
2. errors introduced by the analysis functions

In our schema model, errors are described, computed, and stored by error functions. Error functions are specified as either analysis functions or characteristic functions. We separate error functions from the other functions in order to emphasize their functional and semantic significance.

Error functions can be defined on:

1. the whole data set
2. one particular attribute
3. one data tuple
4. a single atomic data item
5. a function

Since error functions can be defined on data at five different levels, the error of one single atomic data item might be described by more than one error function. For instance, let d be a single atomic data item of attribute A that belongs to a data tuple t in a data set D. The associated error of d might be described by error functions Err_1, Err_2, Err_3 and Err_4 defined on d, A, t and D respectively. Some error aggregation function E has to be defined in this case such that,

$$\text{error of } d = E(Err_1(d), Err_2(A), Err_3(t), Err_4(D))$$

For derived data computed by analysis functions, we also have to specify a meaningful way to integrate the errors of data on which the function is defined and the errors introduced by the function itself. Another important issue concerns the error propagation through analysis functions. All these issues constitute important research subjects for scientific data analysis.

Derivation Histories During the course of exploratory data analysis, lots of derived data sets are generated from the repository data set. Every derived data set has an associated derivation history. The derivation history serves two purposes:

1. it describes the interrelationships among data sets, and
2. it explains, justifies and validates the final analysis results.

For a repository data set, the derivation history consists of information about its origins. It includes the information required to answer questions such as the following:

1. Who collected the data?
2. When were these data collected?
3. What were the data collection methods?
4. What are those parameters?
5. How accurate are these data?
6. What kind of preprocessing has been applied to the data?

For a derived data set, the derivation history is stored as a *dataflow derivation record* which is generated automatically by the dataflow network and its associated modules. In fact, by using the dataflow derivation record and associated source data sets, we can regenerate the derived data set. These issues are beyond the scope of this paper. Nonetheless, derivation history itself is an important research topic for scientific data analysis.

9 Conclusion and Future Work

Several major issues faced by today's scientific database researchers are identified in [Fren90]. Most of them are caused by the absence of uniform data representations at all levels for scientific data, and the lack of an integrated environment for data storage and analysis. This paper describes a step toward the solutions of those problems.

We are integrating a database system, dataflow visualization, and other analysis tools in a highly interactive environment. This environment will serve as the foundation for multidisciplinary collaborative scientific research. We believe that such an integration is the blueprint for the next-generation scientific database systems. The on-going Flexidesc Project is our first attempt to realize the idea and it also serves as a testbed for identifying various research issues.

In this context, we present a schema model for the storage and analysis of scientific data. Our schema model consists of data structure models, syntactic metadata, and semantic metadata. Heterogeneous data structure models can be incorporated into the same schema model.

A major part of this paper is devoted to the definition of scientific metadata. The definition presented also serves as the schema model for metadata.

Our metadata definition is sufficiently flexible and generic for exploratory data analysis in the proposed scientific database system.

The contribution of this paper lies in the framework it provides for multi-disciplinary scientific data exploration. The existence of the schema model is justified as a way for the database system to have a uniform way to store and analyze data. Immediate goals in the future include a further refinement of our schema model and validation of its capabilities in our Flexidesc Project.

References

[AVS92]   *DEC AVS: User's Guide for Ultrix Systems*, DEC, May 1992.

[Beha90] Behari, A., "Flexvis – A Flow-based Visualization System", *Technical Report 90-17*, Department of Computer Science, University of New Hampshire, May 1990.

[Berg89] Bergeron, R. D., and Grinstein, G. G., "A Reference Model for the Visualization of Multi-dimensional Data", *Proc. Eurographics '89*, Hamburg, F. R. G., September 1989, North Holland Publishing Company.

[Cald91] Calder, B. H., "An Interactive Scientific Visualization Application Development Environment", *Technical Report 91-09*, Department of Computer Science, University of New Hampshire, May 1991.

[Camp92] Campbell W. J., et al., "Techniques for Managing Very Large Scientific Databases", *Proc. IEEE Visualization '92*, Boston, Massachusetts, October 1992.

[Dint84] Dintelman, S. M., "Data Models for Statistical Database Applications", *IEEE Data Engineering*, Vol. 7, No. 1, March 1984.

[Elma89] Elmasri, R., and Navathe, S. B., *Fundamentals of Database Systems*, The Benjamin/Cummings Publishing Company, Inc., 1989.

[Fren90] French, J. C., Jones, A. K., and Pfaltz, J. L., "A Summary of the NSF Scientific Database Workshop", *Proc. the 5th International Conference on Statistical and Scientific Database Management*, Charlotte, North Carolina, April 1990.

[Gelb90] Gelberg, L., Kamins, D., Parker, D., and Sacks, J., "Visualization Techniques for Structured and Unstructured Scientific Data", *Proc. ACM SIGGRAPH '90*, 1990.

[Gent84] Gentle, J. E., and Bell, J., "Special Data Types and Operators for Statistical Data", *IEEE Data Engineering*, Vol. 7, No. 1, March 1984.

[Goug88] Gough, M., et al., *CDF Implementer's Guide*, National Space Science Data Center, NASA Goddard Space Flight Center, Greenbelt, Maryland, 1988.

[Habe91] Haber, R. B., Lucas, B., and Collins, N., "A Data Model for Scientific Visualization with Provisions for Regular and Irregular Grids", *Proc. IEEE Visualization '91*, San Diego, California, October 1991.

[IBM91]   "Data Explorer: Understanding the Data Model", *preliminary*, IBM Yorktown, October 22, 1991.

[IBM92]   *IBM AIX Visualization Data Explorer/6000 User's Guide*, IBM, 1992.

[IRIS92] *IRIS Explorer 2.0*, Technical Report, Silicon Graphics, Inc., July 1992.

[Kao92]   Kao, D. T., Sparr, T. M., and Bergeron, R. D., "Towards a Schema Model for Scientific Data", *Technical Report 92-19*, Department of Computer Science, University of New Hampshire, December 1992.

[Kim90]   Kim, W., *Introduction to Object-Oriented Databases*, The MIT Press, 1990.

[Kort86]   Korth, H. F., and Silberschatz, A., *Database System Concepts*, McGraw-Hill Book Company, 1986.

[Luca92]   Lucas, B., et al., "An Architecture for a Scientific Visualization System", *Proc. IEEE Visualization '92*, Boston, Massachusetts, October 1992.

[Lund84]   Lundy, R. T., "Metadata Management", *IEEE Data Engineering*, Vol. 7, No. 1, March 1984.

[Mont94]   *Montage Object-Relational DBMS, Montage Server Product Description*, Montage Software, Spring 1994.

[NCS89]   *NCSA DataScope Reference Manual*, NCSA (National Center for Supercomputer Applications), University of Illinois, Champaign-Urbana, Illinois, 1989.

[POS92]   *The POSTGRES 4.0 References*, EECS Dept., University of California, Berkeley, California, 1992.

[Rew90]   Rew, R. K., and Davis, G. P., "NetCDF: An Interface for Scientific Data Access", *IEEE Computer Graphics and Applications*, 10, n.4, July 1990.

[Rhei92]   Rhein, J., Kemnitz, et al., *The POSTGRES 4.0 User Manual*, EECS Dept., University of California, Berkeley, California, 1992.

[Riba92]   Ribarsky, W., Brown, B., Myerson, T., Feldmann, R., Smith, S., and Treinish, L., "Object-Oriented, Dataflow Visualization Systems – A Paradigm Shift?", *Proc. IEEE Visualization '92*, Boston, Massachusetts, October 1992.

[Spar70]   Sparr, T. M., and Hann Jr., R. W., "A Water Quality Storage and Retrieval System for Regional Application", *Proc. of National Symposium on Data and Instrumentation for Water Quality Management*, Madison, Wisconsin, July 1970.

[Spar81]   Sparr, T. M., "Units and Accuracy in Statistical Databases", *Proc. Workshop on Statistical Database Management*, Menlo Park, California, December 1981.

[Spar93]   Sparr, T. M., Bergeron, R. D., and Meeker, L. D., "A Visualization-Based Model for a Scientific Database System" *Focus on Scientific Visualization*, Springer-Verlag, 1993.

[Sper91]   Speray, D., and Kennon, S., "Volume Probes: Interactive Data Exploration on Arbitrary Grids", *Computer Graphics*, Vol. 24, No. 5, November 1991.

[Ston86]   Stonebraker, M. R., and Rowe, L. A., "The Design of POSTGRES", *Proc. 1986 ACM-SIGMOD Conference on Management of Data and International Conference on the Management of Data*, June 1986.

[Ston93a] Stonebraker, M. R. and Dozier, J., "The Sequoia 2000 Architecture and Implementation Strategy" *Sequoia 2000 Technical Report 93/23*, University of California, Berkeley, California, 1993.

[Ston93b] Stonebraker, M. R., Chen, J., Nathan, N., and Paxson, C., "Tioga: Providing Data Management Support for Scientific Visualization Applications", *Proc. 1993 International Conference on Very Large Databases*, Dublin, Ireland, August 1993.

[Trei87]   Treinish, L., and Gough, M., "A Software Package for the Data-independent Management of Multidimensional Data", *EOS Transactions of the American Geophysical Union*, Vol. 68, No. 28, July 1987.

[Tuke77]   Tukey, J. D., *Exploratory Data Analysis*, Addison-Wesley Publishing Company, Reading, Massachusetts., 1977.

[Upso89]   Upson, C., et al., "The Application Visualization System: A Computational Environment for Scientific Visualization", *IEEE Computer Graphics and Applications*, Vol. 9, No. 4, July 1989.

Data Integration for Visualization Systems

Karen L. Ryan
Cray Research, Inc.
655E Lone Oak Drive
Eagan, Minnesota 55121

Abstract

This paper discusses integration issues and metadata requirements exposed by integrating independently developed molecular simulation codes into a single package. We discuss the use of a structured data model as compared to programming language data structures for data integration. As an example we consider the architecture of a commercially available simulation and visualization system for quantum chemistry. The system architecture currently uses a fairly low level approach to integration using a physical integration scheme much like CDF or HDF. Extensions and trade-offs in moving towards a more structured model are presented. We also present requirements for metadata in scientific data systems. Issues of theory dependencies and implementation dependencies must be addressed when integrating scientific data systems. We argue that appropriate treatment of metadata such as theory dependencies and implementation dependencies is critical to the long term success and extensibility of scientific data systems.

1 Introduction

Integration of scientific simulation applications and associated visualization systems require approaches to data modeling that address both issues of visualization requirements for very high volumes of data and integration issues involved in managing data from multiple applications. We consider trade-offs between structured data model and programming language data structures to adequately manage the integration of a set of independently developed molecular simulation packages.

Within the scientific applications domain integration modeling issues show up in the metadata requirements for such systems. Two different categories of metadata are discussed in the context of the context of different commercial chemistry codes: theory dependencies and implementation dependencies. Theory dependencies arise when integrating applications based in different theoretical approaches. Theory dependencies create missing data problems and problems in incompatible data between applications and across executions of a single application. Implementation dependencies often create problems for setup or visualization of final results from a simulation code execution.

Failure to adequately model such metadata will lead to scientific data systems which are limited in scope and difficult to use. Adequate treatment of such metadata is more important to the overall success of scientific data system than the particular choice of data model used to express the information.

2 Example Architecture

UniChem® an integrated quantum chemistry package, provides a single interface to multiple independently developed applications. As a currently commercially available scientific simulation and visualization system, UniChem®, provides a good example of requirements for scientific data systems.

The system provides a uniform interface for setting up computations and visualizing result data and facilities for visualizing a variety of scalar and volumetric results of quantum chemistry simulations.

The UniChem® design goal is to support simulation job preparation, execution control and result analysis from a single interface for quantum chemistry applications. The user interactively prepares a simulation job and submits it from a graphical user interface. The simulation codes generate data which is automatically streamed back to the interface for monitoring. The codes also generate data written to both ascii and binary files. The data from the ascii and binary files is used to analyze the results and restart the job if necessary. Typical jobs can generate up to 2-3 gigabytes of data Typical users may run anywhere from 1 to 20 jobs per day.

 The analysis portion of the interface provides facilities for visualizing simple scalar results, 2D plots of data and 2D, 3D and annotated 3D displays of volumetric data including molecular orbital surfaces, total electron density and electrostatic potentials. The application integrates multiple independently developed quantum chemistry super-computer simulation packages.The packages span a range of current simulation methods including:

- semi-empirical
- density functional
- Hartree-Fock
- classical dynamics integrated with quantum methods

The applications vary in algorithmic complexity and in corresponding precision of the simulation. Semi-empirical codes are roughly n^2 algorithms, density functional algorithms are n^3 and Hartree-Fock algorithms are n^4, where n is the number of atoms in a structure.

Typical jobs may run for several hours on supercomputer platform. Semi-empirical codes are used with up to 500 atoms, density functional with up to 100 atoms and Hartree-Fock codes with less than 50 atoms.

Despite algorithmic differences, the codes are integrated in such a way that the input and result data appear the same for all codes.

The overall architecture is shown in Figure 1.

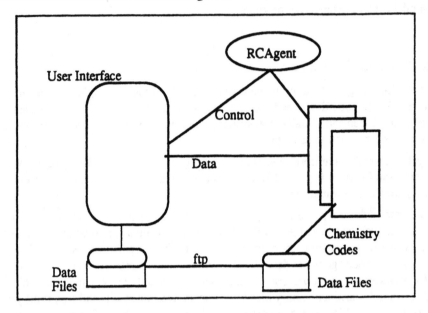

Figure 1 UniChem Architecture

The user interface prepares a job script on a workstation which is sent to the Cray platform for execution. The job script includes input files for the chemistry codes and ftp directives to move output files back to a user designated location on job completion

Each job corresponds to a molecular structure and associated setup and result data. A user opens result files from the workstation interface to view graphical representation of a final molecular structure as well as 2 and 3D renderings of volumetric properties (e.g., molecular orbitals).

Data is generated on Cray platforms and transferred either directly through sockets or via files to the user interface running on an workstation platform. Data messages are used interactively to send data from the chemistry codes to the interface. The messages are also used by the chemistry codes to write data files which are later read by the interface. This facilitates the asynchronous transfer of data between the chemistry codes and interface during job execution.

We use XDR to encode and decode the binary data in transporting it from the Cray platform to the workstation platform. This use is similar to the approach taken by HDF, CDF and netCDF to move data from one platform to another, [1,2]. Unlike HDF or CDF, we do not use a self describing approach to encode the data.

Utilities within the interface unpack the messages and instantiate data structures used by the interface utilities to manipulate the data. There are no utilities within the interface to directly browse or query the data sent back. All information is exposed only through predefined user interfaces. For example, the volumetric data can be viewed through interface which allow the user to select a threshold value and graphically display the data at a given threshold. 2D data can be queries directly to obtain contour values.

The architecture is intended to provide a comprehensive platform for running simulations and viewing results from a variety of quantum chemistry applications. The emphasis in the architecture is on shielding the end user from details of running jobs on the Cray and details of transferring data between Cray and workstation platforms. Data for all codes appears the same to the end user even though there are considerable differences in the syntactic form of the data accepted and produced by individual simulation applications.

2.1 Data Model

The chemistry specific messages used to transfer data between platforms form the basis of the data model currently used by the application to integrate chemistry codes and support visualization of final result data. The current approach is to implement that data model using programming language data structures rather than a structured data model. In this section we will consider the current state of the model, some of its development history and the utility of a structured data model in this context.

Some examples of basic message types are given in Figure 2. With some changes these messages could be expressed in a structured data model. There are about 25 messages currently used with the overall system.

```
UC_GEOMETRY(coord[][3], elements[], *atoms, *units)

UC_MOMENTS (*type, orig[3]. data[15], *orig_units)

UC_CHARGE(*type, *num, charge[])
```

Figure 2 Example Messages

UC_GEOMETRY encodes the cartesian coordinates for atoms in a structure. It includes an array coordinates, an array of atom names, the total number of atoms and the units of the coordinates.

UC_MOMENTS encodes permanent moment data for a structure. Permanent moments may be on of four different types (e.g., dipole, quadrupole, octupole, or hexadecapole). Each message includes data for only one type of moment. Each message includes data for the origin used in the moment calculation, the actual moment data values, and the units for the data. There is at most one moment of each type associated with a result structure.

UC_CHARGE encodes charge data for an entire structure. Charges may be of two different types (Mulliken or Lowdin). The message includes data about the type of charge, total number of charges and the actual charge values. There is one charge value per atom in a structure.

The message types in Figure 2 are organized as data about an individual structure. The example in Figure 3 have much less well defined semantic content.

$$UC\_VOLDATA(res[3], data[])$$

Figure 3 UC Volumetric Data Message

$UC\_VOLDATA$ is used to send block of volumetric data for multiple properties (e.g,. molecular orbitals, electrostatic potentials). The data are essentially uninterpreted values at grid points defined by the values in the resolution array, res.

2.2 Data Model Evaluation

The messages are organized and defined for convenience in preparing and sending data from the chemistry applications to the interface. They are not organized as flat relational structures or as instances of individual objects. Several changes to the structure of the messages would be necessary to express them in a structured data model. For example, there is no explicit connection in the UC_CHARGE or $UC\_MOMENTS$ messages to the result structure data in the $UC\_GEOMETRY$ message. The connection is currently maintained implicitly by the fact that the data is written to the same result file or to the same socket (in the case of the interactive dumping of data).

The examples in Figure 2 could be implemented using common data modelling techniques. For example, we could define a set of 3 relations corresponding to the current message types. Alternatively, we could define structure and atom objects and associate appropriate data with each; i.e., a structure object would have a collection of atoms and moments data. An atom object would have cartesian coordinate and charge data. The latter alternative corresponds closely the internal data structures used by the interface.

The example message in Figure 3 would be much less usefully expressed in a structured data model. It is not critical to access or edit the data values at individual grid points. The primary utility of the data is in visualization of the data at a given threshold. There is no direct relationship expressed between particular grid points and atoms in the structure. That relationship is only implicitly maintained and exposed through the graphical rendering of surfaces over a display of the result structure.

The data model expressed as a set of programming language data structures is effective for the task of integrating a fixed set of applications. The overall number of data message types is relatively small (<25). This means the messages can be used effectively as an external API as well as an integrating mechanism in the application itself.

As the complexity of the data grows this approach to managing information becomes less effective. Already we have encountered requirements to extend the message types; creating new versions of messages such as $UC\_GEOMETRY$ to include additional data. $UC\_MD\_GEOMETRY$ was created to send back data about force field atoms as well as quantum atoms to support new extensions in functionality to the chemistry codes. A more highly structured data model, such as an object oriented model, would have simplified the process of creating a new, message type. Instead at this point, there is no formal connection between UC_GEOMETRY and UC_MD_GEOMETRY even though both are interpreted similarly by the interface.

Currently the set of messages is growing slowly. As the software continues to expand we only add about 5 new data message types a year. Many of these are isolated in applicability to a single application. We conclude that expandability alone is not a sufficient reason to move from a set of data structures to a structured data model in this application.

The current mechanism also cannot support arbitrary querying by end users or comparison of results across molecular structures. While multiple structures can be active (open) within the interface at one time, the interface is not set up to search arbitrarily large numbers of structures for analysis or comparison of results. Evolving requirements in this area will eventually push us to a more structured data model.

It is also important to note here that an integrated simulation and data management system may work only in a limited sense for simulation requirements such as those the UniChem application addresses.The emphasis is on high speed simulation for the chemistry codes integrated by the UniChem application. Analysis of results is moved off the supercomputer platform and managed entirely independently of the simulation codes. Fine grained data flow control of the simulation codes is impractical for jobs which take hours (to days) to run on a supercomputer. Such integrated data analysis and data management approaches would work once the data simulations were complete. This is analogous to applying integrated data flow paradigms to earth sciences data after the data has been originally generated and collected from various sensor sources.

3 Data Integration Issues

Since UniChem® integrates multiple independently developed applications there are constantly integration issues to address. Standard concerns of data volume, format and granularity are managed by requiring all data to use the predefined data message format (a single level of abstraction where the application takes care of format translation to the message format type). We encounter additional data modelling concerns as we extend the coverage for the data messages to new domains and new data within the same domain. The semantics of the chemistry applications being integrated by UniChem® has a strong influence on the effectiveness of the existing data messages.

There are two major areas of concern:

- theory dependencies
- implementation dependencies

3. 1 Theory Dependencies

Theory dependencies occur when applications using different theoretical approaches are integrated into the same system. The UniChem interface defines a common intersection between different levels of theory (semi-empirical, density functional, and Hartree-Fock) and across different techniques (e.g., quantum based methods and force field methods). Data which is not important in one theory may be significant in another. A single data model representing data across multiple applications (possibly from multiple theoretical approaches) must be able to deal with the fact that data may not be preserved, or may be modified or even invalidated as a side effect of application execution.

As a simple example, consider molecular bonding information. While integral to data for force field approaches, bond data is not preserved in quantum applications and may even be changed as a result of execution of a quantum application. Connectivity information is a useful approximation employed in understanding a structure but it has no direct representation in a quantum system. The data is approximated in the interface by using atomic distance information. All atoms within a certain distance are represented as bonded by the interface. In the case of a quantum optimization, the relative positions of individual atoms can change, sometimes enough to move the atoms outside a predefined bond range. The problem is that end users want to see the original bonding information in an animation of a quantum dynamics results, since similar representations of results from force field based approaches do maintain the bonding information The original bonding data cannot be calculated from the final result data since there is no guarantee that originally bonded atoms will be close enough to each other to yield a bond from a distance calculation.

We have dealt with this particular case by defining a separate message type for bond information which is independent of the messages which send back quantum and classical geometry data (i.e., UC_GEOMETRY and UC_MD_GEOMETRY). The quantum calculations accept the bond data as input and immediately echo it back to the interface. The bond data is not used by the calculation; rather it is passed through the simulation code back to the interface to facilitate interpretation of final results.

Theory dependencies will be a persistent problem for any sort of scientific data application. As the range of integration effort extends across theoretical approaches within a domain, such problems will inevitably appear.

This problem is also related to some problems of "missing data". Data can be missing relative to a particular schema for a number of reasons. Missing data problems have been discussed in many contexts, e.g., [9, 10, 11, 12]. Theory dependencies can cause missing data since not all theories express the same information. Integrating systems based in different theoretical approaches will produce cases of missing data.

It is interesting to note that theory dependencies may also be an issue for systems which provide access to essentially uninterpreted data. Earth information systems are good examples of systems which provide access to sensor data, imposing particular theoretical point of view of the data. Any system which integrates incompatible theoretical viewpoints will almost certainly need to address some sort of theoretical dependencies expressed as missing or partially specified data.

3.2 Implementation Dependencies

Implementation dependencies are frequently dismissed in integration discussions as irrelevant low level details. But algorithm semantics expressed in the implementation a particular application can have major effects in the integration of multiple applications. In many cases, data may be irrelevant for the semantics of an algorithm but important for the setup or visualization of final results. Simple examples include atom names (as a means to identifying individual instances) and structure orientation.

Atom names are surprising difficult to preserve across integration of independently developed systems. Tracking of individual atoms across simulation code executions is commonly done through atom order in an input deck. We have seen a number of implementation level issues associated with atom names in our system. Atom names in the interface are determined by either:

- the order used to interactively build or edit a structure

or

- the order of atoms in an external file.

The order of atoms seen by a simulation code is affected by the order of atoms in an input deck. The input deck order can be affected by:

- the order of atoms in the interface (either file or build order)

or

- the ordering imposed in building a z-matrix (an alternative to a list of cartesian coordinates) of a molecule

or

- the type of calculation

The input deck is affected by building a z-matrix in that the order of atoms in the deck may be the same as the order of atoms in the zmatrix if a calculation accepts a zmatrix as input. All codes accept either a set of cartesian coordinates or a z-matrix (also called a set of internal coordinates).

The type of calculation for certain codes can also affect the number of atoms in the input deck. For at least one code, running a simulation using symmetry information means that symmetry redundant atoms are not present in the input deck. The atoms are regenerated for the final result geometry that is returned to the interface, but there is no guarantee that the order of atoms in the result file will be the same as the order of atoms in the original input structure. If the order changes in the current system, the atom name changes. This causes difficulties for some users in tracking the precise behavior of an individual atom.

Another implementation dependency seen in the current system is caused by differences in structure orientation. Structures are submitted to a simulation code in a particular orientation. Volumetric data are computed to fit in a "box" whose dimensions are computed based on the input structure orientation. In the case of one code loosely integrated into the system, the structure may be reoriented if symmetry information is used as part of the simulation. But the reorientation occurs after the box dimensions have already been computed. Structures can be reoriented without affecting the computation of volumetric data for density surfaces but the reorientation, if not managed properly, may result in incorrect visualization of results. The possible solutions in this case were limited by the fact that the application is only loosely integrated with the rest of the system. The only options, given the current data model were to disallow symmetry computations when computing volumetric properties or to anticipate, ahead of the computation, the precise structure reorientation to be imposed by the simulation code. A better option would be to associate the orientation information with the volumetric data in such a way that the data could be recomputed if the orientation changed.

4 Data Model Implications

Many researchers currently advocate a position of more tightly integrating the data model, data analysis, and in this case data simulation tools, so that all tools share the same highly structured model, e.g., [3,4]. Similar proposals have been made in other application areas as well, e.g., [5,13]. These approaches seek to address the issues of theory and implementation dependencies by developing a sufficiently expressive model so that all dependencies are directly represented. The key to these approaches is that all analysis tools are written to take advantage of a single uniform model. The UniChem application cannot directly utilize this approach since we are dealing with independently developed applications; application which do not shared the same assumptions about data or the same data model.

Other proposals focus on the importance of meta-data and inclusion of meta-data in a model for scientific visualization systems, e.g., [6]. Recent work in object oriented databases suggest approaches to manage interoperability between independently developed object models, by managing separate class and instance hierarchies [7], and by providing a "RISC" object model [8], in which other models can be expressed. Other approaches deal with the problems of unanticipated data model extension requirements by proposing techniques to support flexible object typing e.g., [14].

The experiences of the UniChem application suggest that it is not possible to develop a single, correct, all-encompassing data model to meet the requirements of integrating independently developed simulation codes together with a single visualization interface. Particularly in the case where the simulation codes have been independently developed, it will almost certainly be true that the data models used will not be easily integratable in all aspects. The issues discussed in the context of the UniChem application present meta-data requirements that should be considered when developing data models. Theory dependencies are an important source for meta-data requirements. It is important to recognize that a data model encoding of any scientific theory will need to address theory specific issues and that there will be missing data issues whenever models are extended to support tools based on different theoretical approaches. Implementation dependencies discussed in this paper suggest additional types of meta-data that need to be represented. In particular, instance level issues, such as mismatches in instance level (e.g., individual atom) identity, are frequently caused by implementation dependencies. Approaches such as those outlined in [6, 7, 8] need to take theory and implementation issues into account and provide sufficient formalism to capture such information. It is also important to explore theory and implementation dependencies for additional understanding of meta-data requirements.

Our primary concern is that in cases where there is no control over how an application generates data to be exchanged, the data will be at the wrong level of abstraction, in the "wrong order", or be in a form which is too expensive to modify to conform to a standard data model. An ideal model must be able to minimize these concerns by providing an encoding which is sequence independent, at an appropriate level of abstraction, does not demand modifications to the algorithms or implementations of the integrated applications, and support efficient inter-translation of data between applications.

Acknowledgments

The UniChem product is the result of a combined effort by many people including: Scott Borton, Ilene Carpenter, Han Chen, Brad Elkin, George Fitzgerald, Rich Graham, Cathy Guetzlaff, Chengteh Lee, Russ Loucks, Justo Perez, Thomas Raeuchle, Karen Ryan, Cary Sandvig, Shep Smithline, and Eric Stahlberg.

References

1. HDF 3.3 Reference Manual, Draft version 3.3, NCSA, University of Illinois at Urbana-Champaign, 1993.

2. M. Gough, et. al., "CDF Implementors Guide", NASA Goddard Space Flight Center, Greenbelt, Maryland, 1988.

3. M.R. Stonebraker, J. Chen, N. Nathan, and C. Paxson, "Tioga: Providing Data Management Support for Scientific Visualization Applications", University of California - Berkeley EECS Technical Report, 1993.

4. B. Lucas, et.al. An Architecture for a Scientific Visualization System, IEEE Visualization '92, Boston, 1992.

5. P. Patel Schneider, R. Brachman, H.Levesque, "ARGON: Knowledge Representation meets Information Retrieval", IEEE Conf. on AI Apps, pp. 280-286, 1984.

6. David T. Kao, T. Sparr, R. Daniel Bergeron, "An Extended Schema Model for Scientific Data", IEEE Workshop on Database Issues for Data Visualization, IEEE Visualization 93, workshop notes.

7. S.E. Bratsberg, "Integrating Independently Developed Classes", in Distributed Object Management, M.T. Ozsu, U. Dayal, P. Valduriez, (eds.), San Mateo, CA: Morgan Kaufman, 1993.

8. F. Manola, S. Heiler, "An Approach to Interoperable Object Models", in Distributed Object Management, M.T. Ozsu, U. Dayal, P. Valduriez, (eds.), San Mateo, CA: Morgan Kaufman, 1993.

9. W. Lipski, Jr. "On Semantic Issues connected with incomplete information databases", ACM Transactions on Database Systems, vol 4, September 1979, pp 262-296.

10. Joachim Biskup, "A Foundation of Codd's Relational May-be Operators", ACM Transactions on Databases Systems, vol 8, No 4, December 1983, pp. 608-634.

11. Peter Buneman, Susan Davidson, Aaron Watters, "A Semantics for Complex Objects and Approximate Queries", Univ. of Penn., Dept. of Comp and Inf. Sci. Technical Report, MS-CIS-87-99, November, 1988.

12. Linda Demichiel, "Resolving Database Incompatibility: An Approach to Performing Relational Operations over Mismatched Domains", IEEE Transactions on Knowledge and Data Engineering", vol 1, no 4, December, 1989.

13. Gio Wiederhold, Robert L. Blum., Michael Walker, "An Integration of Knowledge and Data Representation", in On Knowledge Base Management Systems, Michael L. Brodie and John Mylopoulos (eds.), Spinger Verlag, New York, 1986, pp 431- 444.

14. Stanley B. Zdonik, "Incremental Database Systems: Databases from the Ground Up", Proceedings of 1993 ACM SIGMOD, International Conference on Management of Data, Washington, D.C., May 1993. pp 408-412.

Inherent Logical Structure of Computational Data: Its Role in Storage and Retrieval Strategies to Support User Queries

Sandra Walther

Center for Computer Aids for Industrial Productivity (CAIP)
Rutgers University, Piscataway, NJ 08855-1390

Abstract. This paper describes a data management strategy which implements the thesis that the design of object-oriented, scientific databases (e.g., the data structures, hashing procedures) should incorporate the domain-specific relations of objects in the database to facilitate extraction and extrapolation services required by user queries. The strategy has been used to create object-oriented databases from data sets computed by iterating over meshes, incorporating a variety of geometries and coordinate systems. One set of data structures defining the data object and the hashing maps is sufficient to manage this type of data (multiple scalar and vector quantities at nodes in an n dimensional mesh) for interactive examination on both serial and massively parallel facilities.. The question raised is: can this approach which exploits the inherent logical relations of meshed data generated by simulations of fluid flows be applied to scientific data from other domains with different inherent relations?

1 Introduction

During the past five years, we have been developing an object-oriented distributed scientific modeling environment, SCENE (Scientific Computation Environment for Numerical Experimentation), featuring a data management strategy that uses the *inherent computational structure of the data* to establish logical (hashing) maps. These maps control access to all scalar and vector values, computed at a specific meshpoint, as "data objects" in an object-oriented database. The maps function as a control grid which supports user queries about data relationships. These queries can effect searching and visualization of selected values or the extrapolation of new data values representing data behavior. Newly defined data is automatically registered in the logical maps and incorporated into the database's exploration and visualization services. Our hashing technique has been successfully applied to data sets computed in Cartesian and curvilinear coordinates. We have constructed distributed object-oriented databases for data sets representing various flow models for interactive exploration by their respective researchers. Serial versions of SCENE have been employed regularly on datasets from grid sizes averaging 50 x 45 x 54 (121,500

*Research supported by NSF grants IRI-9116558 and ECS-9110424.

data objects with 10 values each). A parallelized version is under development that interactively handles a data set of grid size 256 x 256 x 256.

SCENE has been the subject of a number of papers and has been discussed from the standpoints of its use of Smalltalk[4], its object-oriented structure[1], [4], [6], its parallel/distributed strategies[7], its symbolic and numeric methods[5], and its scientific user interface [2], [3], [6]. In this paper, we would like to discuss it in terms of its logical structure and its implications for a general approach to the incorporation of intrinsic logical relations in the management of data. By "intrinsic logical relations", we mean relations that are *necessarily* a part of the meaning of that data and that are "given" or implied in the data itself (*apriori*) rather than imposed by outside considerations. In that respect, we consider the *use* of the data (the queries or accesses that yield information) to be an indication of logical structure while the constraints that may be introduced by the programming language of an implementation, the physical layout of facilities, the architecture of processors or algorithmic requirements of collateral software, e.g., communications and/or graphics packages, are external *a posteriori* factors.

2   Logical Structure of Meshed Data

The underlying assumption of our approach is that *storage of scientific information should incorporate the logical structure of the queries made by domain users to answer domain questions.* This data management strategy was developed to support interactive exploration of large 2D and 3D data sets representing models of fluid flows at one or more time steps; specifically, it evolved out of the data access requirements of particle tracking initiated by user probes (selected graphically through mouse designation) of interesting places in a vector plot of some flow field whose values were computed originally by iterating through a mesh. In this case, the user selects the starting point from which the "track" or path line will be extrapolated; the "extrapolation" of each point in the path is computed by some algorithm (there are various options depending on the type of flow) that *necessarily* includes the velocities at a set of points that represent the significant neighbors of the selected point.

Enabling users to compute new points in *data* space by designating points in *display* space requires: 1) a procedure for decoding screen points into data points; 2) a procedure for searching the data set to find the closest actual data point (node) in data space to the decoded point; 3) a procedure to retrieve the relevant data already computed at this point (certainly the velocities but it could require other scalar and vector values as well); AND 4) a procedure to implement new computational relationships between such selected values and other values in the data set. While many data management strategies can effect 1), 2), and 3) with varying degrees of efficiency using methods to cross reference arrays of variables, item 4 requires that the cross referencing incorporate the logical relationships among the elements that produced the data in the first place. In other words, to continue computing with a data set that is the result of a computational model, one must re-establish the data relationships that supported the computational relationships incorporated in the algorithms implementing the modeling equations.

In the case of data computed by iterating through a mesh, the relationship of each element in that mesh to every other element must be reconstituted so that it can be employed in more complex computational expressions as if the original data relationships were still in place. One way to approach this is to ask what the new computation would look like as program code if it were treated as a subroutine called from the main computation. Looked at in this way it is evident that the mesh relationships of the components needed for the new calculation are indispensable; the new computation must reference the already computed elements in these terms.

Consider, for example, a data set of a flow field (e.g., 32 x 32 x 32). Typically, when we program such an operation we write a procedure in which we access the entire data set by iterating through its members in a nested order, (dimension by dimension by dimension). In C pseudocode, the procedure is as follows:

```
let KDIM = size of "z" dimension, JDIM = size of "y" dimension, IDIM = size of "x" dimension.
for (k = 0;  k < KDIM; k++) {
    for(j = 0; j < JDIM; j++) {
        for (i = 0;  i < IDIM;  i++) {
            value[i][j][k] = ...some operation on value[i-1][ j][k+1]
}}}
```

Such a procedure assumes that each appropriate neighbor can be accessed by an index adjustment to the location of the original element's index. Many control factors must be specified before such a procedure can be implemented for a given data set. We must correlate the geometric axes with the logical iterators; in this example, we have correlated the x axis with the i dimension, the y axis with the j dimension, and the z axis with the k dimension. Of course, those assignments are not logical necessities but merely the choices of this computation. The identification of the axes with the looping order is also a choice of the computation. In this example, the outer loop is correlated with the k dimension (and thereby, with the z axis; the middle loop is correlated with the j dimension and the y *axis*; the inner loop is correlated with the i dimension and the x axis.

Logically, there are six combinations for the correlation of axes with looping order ($zyx, zxy, xyz, xzy, yxz, yzx$). Normally, a specific combination is selected for a given computation "arbitrarily"; that is, it may be for historical reasons ("every one who does this problem sets it up this way"), for language reasons (Fortran conventions), or for no special reason. The point is that this logical decision is not connected with the geometry of the problem. Geometrical considerations such as directional relations among components must be specified in addition to these logical commitments.

Moreover, meshes can be implemented in various coordinate systems (rectilinear, curvilinear) and mapped to a variety of geometries. It would be most desirable to develop a strategy that was invariant with respect to these factors. As it turns out, the logical relations of mesh components (their neighbor relations) do hold regardless of the coordinate system or geometry of the data. The one restriction we specified originally is that the number of nodes be invariant for each mesh in a given dimension. This is the defining characteristic of a *structured* mesh. Although we are now applying our techniques to unstructured data, it is illuminating to trace the development of the strategies from their initial implementation with structured meshes.

3 Data Structures Implementing Logical Meshes

Having identified the logical characteristics of our type of scientific data and the logical requirements of our user queries, we sought to identify the program data structures that would be closest in form (isomorphic) to the logical structure of the data. Fortunately, this is not that difficult once the problem is cast as a programming strategy to manage a multidimensional mesh; it suggests the use of multidimensional arrays. We selected as our basic data structure a two dimensional array, (defined as an *XYMap*) whose indices were read as *row* and *column* references. Subsequent dimensions are defined as arrays of arrays of the next lowest dimension. Since the work was done in C language, it was very crisp and simple to define these elements as arrays of pointers to arrays of pointers. Thus, the logical map was implemented as a hierarchy of lists of addresses

Since the actual data sets we were handling were multidimensional in space and time, we named our logical levels in terms of planes, volumes, and timeseries. A *plane* is a 2 dimensional array whose row and column references identify the basic address of a data object (a computational node with all its values (fields). A *volume* is a set of planes ordered by proximity (an array of pointers to planes); a *timeseries* is a set of volumes. Macros defining the accessing of an item in a plane, *planeAt(r,c)* and in a volume *volumeAt(r,c,p)* were also defined so that program statements were somewhat self documenting.

In addition, we defined data structures to manage the informational objects which are the data objects (records) of the data set (or object-oriented data base). For the data sets we dealt with, a data object is a record comprising all the scalar and vector quantities computed at a coordinate position in a mesh. The actual declaration statements are as follows:

```
typedef struct {float x,y,z;} Point 3d;
typedef struct {int r,c,p;} gridAddress;
typedef struct {int index;                    /* index into basic object array */
    gridAddress map;                          /* row,column,depth indices in logical map */
} BasicHashObject;                            /* required control fields for every object */
BasicHashObject *hashObjects;                 /* the main storage array malloc'ed */
typedef struct {int *plane;} XYMap;           /* matrix of indices to objects on a plane */
XYMap **volume;                               /* array of pointers to malloc'ed planes */
#define planeAt(r,c)  p->plane[(c)+(columns*(r))]   /* r,c, are I row, column indices */
#define volumeAt(r,c,p)  volume[(p)]->plane[(c)+(columns*(r))]
        /* p is a specific plane */
**objectfield;                                /* array of addresses of field arrays */
```

These data structures are applicable to any structured mesh regardless of coordinate system, topology, or size of the data set. For any given data set, space for the actual data objects and for the logical maps is allocated at run time based on the user supplied dimensions of the data set. Data can be loaded into the object format as it is computed or from precomputed files; in either case, the row, column, depth indices are the mesh indices from the computational iteration (i,j,k loops) that generated the data and are embodied in the data order (incorporated in the control variables OUTER, MIDDLE, INNER as shown below). The database for a given data set is constructed automatically through an interactive tool, the ObjectEditor, which prompts the user for the information needed to configure the generic database services to the specific situation. This procedure is explained in more detail in [6]. Basically, the user indicates the size of the mesh in each dimension, the looping order, the relationship between loops and axes, and names the fields that are included for each data object. From these specifications, the database automatically configures its control procedures to implement the logical relations they imply.

In terms of actual storage, the data is carried in a set of arrays, one for each field value. Currently, each field array is of type *float*; a vector quantity such as *velocity* is stored in three arrays, one array for each scalar component (u,v,w). The *logical* data object (the struct BasicHashObject) carries only its logical (map) coordinates (its grid address) and its own "home" address (its own index in the array of logical objects, the array hashObjects). The logical objects, the logical object array, and the logical maps are constructed at runtime. The r,c,p values for each logical object are stored in its map field; the index of the logical object in the array hashObjects is stored in its index field; that index is also stored in the hashing map at the r,c,p indices of the logical object.

Most importantly, the index of each logical object in its logical array is the key for retrieving its actual data fields in the field arrays. For example, consider a data object whose logical position in the mesh is described as $r = 21$, $c = 17$, $p = 32$ (the object at the 21st row, 17th column, 32nd plane). Suppose that it is item 3208 in the list of logical objects (or index 3208 in the array of logical objects). Suppose that it has nine data fields (x position, y position, z position, u,v,w, temperature, pressure, and density). Each field component will be at index 3208 in the array of all values for that field. The logical objects and the logical maps are cross referenced so that we can start with knowledge of a logical place (e.g., [r,c,p] = [21,17, 32]), access its fields, proceed to a neighboring logical place (e.g., [r,c,p] = [22,17,32]) and retrieve all the values for that logical object. The code for constructing the hashing maps from the array of objects is shown below:

```
mapObjects()                              /* construct map based on data order */
{ int d,p,r,c;
 BasicHashObject V;
 d = 0;
 for(p = 0; p < OUTER; p++) {
        for(r = 0; r < MIDDLE; r++) {
         for(c = 0; c < INNER ) {
            V.index = d;                  /* object knows its own array index */
            V.map.c = c;                  /* object knows its logical column */
            V.map.r = r;                  /* object knows its logical row */
            V.map.d = d;                  /* object knows its logical plane */
            volumeAt(p,c,r) = d;          /*object index stored in logical map */
            hashObjects[d++] = V;         /* store mapped object */
}}}}
```

The loop controls OUTER, MIDDLE, INNER are the ordering terms defined by the user with respect to the dimensions of the computation.

These data structures supply the search and retrieval mechanisms that support *all* graphic and computational services. Essentially, most services require algorithms that "walk" the computational mesh, retrieving object values for presentation in their mesh relationships. A contour plot of objects on a given plane with respect to a given field (e.g., density at plane 52) requires the construction of triangles at adjacent rows and columns; a wireframe plot represents rows of values as surface lines along one axis, and columns of values as surface lines along the other axis in a plane. Interpolation of path or stream lines requires retrieval of values in terms of "mesh neighbors". *Most queries to the data base are in fact resolved into queries about the logical maps.* For example, the directive "do a surface plot of all planes where temperature is greater than t while pressure = p" calls for a loop through all planes, inspecting the relevant field values of the objects in a given plane, and forming a collection of those objects that meet the test parameters. Some queries (e.g., interpolating velocity behavior from a selected coordinate position) require that an object find its mesh neighbors; it can do this because it carries its own map coordinates as a field.

In the serial implementation, the maps store the index of the logical object in the storage arrays; in the parallelized implementation, they store the *process ID* for the object in partitioned data space (distributed memory). This version is described in more detail in [7] and in section 5 below. In fact, this incorporation of the logical structure of data in its storage provides a very simple transition to parallelizing and distributing visualization services.

4 User Queries

Two specific requirements of SCENE's user interface are accommodated easily under this data management strategy, namely, query by mouse selection of a region and query by equation.

4.1 User Query by Mouse "Pick" in Display Space

SCENE supports a number of user queries that are initiated by mouse selection of a point on a graph. Samples are shown in Figs.1 to 4. For example, by designating a specific place on a contour map, a user can request a plot of the featured dependent variable at a constant coordinate on any axis. In Fig.1, the user has indicated a point and requested a plot of the vorticity magnitude for every y at a constant xz (a "column plot"). In Fig.2, the user has indicated a point and requested a plot of density for every x at a constant yz. Note that in this case the data is in curvilinear coordinates. In Fig.3, the user has indicated a point and requested a plot of pressure at that point on every plane. In Fig.4, the user has indicated a point and received the *actual data values of all fields at this location in the database.* In Fig.5, the user has designated locations from which particle paths are computed. Interpolating the particle's subsequent positions requires velocity data from four neighbors (2D data) or eight neighbors (3d data).

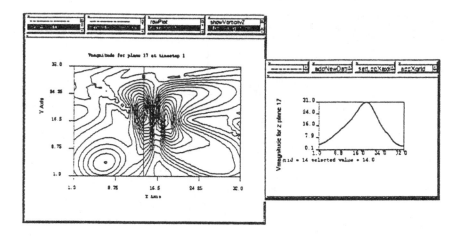

Fig. 1. Contour plot of vorticity magnitude on plane 17 of a 32x32x32 data set. The user has indicated a point (black square) at which a profile of vorticity magnitude is to be extracted.

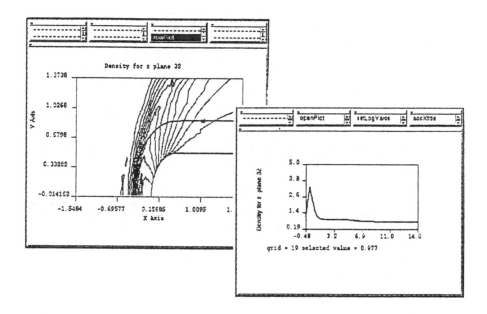

Fig. 2. Contour plot of density on plane 32 of a 40x32x32 data set in curvilinear coordinates. Note the shape of the grid at the user selected point.

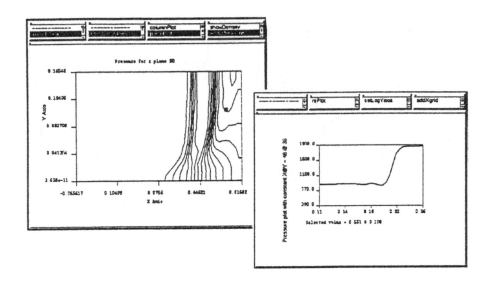

Fig. 3. Contour plot of pressure on plane 50 of a 54x42x53 data set. The user designated probe has produced a profile of pressure at that point across all planes.

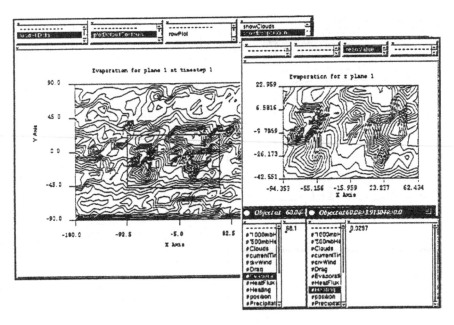

Fig. 4. Contour plot of evaporation for a 2d climate model. The user has "picked" a zoom region (box in left tool) and selected a point at which values are to be inspected. At the right, tools show the zoomed view and the selected data object.

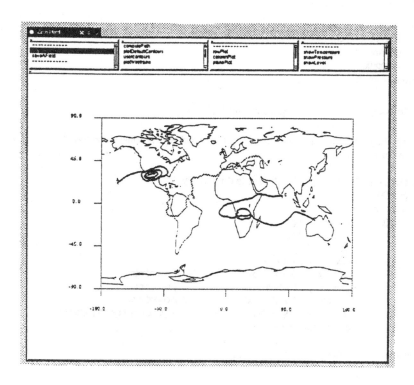

Fig. 5. Particle trajectories have been traced using the climate data set shown in Fig.4. The user designated one starting point (A) near Hawaii and the particle track was computed for 100 intervals to a point over the south western U.S. .Another particle (B) was tracked from the Yucatan to central Asia. A third particle (C) was tracked from India westward across Africa and then eastward to Australia.

These retrieval procedures are implemented by transforming the requests from points in display space to points in data space and then searching a regional map to find the closest actual data point in the region to the selected point. The visualization tool decodes the mouse equivalent display coordinates from "window space" to "data space" and requests the database to extract the set of xy coordinates of objects in the requested plane along with the map location of each coordinate pair (a transient regional map produced by collecting the spatial coordinates and the logical index of all logical objects in the plane). The database computes the distance of that selected point to the position fields of the objects in that plane to find the data object closest to the selected position. That object "knows" its mapping coordinates - the plane, row, and column parameters which are used to retrieve all its data fields. Thus, queries about the data in terms of physical coordinates can be resolved into accesses of object fields in terms of their logical mesh relationships and queries in terms of mesh relationships can retrieve physical information.

The code to access a regional map illustrates the utility of the logical map. A region object is defined as:

```
typedef struct {
    Point3d position;
    gridAddress map;
    int index;
} regionObject;
```

The code to construct a regional map follows:

```
int getRegionMap(p1,p2,r1,r2,c1,c2) /*    get all logical objects within parameters */
int p1,p2,r1,r2,c1,c2;
{
regionObject *regionMap;         /* allocate dynamically */
regionObject R;
int r,c,p, index,n;
    for(p = p1; p < p2; p++) {
        for(r = r1; r < r2; r++) {
            for(c = c1; c < c2; c++) {
                index = volumeAt(r,c,p);
                R.position.x = fieldX[index];          /* x coordinate */
                R.position.y = fieldY[index];          /* y coordinate */
                R.position.z = fieldZ[index];          /* z coordinate */
                R.map = hashObjects[index].map;        /* logical object's map indices */
                regionMap[n++] = R;
    }}}
return(n); /* size of this map */
}
```

4.2   User Queries Expressed as Equations

Most significantly, this approach supports user queries framed as equations requiring higher order interpolations. Frequently, when scientific users are exploring their data through visualization tools that extrapolate behavior of the computed data, they identify a quantity or set of quantities that could be computed based on the existing data. The SCENE visualization tools allow a user to specify a computational procedure that adds a scalar or vector field to the data base. In the current iteration, a user can describe a field and can enter a mathematical expression *referencing other data fields (i.e., neighbor objects in the computational mesh)*. New data can be computed using expressions including the following operations: differentiation, functional transformation, and vector operations like gradient, curl, divergence, and laplacian. Tensor operations are planned in future SCENE versions.

For example, the data set shown in Fig.3 can be extended to add the quantity "total pressure". This new field is defined as

$$P_t = p \left(1 + \frac{\gamma-1}{2} \, rho \, \frac{|v|^2}{\gamma p} \right)^{\frac{\gamma}{\gamma-1}} \tag{1}$$

where *p, rho, and v* are the symbolic names assigned by the user to the pressure, density and velocity fields of the original data. This capability, which we call "user-added filters" has been described in [5] and [6]. The newly computed data is added to the database and "registered" in conformity with the above data management structures. The entire transaction is "arranged" through the ObjectEditor tool which records the user's designated symbol for the old and new fields in all the relevant storage lists, linking each symbolic name with the address of the array (or in the case of a vector, the addresses of the arrays) holding the actual data values.

5   Parallelizing the Data Management Paradigm

A version of the data management code in which objects are distributed among processes has been implemented under a parallel processing environment incorporating a Linda type paradigm. The Linda[8] model of process management in tuple space (distributed memory) supports the distribution of data among processes so that searches and accesses can be done concurrently. Versions have been prototyped under Kernel Linda on a 30 processor Cogent Technologies system and on a group of SPARC workstations running Harness, a Linda like distributed environment. Our strategy has been to parallelize the data structures that support the mesh definitions, namely, the hashing maps and the procedures that access objects through their row, column, plane relationships. For the parallel version, we have developed algorithms that divide a three dimensional hashing map into submaps with overlapping edges. Each process is assigned a submap and its associated data. A master process maintains a table of all process to submap assignments and constructs a metamap so that references to the row-column-plane indices in the global map are translated into references accessing the appropriate subcube in its own process.

Certain types of searches and data manipulations parallelize very well under this strategy. For example, a data set in which each data object comprises several scalar (e.g., temperature, density, pressure), and several vector (e.g., velocity, vorticity) values can be queried to produce an isosurface concurrently; the master process sends the same message "return all points where temperature = t and pressure = p" to each process. Queries calling for the construction of triangles or polyhedra also operate well concurrently for structured meshes under this scheme. In this case, the logical subcubes manage physically adjacent objects so each process can be directed to form geometric structures using values from nodal objects (e.g., triangularize pressure). Because the subcubes have been partitioned with overlapping boundaries (i.e., "boundary objects" are repeated in each subcube that is adjacent), their data is selfcontained for such procedures and the processes can operate autonomously (no interprocess transactions). However, other types of queries, (e.g., tracking pathlines) require interprocess messaging when the interpolated trajectories cross subcube boundaries.

This format of mesh partitioning into overlapping domains has been used in parallelized computations on hypercubes but, to our knowledge, has not been employed as a strategy for managing object-oriented scientific data. Moreover, the partitioning of the total data spatial domain into spatial subcubes can be extended to unstructured spatial data by associating the logical subcubes with a *data range* and constructing local hashing within the subcubes on the basis of "bins" rather than "points".

6 Conclusion

In the above discussion, we have described how we identified and used the logical structure of datasets based on structured meshes to develop a set of data structures and procedures general enough to be employed on a variety of geometries and coordinate systems, dynamically configurable to the size of the dataset, and supporting user queries that extract and extrapolate data graphically and computationally. We believe the object oriented paradigm and the multidimensional logical mapping strategy can be applied to other types of data for which an inherent logical structure can be identified that is *isomorphic* to its query structure. In the case at hand, the computational relations required by the computational queries can be represented by the storage management structures. The spatial relations featured in the visualizations can be incorporated in the data management.

The limitation of "structure" guarantees a one to one correspondence between objects in the data base and indices in the logical map but the strategy can be applied to unstructured data by treating the logical indices as "bins" with ranges that define the scope of items residing in the bin. Bins could be defined in terms of spatial regions, alphabetic regions, or properties that express combinatorial qualities. We are currently working on unstructured spatial data and welcome samples of other types of data to see whether our approach can be extended to their domain.

For a comparison of SCENE to other interactive scientific tool environments, see [10], [11], [12], [13] and [14]. Similar interests in generalized data structures for meshed data sets can be found in [9] and [15].

References

1. Walther, S., Peskin, R.: Object-Oriented Visualization of ScientificData. J. Vis. Lang. and Computing 2 (1991) 43-56
2. Peskin, R., Walther, S., Froncioni, A. M., Boubez, T.: Interactive Quantitative Visualization. IBM J Res. and Dev. 35 (January, 1991) .205-226
3. Walther, S.,Peskin, R.: Object-oriented data management for interactive visual analysis of 3-D fluid flow models. Proc. SPIE Conf. on extracting meaning from complex data, San Jose, CA. 1459 (February 1991) 232-243
4. Walther, S., Peskin, R.: Object-oriented Graphics for Interactive Visualization of Distributed Scientific Computations published in Computer Graphics Using Object-oriented Programming. John Wiley & Sons (1992) 213-234
5. Peskin, R., Walther, S., Boubez, T.: Computational steering in a distributed computer based user interface system published in Artificial Intelligence, Expert Systems, and Symbolic Computing. IMACS Trans. on Scientific Computing, Elsevier Science Publishers B.V. (North Holland 1992) 104-113
6. Walther, S., Boubez, T., Ghazi, K.: Object-Oriented Data Management for Distributed Scientific Simulations. Soc Comp. Sim Proc. Object-Oriented Simulation Conference (1993) 170-175
7. Walther, S., Peskin, R.: Parallelized Interactive Data Management of Large, Scientific Data Sets. Sixth SIAM Conf. Parallel Processing for Scientific Computing (1993) Proceedings.
8. Carriero, N., Gelertner, D.: Linda in Context. Commun. ACM 32 (1989) 444

9. Globus, A.: Octree Optimization. Proc. SPIE Conf. on extracting meaning from complex data, San Jose, CA. **1459** (February 1991) 2-10

10. Bitz, F., Zabusky, N.: DAVID and Visiometrics: Visualizing, Diagnosing, and Quantifying Evolving Amorphous Objects. Computers in Physics **4** (1990) 603-613

11. Felger, W., Astheimer, P.: Visualization and comparison of simulation results in computational fluid dynamics. Proc. SPIE Conf. on extracting meaning from complex data, San Jose, CA. **1459** (February 1991) 222-231

12. Moquin, B., Brasseur, P.: Application of a New, Fully Object-Oriented Programming Methodology to the Analysis of Multidimensional Turbulence Data. Bull. Am. Phys. Soc., Div. Fl. Mech., **37** (1992) 1781,

13. Goodrich, M.T., Salzberg, S., Ford, H.: A Geometric Framework for the Exploration and Analysis of Astrophysical Data. Wkshp on Advances in Data Management for the Scientist and Engineer. AAAS Boston, MA (1993)

14. Coburn, J.F., et.al: An Object-Oriented Environment for Chemical Process Simulation. Am. Inst. Chem. Eng. (1990) Orlando, Florida.

15. Fornter, B.: The Data Handbook - A Guide to Understanding the Organization and Visualization of Technical Data. Spyglass, Inc. Champaign, IL. (1992).

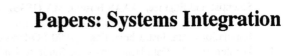

Papers: Systems Integration

Database Management for Data Visualization

Peter Kochevar

DEC/San Diego Supercomputer Center
La Jolla CA 92037, USA

Abstract

Visualization management systems which integrate database management, data visualization, and graphical user-interface generation into one package are becoming essential tools for conducting science. Unfortunately, the link between data management and data visualization is not very well understood. To make matters worse, most database management systems available today are not well-suited for handling large, time-sequenced data sets that are common to many scientific disciplines. The reason for this shortfall is that most database systems do not use an appropriate data model, are not geared toward real-time operation, and they have inadequate user-interfaces. Hints as to how database systems can fix these problems are given so that effective visualization management systems can be constructed.

1   Introduction

Database management systems (DBMSs) are essential for doing research in fields which require the handling of large amounts of data. No where is this statement more true than in the Earth sciences where the study of global environmental change places great demands on information systems. To Earth scientists, the search for and ready access to data is as important as is their actual visualization. Frequently, scientists do not know precisely what they are looking for when conducting a study. The browsing of databases on the basis of data set contents is a much desired capability for many scientists and DBMSs, in principle, are particularly well-suited for this task.

Browsing requires close integration with data visualization systems. DBMSs are not very useful if the results of queries cannot be presented to users in an effective manner. Data visualization must address the presentation of all forms of data whether it be "raw" scientific data like satellite imagery, meta-data describing raw data, or a list of data sets that result from a database query.

For effective browsing, a visualization system must do more than just present information visually. Users must be able to interact with screen visuals as a way of customizing visualizations and interfacing with the DBMS. What is needed are *visualization management systems* which integrate DBMSs, data visualization systems, and graphical user-interface builders into one package.

From the standpoint of data management, *there are no good DBMSs for dealing with scientific data of the kind found in the Earth sciences*. The relational model is inadequate as a basis for a DBMS because most of the data that resides in scientific databases is simply not relational in nature. In the Earth sciences, much data is in the form of satellite imagery which does not easily fit the relational model of an unordered set of data elements. To store such data, relational DBMSs usually resort to the use of *binary large objects (blobs)* whose internal structure is completely opaque to a database's access machinery. Even worse is data associated with polyhedra, for example, river basins are often modeled as 3-space graphs in which data is associated with both graph vertices and graph edges. Relational systems are particularly bad at storing topological information required to fully describe such networks.

Object-oriented DBMSs are promising but it is too early to tell if they can serve as good scientific database managers. In general, most current DBMSs are lacking in their data models, in their ability to handle large, time-sequenced data sets at real-time rates, and they are lacking in their means of interacting with users. This paper begins to address some of these issues so that complete visualization management systems can be constructed which effectively and efficiently serve the scientific community.

2   A Data Model

An appropriate data model is an essential part of a DBMS. The fact that relational DBMSs use the notion of the relation as their theoretical underpinning is both their strength and their weakness. The mathematical notion of the relation gives rise to the relational calculus, has implications on storage strategies, and it has bearing on how data is to be visualized. But, the idea of the relation is too ackward a concept to adequately deal with a large variety of scientific data particularly when topological relationships exist between data elements.

For scientific data, the notion of the *fiber bundle* [3, 4, 7] is more appropriate as a basis for a data model than most other theoretical concepts. Fiber bundles contain the notion of the relation as a proper subset yet they are quite rich in their expressibility of varied data structures. The downside is that fiber bundles, with all their generality, are more complex entities than relations thus entailing a more complex set of manipulation operators.

Mathematically, a fiber bundle represents a space which is the Cartesian product of two other spaces; a *base space* and a *fiber space*. Conceptually, a copy of the fiber space is attached to each element of the base space. For each base space element, this copy is referred to as a *fiber*. A *fiber bundle section*, or simply a *section*, is the identification of one element from each fiber in the bundle. As an example, Figure 1 shows a 3D fiber space attached to a point in the spherical base space of a bundle. A section for this fiber bundle is illustrated in Figure 2 where each element of the section is a 3-vector.

Fiber bundles are a generalization of the concept of graphs of functions. In this sense, a base space of a fiber bundle is analogous to the independent variables of a function while its fiber space corresponds to the function's dependent variables. A fiber bundle section is represented by the function itself whereas the entire fiber bundle is the space where the function would be graphed.

Although it is often convenient to associate independent and dependent variables of functions with base and fiber spaces, the definition of fiber bundles makes no assump-

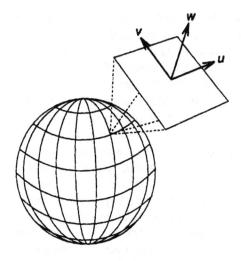

Figure 1: A fiber associated with a point in a base space.

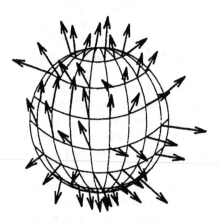

Figure 2: A fiber bundle section.

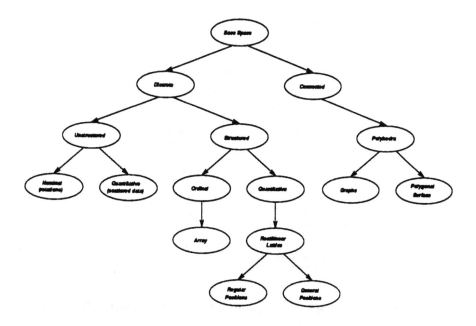

Figure 3: A partial taxonomy of fiber bundle base spaces.

tions about the structure of these spaces. Both base and fiber spaces can be arbitrary topological spaces which may or may not be metric spaces, that is, there may or may not be any coordinates defined for them. For instance, a base or fiber space can just be a finite set of elements in which there is no implicit relationship between members of the set. With so little structure, the only meaningful operation on spaces of this type is the formation of subsets from among the elements.

In practice, each element of a fiber bundle section can be thought of as a simple scalar type, a record, or an entire fiber bundle section. Fields in a record can themselves represent a scalar, another record, or a fiber bundle section as well. Note that the *relation* which forms the theoretical underpinning of relational DBMSs is a special case of a fiber bundle. Such a structure has a base space consisting of an unordered set of elements and a fiber space which is the Cartesian product of the domains of the fields in a record.

A partial taxonomy of fiber bundles can be constructed which is based on the structure of their base spaces (see Figure 3). This taxonomy can be used to fashion an inheritance hierarchy from which an object-oriented implementation of fiber bundles can be made (see Figure 4). Depending on where a data set falls within the taxonomy, only a certain set of visualization techniques can apply. For instance, suppose a data set consists of a base space which is a 3D rectilinear lattice whose axes represent latitude, longitude, and altitude, and whose fibers represent the range of some scalar value. For such data sets, visualization techniques are limited to taking cutting planes, forming iso-surfaces, doing volume rendering, and so on.

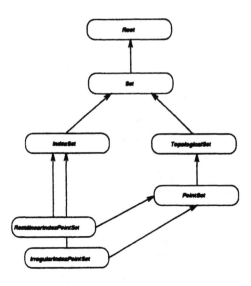

Figure 4: An inheritance graph for an object-oriented implementation of fiber-bundles.

3   Real-Time DBMSs

By its very nature, the field of global environmental change relies on and hence needs access to time-sequenced data. The most appropriate format for visualizing such data is as animations so that environmental changes become readily apparent. To complicate matters, scientists want to visually navigate through the scenes representing the global data as the data is being animated. Therefore, it is not sufficient, in general, to simply replay an animation loop of pre-computed images.

Data comprising each time step of a time-sequenced data set can be very large since their coverage may range over the entire planet. To effect animation, database queries for these times slices must be handled many times per second. Unfortunately, most existing DBMSs are not equipped to process transactions at frame-rates for such large data items.

From a database, data must be sequenced into a set of rendering engines which construct images for eventual display on a monitor. To support the timely access to time-sequenced data, data must be distributed or "striped" across many inter-connected storage servers. Nonetheless, these collections of servers must appear to the end-user, as well as applications programs, as a single, unified database. The DBMS must keep track of the whereabouts of the data, the compute servers, and the end-user's display system so as to minimize data traffic across the network.

To further maximize bandwidth, data should only be drawn out of a database at a level-of-detail that is compatible with the resolution of the display on which it is to be viewed. For instance, a 6K by 6K AVHRR satellite image is far too large to view altogether at its full resolution on a typical workstation. But, the entire image can be viewed at once if the viewpoint is pulled far enough back from the image. In this case, an appropriately sub-sampled rendition of the image suffices for its screen representation. As the viewpoint is brought closer to the image, a fuller resolution version of the image would need to be displayed. But to compensate in this case, large portions of the original image could be clipped away by the specification of a viewport commensurate with a display's resolution.

Level-of-detail management of the kind just described should be performed transparently to an end-user both during retrieval and during the storage of data. As a user navigates through a virtual environment representing data, level-of-detail swapping should occur automatically and seamlessly as data objects loom up and recede within a user's field of view [6]. In this regard, a visualization management system acts much like a flight simulator. At the heart of this simulator is the DBMS which must be able to support the access to varied levels-of-detail. To unburden users as much as possible, the DBMS should automatically sub-sample array data and it should automatically decimate polyhedral data when coarser levels-of-detail would suffice during a visualization.

Finally, real-time database support should not be limited to data retrievals since a DBMS must be able to ingest large data sets at real-time rates as well. For instance, sensor data such as satellite imagery is frequently generated in a continuous manner yet it still must be properly stored for future access. Similarly, output from simulation programs running on supercomputers or workstation farms can produce large data sets many times a second. Again, such data should be stored in a database so that the results can be analyzed by researchers at later times.

4 Interacting With a Database

Database interactions should fall under the aegis of visualization management systems which seek to integrate data rendering, data browsing, and data understanding into one package. The primary focus of such systems should be the creation of a methodology which lets non-visualization and non-database experts easily perform their own sophisticated interactive visualizations and complex database interactions. End-users should not have to write visualization programs to render every data set that results from a query. This idea should also hold not only for data sets that are used frequently and are familiar to a user, but also for data sets that are completely unfamiliar to them.

In Kochevar et al [8], a very simple visualization management system called the Visualization Executive is described which links the Postgres DBMS [11] with most any visualization package. The design of the Visualization Executive was intended to be somewhat analogous to that of the Apple Macintosh folder browser. On the Macintosh, a user traverses the folder tree until a document of interest is eventually located. The browsing of the folders proceeds visually by pointing and clicking on iconic representations of folders and documents. When a desired document is located, the user selects a representative icon and the document is then "visualized" within the application which created the document.

In a similar fashion, a user of the Visualization Executive navigates through the database by pointing and clicking on iconic representations of the database's contents. Once a data set of interest is located, a user selects a data set's icon and the corresponding data set is then visualized. The key idea which make this functionality possible is that information as to how to visualize each data set is stored in the database along with the data set itself.

To aid in the navigation of a database's contents, one example of a domain-specific, graphical query tool is provided within the Visualization Executive. The intent of this tool is to allow non-database experts to make complex queries of the database in a way that is more natural and intuitive given the kind of data that is being sought. For example, a frequent query of Earth science databases is for data sets that pertain to a particular region of the planet. Rather than forming a textual query in an arcane database query language, the Visualization Executive provides a world map on which a user can mark regions of interest.

Although far from a production system, the visualization management system that was developed was successful because of the insight that was gained from its design and implementation. Some of the things learned that have bearing on the interplay of visualization and database management include the following:

Visualize all forms of data. The results of general database queries should be visualizable just like any other scientific data. One appropriate visualization technique for data of this kind is the positioning of icons onto an "informational landscape". In this way, the visualization encodes additional information that can be utilized by a scientist. For example, queries for data sets pertaining to regions of the Earth might be positioned above a world map or globe so that a "light cone" highlights the exact area of a data set's coverage. In addition, the visualization of query results must be able to handle the screen clutter which can result when queries generate thousands of items. The hierarchical display of data, such as the case with folders on the Macintosh, is one visualization technique for dealing with the clutter.

Provide for interactivity. Interactivity is important in data visualization as a means for both exploring the information content of a chosen data set and for extending links back into the database. Objects that appear in a visualization can be thought of as "widgets" when various behaviors are assigned to screen visuals. These behaviors might be elicited when pointed at with a picking device via a callback subroutine, say. Such behaviors can trigger additional database interactions and visualizations, thus affording a mechanism with which to do database browsing. As an example, consider a query for all snow gauges in the Sierra Mountains of California which results in a collection of icons representing each gauge displayed on a map. When an icon is pointed at, a history of snow measurements for that site could be displayed as a 2-D graph with time as the independent axis and snow depth as the dependent axis. If, in addition, icons are provided to allow further database queries, a scientist might then request climate data for the same area and period of time in order to visually explore the possible correlation of mean temperature and snow depth.

Eliminate needless programming. Scientists should not be required to write visualization programs either themselves or through visualization experts acting as intermediaries. A scientist should only have to identify what is to be viewed via browsing and then let the visualization management system figure out how to do the visualization. To have this capability, a visualization management system requires built-in intelligence and access to a knowledge base that contains rules and definitions pertaining to data visualization. Simple systems have been developed which address the automatic visualization of certain kinds of data [2, 5, 9, 10] and these systems need to be extended to fully serve general scientific applications.

Account for end-user's tasks. A data set can be visualized in a variety of ways. When scientists visualize data they are making use of the large bandwidth of the human visual system to make a visual computation. Exactly how a scientist wishes to participate in the computation is information that can be used to structure an appropriate visualization for a particular task. At times scientists may wish to select one item from many possibilities, they may want to correlate or compare data in different data sets, they may want to search for patterns or anomalies, and so on. In general, a visualization should make the visual computation as efficient as possible. Having a list of predetermined visualization programs associated with a data set is too limiting in that it may hinder exploration and preclude the data reusability and sharability.

Utilize self-describing databases. Databases, augmented with knowledge bases, need to be self-describing, in other words, the schema design and a complete characterization of all data classes must be stored in the database along with the data. Having this information on-line allows a visualization management system to "learn" about the structure of a database thereby giving it the flexibility to dynamically create graphical interfaces tailored to the information that a user seeks. Information about classes of data and their relationship to one another should go beyond the mere description of syntactic structures. The semantics associated with classes of data is important information that needs to be stored in the data/knowledge base as well. Such information can be used to give a domain-specific look and feel to interactive visualizations.

Aid applications programmers. From a developers standpoint, it is preferable to interact with a DBMS by building persistence into existing programming languages. Within programs written in an extended programming language, designated data objects would continue to exist once the scope of the program ends. Such data objects would be used just like any traditional data object in a program except that their storage resides in a database managed by a DBMS. The ODE system from AT&T is one such DBMS which uses an extension of C++ as its interaction language [1].

5   Conclusion

Computation is an integral part of conducting science today. As a result many scientific disciplines, particularly the Earth sciences, are awash in data that must be managed. Unfortunately, database management systems currently available are inadequate for handling most forms of scientific data. Some of the areas in which database systems are lacking were discussed and hints as to how these shortcomings can be alleviated were offered. In general, those in the field of scientific visualization are among the first to grapple with the problem of managing scientific data. As such, the scientific visualization community must push the database field to satisfy its needs. This paper has been one small nudge in what is hoped is an appropriate direction.

References

[1] R. Agrawal and N. H. Gehani. ODE (Object Database and Environment): The language and the data model. In *Proc. ACM-SIGMOD 1989 Int'l Conf. Management of Data*, May 1989.

[2] Clifford Beshers and Steven Feiner. Automated design of virtual worlds for visualizing multivariate relations. In *Proceedings Visualization '92 Conference*, pages 283–290, 1992.

[3] D. M. Butler and M. H. Pendley. A visualization model based on the mathematics of fiber bundles. *Computers in Physics*, pages 45–51, Sep/Oct 1989.

[4] David M. Butler and Steve Bryson. Vector-bundle classes form powerful tool for scientific visualization. *Computers in Physics*, 6(6):576–584, Nov/Dec 1992.

[5] Stephen M. Casner. A task-analytic approach to the automated design of graphic presentations. *ACM Transactions on Graphics*, 10(2):111–151, April 1991.

[6] Thomas A. Funkhouser et al. Management of large amounts of data in interactive building walkthroughs. In *Proceedings Workshop on 3D Interactive Computer Graphics*, Boston, MA, 1992.

[7] R. B. Haber, B. Lucas, and N. Collins. A data model for scientific visualization with provisions for regular and irregular grids. In *Proceedings Visualization '91 Conference*, 1991.

[8] Peter Kochevar et al. Bridging the gap between visualization and data management: A simple visualization management system. In *Proceedings Visualization '93 Conference*, 1993.

[9] J. D. Mackinlay. Automating the design of graphical presentations of relational information. *ACM Transactions on Graphics*, 5(2):110–141, 1986.

[10] Hikmet Senay and Eve Ignatius. VISTA: A knowledge based system for scientific data visualization. Technical Report GWU-IIST-92-10, George Washington University, March 1992.

[11] Michael Stonebraker et al. The implementation of POSTGRES. *IEEE transactions on knowledge and data engineering*, March 1990.

Data Exploration Interactions and the ExBase System

John Peter Lee
Institute for Visualization and Perception Research
Computer Science Department
University of Massachusetts Lowell
jlee@cs.uml.edu

Abstract. This paper describes elements of data exploration interactions and the design philosophy of the ExBase (*Exploration of DataBases*) system. The ExBase system integrates a database management system with data visualization and analysis, for interactive data exploration. Knowledge about the interactions between user, data, and the system will be automatically recorded by the system for subsequent analysis. This approach will help define the user and system interface requirements for future data exploration environments. Our top-down design focuses on supporting user interactions and accommodating new technologies as they appear. We believe that new avenues for data exploration will be enabled because of this coupling.

1 Introduction

Data exploration is the search for important structures and patterns within a data set. It possesses elements of data space navigation, data subsetting, data analysis, and data visualization. Data exploration can be undertaken at a high level for cursory information, or at a lower level for in-depth insight. To facilitate data exploration, it is important for software environments to accommodate the types of data interactions that a user must perform over a data set.

Current commercial database management systems (DBMS) excel at storing, accessing, and interrogating tabular data for complex relationships. Unfortunately, their style of interaction prohibits an active dialog between user and data, because the DBMS does not manage retrieved data. Current data visualization systems have powerful image composition capabilities, and are useful at displaying huge amounts of data for rapid assimilation. They lack data interrogation capabilities, such as a standard interface and implementations for accessing a particular subset of data based on complex data relationships. Data analysis systems operate over user-defined packages of data, but generally not over data visualizations. There exists a need for combining these three components to provide a data exploration environment that permits data retrieval, data analysis, and data visualization. While exploring data, the user should be able to interact effortlessly with data via an assortment of interaction paradigms that are suited to specific tasks, yet are seamlessly integrated.

The ExBase system (*Exploration of DataBases*) under development at the University of Massachusetts Lowell attempts to provide a system interface layer between the components mentioned above, and a user interface to support interactions with each component. Our primary goal is to provide data exploration services in a single environment by constructing an object-oriented data processing core with well-defined interfaces for the peripheral functions (DBMS, analysis and visualization). Additionally, a history mechanism will record interactions between user, data representations, and the system components. This is done to gain knowledge about the data exploration process - the dominant interactions, sequences of actions, services used, etc., that will form a requirements manifest for future data exploration environments. These systems are in an early stage of evolution, and our approach will serve as a testbed for the evaluation of new technologies, suitable user interfaces, and data interaction metaphors.

This paper is organized as follows: Section 2 gives background on data interactions and integrating database and visualization systems; Section 3 discusses foundations of the ExBase system design to support data interactions; Section 4 discusses what we feel are the key issues to be addressed in the evolution of data exploration systems; Section 5 concludes with a summary of the important aspects of our approach.

2 Background

The ExBase system is intended to support a wide variety of user interactions with data. Interaction with data takes many forms; we have mentioned navigation, subsetting, analysis, and visualization earlier. This section discusses data interaction concepts and data interaction in database and visualization systems.

2.1 Goals, Interactions, and Tasks

Data exploration is an *interactive* process, in which the researcher engages in an active dialog with various representations of data through the application interface. In this process, subsets of the entire data set are browsed, edited, sampled, and tested against hypotheses. After this exploratory phase, the entire data set can be manipulated, but with only a few of the attributes retrieved [Khoshafian85] for in-depth study.

Support for data interaction requires consideration of the human user. The user undertakes a cognitive effort to transform a research goal to a physical system activity. Likewise, physical output from the system must be interpreted by the user and evaluated as to satisfying the goal [Norman86]. Typically, the user concept of data is different from that of the system, so the system must provide intuitive data interaction metaphors. In this way, the cognitive effort in translating and evaluating goals and actions can be minimized. This implies a tight *conceptual* coupling between the user and data, but perhaps a loose physical coupling between data and its representations.

The user *goal* is an abstract concept that describes the research objective. A goal is broken down into a sequence of *interactions* over the data. Interactions describe the data manipulation activities. Examples are data subset retrieval, structure-finding operations, geometric representation transformations, and visualization setting specification. Interactions are then transformed into *tasks* to be performed. A task is a collection of activities in a domain with a goal [Paulin90]. Tasks are concrete entities that are both domain and data organization dependent. Examples are a database query with spatial attributes, or a point cloud visualization for a fluid flow. Once the interactions are specified to address a goal, they must be implemented as tasks in different domains.

Determining the data interactions and the domain tasks for data exploration is a formidable undertaking, given the variety of interactions, data representations, and exploration methods available. Formal psychological interaction studies and task analyses for data exploration and visualization are few. Direct observation of tasks, operation frequency counting, and structured interviewing are among the methods used to create user, dialogue, task, and application models for various systems [Browne90]. Such studies need to be conducted for the data exploration process.

Informal psychological studies on visualization display design [Wickens93] hypothesize that there is a complex relationship among data structures, task demand and the human perceptual system for utilizing a suitable visualization technique. Tasks possess levels of "uncertainty", where the uncertainty level deals with the confidence of an investigation or visualization. Tasks were listed to include *searching* for a predefined value (value, cluster, pattern, discontinuity or gradient), *comparisons* (ordering, magnitude of difference), and *understanding* (the relation at hand).

An important empirical study of data interaction processes for the goal of data analysis [Springmeyer92] revealed four main categories of interactions: *interacting with representations* (generation, examination, orientation, querying, comparisons and classifications), *applying math* (estimation and transformation calculations, derivations, and statistics generation), *maneuvering* through data spaces (navigation, data management, and data culling), and *expressing ideas* (recording and describing). These processes form a solid core of concepts that characterize most data exploration interactions, because the tool used was disregarded during the analysis.

With this knowledge, we know there are a wide variety of interaction processes that could be performed and a larger number of tasks in each domain. Our concern is to understand database navigation and querying, statistical analysis techniques, and data visualization. From this, domain task support will be developed.

2.2 Database Navigation and Querying

Navigating through a data space will become more important as larger databases are explored (for an immediate example, consider navigating the World Wide Web). There are a number of database navigation methods. In [Larson86], four basic visual browsing operations of structuring, filtering, panning, and zooming were introduced. An earlier, but more in-depth study used graphical methods to portray database navigation [Canter85]. User interaction patterns were recorded and rendered as paths through this network. This study revealed five navigation strategies: scanning, browsing, searching, exploring and wandering. The strategies were recognized by "graphical indices": paths, rings, loops, and spikes.

Undirected database exploration was among common information search strategies revealed in the recent empirical study of [O'Day93]. A single search started with an orienting overview that provided indices to points of interest in the database. This overview often resulted in a series of interconnected searches that were controlled by the database content. Thus, the content of incremental database search results guided further exploration.

Querying is often the sole method for database navigation. The interaction between a query and a database is well-known, as is explained in any standard database system textbook [Korth92]. Query languages emphasize ease of use over physical access efficiency, thus permitting a *view-level* interaction with data semantics rather than a *physical* interaction with its storage representation. In typical business applications, queries are very specific and operate over a well-known database, whose structure, or schema, is known to the user. The amount of retrieved data is usually small, and exactly matches the query. For data exploration, however, the database schema and underlying structure might be unknown, and queries may return large amounts of data for visualization purposes.

An interesting development is the Dynamic Query paradigm [Shneiderman93] to enhance rapid, incremental, and reversible querying over data resident in main memory. Range selections can be easily made on attributes via graphical user interface sliders. With each slider adjustment, the display screen, a scatterplot display, is continually updated to reflect the new query conditions. This method is useful for rapid exploration and detection of patterns and exceptions of data. The method is limited to simple queries that are conjunctions of disjunctions. Query targets can be compared against a subset of their respective ranges, but not against each other.

The interaction between a user and database is less well-known. Querying is a domain-dependent process. One can envision an abstract set of queries that can be applied to a generic data model. These abstract queries form the basic operations (interactions) by which a data set is explored. The domain-dependent aspect (tasks) is incorporated into the implementation of the query. Thus, there are generic queries for data exploration, and refinements of these queries for each particular application domain. A major challenge is to support these data exploration queries posed to the database for each domain.

2.3 Data Visualization

Data visualization techniques allow large quantities of data to be inspected simultaneously. This allows the investigator to ask more questions (queries) of the data. The "question-answer" method of traditional database querying can evolve into an "answer-question" scenario (as in [Owen86]) once visualization is introduced. An interesting data rendering should compel the user to ask more questions about the data. Thus, visualization provides the input for some exploration from the output of another. *Direct manipulation* [Shneiderman83] techniques can improve the user interface for this scenario. With direct manipulation, a portion of a visualization can be graphically specified and manipulated as input into another process.

Visualization interactions involve the production and manipulation of imagery and geometry. The classical visualization pipeline model of [Haber88], which is implemented in commercial systems such as AVS [Upson89] and IBM Data Explorer [Lucas92], consists of the following general processes:

- simulation data is enriched and enhanced via computational filters (interpolation, noise suppression) to create derived data

- derived data is further transformed via transfer functions and attribute mappings to produce an abstract visualization object

- abstract visualization objects are rendered to the display screen via physical mapping transformations common to computer graphics

Thus, visualization can be though of as the application of filters and mappings over various types of data objects.

An extension to this model emphasizes the user-data dialog by proposing support for interactions and their specification [Bergeron89]. Four basic interactions are discussed: modification of the visualization process, modification of the transformation parameters within a process, interaction with visualization output to change the process, and interaction with the data being processed. An additional pipeline for interactions is developed in [Seetharaman93] for multiple representation spaces.

Once an image or geometry is rendered, the user can interact with the visualization further by applying rotate, pan or zoom operations. The user can also reapply an output filter such as color map for an alternate representation of the same data or alter any of the other visualization display settings. Single-valued probes have been used for fine-grained feedback to display the underlying data at specific locations in the visualization with the aid of a graphic cursor [Felger92]. Slicing through volumes is a similar probing method that displays a range of data values simultaneously [Speray90].

2.4 Data Analysis

Data analysis is the scrutiny of data to obtain some measure about it, deriving data from the original database data. If such describes the structural decomposition of data or summarizes the data based on some measure, it is termed *metadata* [Treinish92]. In many cases, a data analysis output will visualized. For example, a finite element analysis that determines forces over some geometry can have color mapped to the computed force values on the surfaces of the geometry in the visualization. A visualization enables *visual data analysis*.

Data analysis also encompasses the determination of structure in a data set. Such structures are manifested as clusters and hypersurfaces [Tukey77] that can be determined via projection pursuit techniques [Crawford90]. As in database navigation, visualization plays a fundamental role in this process. Current research into *knowledge discovery in databases*, or data mining, focuses on the automated extraction of patterns from data [Piatetsky-Shapiro91]. An algorithmic approach is employed to find structure in data, as opposed to the visual approach taken in data visualization. In our case, we wish support statistical data analysis functions because these have been lacking in extant visualization systems.

2.5 Integrating Databases with Visualization

There are several long-standing reasons for the paucity of database-visualization integration activity. The main reason, as pointed out in [Shoshani84, Treinish91], is that scientific databases (which are the most prevalent types of visualized data) have data structures (such as vectors, hierarchies, and sparse multidimensional matrices) and access patterns (over spatial and temporal data, for example) that cannot be easily accommodated by relational databases. This is often termed the "impedance mismatch" between application data and database data. Another reason that DBMS are not incorporated into data visualization applications is that the overhead involved in data management operations (such as data structure maintenance, query processing, security and concurrency considerations) hinders overall performance [Grinstein92].

There are recent examples of DBMS-visualization integration worth mentioning, and we hope they will favorably impact future data exploration systems. The need for integrated database querying, coupled with visualization and analysis functions will result in new interaction metaphors, improved systems interfaces, and performance enhancements. Such systems will find greater utility within the user community.

The FLEXIDESC project [Sparr92] supports collaborative research, and has similar integration components as our design. It aims to create a scientific data model that accommodates various types of metadata [Kao93], provide a querying formalism based on dataflow networks, and explore the relationship a query has between its input and output data. It utilizes a loosely coupled DBMS that supplies a data subset for visualization system to process further. Subsequent interactions over the data retrieved do not result in further database queries to be executed. This activity uses the Aurora Dataserver [Xidak94] and an AVS front-end.

The Sequoia 2000 system [Stonebraker92] tightly couples the Postgres DBMS [Stonebraker90] to the Tioga visualization front-end [Stonebraker93] for global change research. The visual programming environment allows the construct of visualizations as well as database interaction functions. User navigation through the data space is accomplished by a flight simulator paradigm that results in incremental retrievals from the DBMS. A hierarchy of data *abstracts* is specified to support query result navigation and operations such as spatial zooming.

The Gaea project [Hachem92] attempts to develop an automatic metadata manager for generic metadata, and implement important data modeling relationships in the DBMS. It consists of a spatio-temporal core DBMS for global change research data with provisions for analysis and visualization tools. Of particular interest is data derivation information that is stored within the database and used in subsequent analyses. A Petri Net model implements the derivation history mechanism [Hachem94], which currently uses the ObjectStore DBMS [Lamb91] and AVS.

There has so far been little research results from these projects. One can see that there are different approaches to the problem, emphasizing different aspects, and using different types of software systems. Our architecture is unique because it will record and analyze user and system interactions in order to model the database explorer.

3 Design Philosophy and Components

The ExBase system relies to a degree on existing software components that might not be initially suitable for database exploration. Performance issues, though important, are secondary to the proof of design. We are focusing on establishing the nature of data interactions within the system, developing interaction metaphors, and evaluating implementation tradeoffs in light of the interactions. By adding interaction retention and analysis tools, a user model of the data exploration process in various domains can be constructed. Performance issues will be addressed in the future when we have more complete information on the data flow within the system.

3.1 Software Components

The ExBase system is composed of the following software subsystems:

Exvis - Exvis [Grinstein89] utilizes an iconographic approach to data visualization. Data can be mapped onto the geometric, color, and sound properties of representation primitives called icons. Within Exvis, a dataset residing in a flat file is selected, the relevant fields (dataset attributes) for study are indicated, and all data relating to those fields are completely loaded into application memory. The data attributes are then mapped to the icon attributes, as well as to the horizontal and vertical axes of the display. Global controls are available for various display settings, such as the size of the icons, the amount of jitter or randomness in icon placement (to avoid artifacts), and constraints on the display. The data is displayed as a 2D texture array, an enhanced scatterplot that can be brushed with the cursor to produce auditory textures. A 3D extension has recently been developed.

Orion - Orion [Xidak93] is a general-purpose DBMS that is useful for tabular data, with extensions for reference attribute types and is-composed-of data modeling. Among its strong points is that one can describe an application data structure to the database, issue a query, and have the DBMS transform the data from the database form into the described structure. However, it still requires the application to perform a FETCH loop to retrieve each row of the result set.

Aurora - The Aurora Dataserver [Xidak94] is a hybrid scientific data management system that wraps a spatial data processor around the Orion DBMS. Tabular data in the DBMS may be queried, and may then be sampled over the spatial coordinates (data that are mapped to display axes). Non-spatial data may also be mapped to an axis, and any number of axes could be specified. Data that are mapped to an axis can only be sampled, not queried in the relational sense. Retrieved data is stored in a structure called a Memory Set, a term we use in our design description below.

We wish to retain the Exvis methodology for visualizing data because it can display many data parameters simultaneously and in many output formats. The Exvis display concepts are elegantly simple, and are general enough to apply to most data types. In this way, we can further evaluate the display methods. We wish, however to incorporate a new data management paradigm that will be supported by Orion and Aurora. One of Exvis' chief limitations is the lack of powerful data selection methods, which will be handled by the DBMS technology.

Looking forward, we wish to integrate the architecture with commercial visualization environments such as AVS, because they possess a wide assortment of classical visualization techniques and dataflow programming interfaces. It would be interesting to integrate classical visualization techniques with the Exvis iconic paradigm (say mapping icons onto surfaces) and the DBMS facilities. Thus, we need a modular design with a well-defined interface to enable this future integration.

3.2 User Requirements

User requirements drive the system design; knowing how the system will be utilized will determine the internal functions. Two user groups are identified for this system: domain scientists and interaction analysts. The domain scientist has knowledge of the subject area and terminology of the database, but perhaps little knowledge of the intrinsic data relations. The interaction analyst aims to characterize the data exploration process by recording and analyzing user and system component interactions. In other words, the interaction analyst explores data explorations.

The basic processing model for either user begins with a data selection, followed by a sequence of operations and transformations on the data (which could also include additional data selections). We envision very large databases that cannot completely fit into main memory, thus necessitating DBMS tools for robust data selection. A query is issued to retrieve a subset of the data based on some selection condition. The retrieved data can then be visualized by performing intermediate transformations, graphical representation mappings, and visualization display parameter settings. Based on the visualization, all or part of the process is then potentially modified and repeated. Figure 1 shows the interactions from the user perspective, and the fact that all data is stored within the DBMS.

The user can issue DBMS queries to selectively retrieve domain data or important ExBase data types. Queries can also operate over the retrieved Memory Set, but might be of a different form and tightly coupled to the visualization display. Operations such as statistical functions generally operate over Memory Sets, but could also operate over DBMS-resident data, or be compared to aggregate DBMS data. Operations of a different nature are the specification of data-to-representation mappings and visualization settings. These are related to image production as opposed to data selection and analysis. Finally, the user could interact with the data visualization as described earlier. To accommodate these interactions, the following general tasks must be supported:

For the domain scientist:
- issue a selection query to the database.
- load / store an important query, memory set, representation mapping, or visualization setting.
- perform an operation on a memory set.
- specify a representation mapping or visualization setting.
- display data, from a memory set to a visualization .
- perform an interaction over a visualization.

For the interaction analyst:
- retrieve/store interaction data.
- analyze and display interaction data.

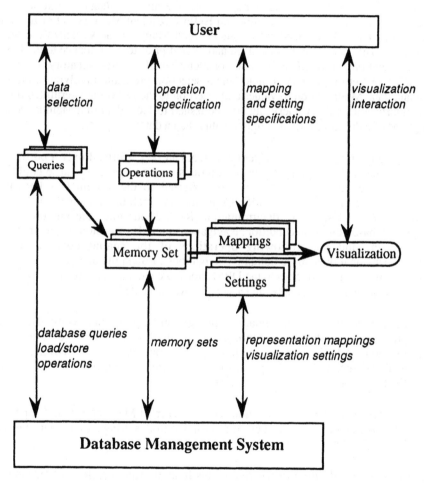

Figure 1 The Primary User Interactions in the System

An ordering of operations is necessary for successful interactions. For instance, to display data, a representation mapping and a visualization setting must be specified. A representation mapping can only occur after a memory set is created and selected, meaning that the Memory Set must be nonempty. A visualization setting may be specified before a Memory Set is created because it deals with global display parameters.

3.3 Primary Functional Units

The previous section described the dominant user interactions with the system. This section describes how the interactions are handled by the system. There are five primary functional units to accommodate both user groups' interactions.

1. *answer (ad hoc) query* - The user specifies some subset of data to be extracted from the DBMS and transferred into either an ExBase-resident Memory Set or to another predefined data object structure (a Query, Icon Mapping, or Visualization Setting structure). This query can be displayed and altered prior to it's issuance to the DBMS. A specification can be made by name or identifier of a stored Memory Set, Query, Mapping or Setting, or can be made via a selection predicate involving portions of domain data. Modification of values and insertion to the DBMS are permitted through this interface as well. A query can also be issued to local data in a Memory Set, but might be of a different form and functionality than a database query.

2. *operate over memory set* - Operations that can be performed over a portion of a Memory Set include computations, restrictions, and navigations. These could send data to some other processing module external to the system (for knowledge discovery), or back to the DBMS. Computations include statistical calculations, correlations, and structure determination. Restrictions alter the amount of data displayed, based on some condition. Navigations include extensions of the traditional pan, zoom, and path-following operations of the spatial domain into the multidimensional data-space domain. Navigations through the data space most often will require additional queries to the DBMS for more data, depending on the semantics of the operation and the context under which it was executed.

3. *specify a mapping* - Two primary mappings can be performed within the system: mapping data attributes to representation attributes and representations to visualizations. Additionally, the mapping space (geometry, color, sound) itself can be specified and altered. Both mappings and settings can be retrieved from and stored to the DBMS, or can be created from scratch.

4. *display memory set* - This function takes the current Memory Set, and applies the current representation mappings and visualization settings to render the data. Displaying could also mean producing a textual report.

5. *process a visualization interaction* - This function supports the specification of a user interaction over a visualization. The interaction could be simple, as in reorienting the image by translations and rotations. The interaction could be made more complex by allowing the user to "brush" the visualization with the cursor to obtain underlying data values and / or portray an auditory data representation. The interaction could be

more complex still by allowing the specification of a region of interest within the visualization that must be sent to another processing module, or to the DBMS for additional data retrieval based on properties of the data that became apparent through the visualization.

3.4 Primary Data Types

There are six fundamental (composite) data types in the system. Data type components can be used in queries.

- Domain Data
- Queries
- Representation Mapping Data

- Visualization Setting Data
- Memory Sets
- Session Data

Domain Data is the base data stored within the DBMS, as well as metadata, and is composed of one or more *tables* of *records*. Each table represents a distinct object of the database, and each record represents a unique instantiation of an object. In relational DBMS terminology, these items are called relation and tuple, respectively. Tables are defined by *attributes*, which have variable values for each record. There are many different types of data models that describe a particular method of data organization and behavior (relational, object-oriented, functional, etc.), and it is not our intent to delve into these issues in our implementation. We will be following a relational model, with extensions as provided by the particular DBMS we are using. It is expected that each database will have a different *schema*, or overall design (*not* necessarily a different underlying data model). Domain Data is retrieved from the DBMS by queries and placed into Memory Sets.

Queries are text strings that specify a data retrieval from the DBMS, in a standard language, typically SQL. A Query data type contains a name or identifier, the actual query text, a listing of the targets of the query (the attributes mentioned in the SELECT statement), a reference to the Memory Set it created, and a comment item for description of the query. The name / identifier, query text, and comments are given by the user; the other items are computed by the application.

Representation Mapping Data specifies a mapping between representation parameters and Memory Set attributes. This data type contains a unique name for the mapping, a mapping type, a table listing Memory Set attributes with associated representation parameters, a reference to the appropriate Memory Set, and a comment for a description of the mapping.

Visualization Setting Data contains all of the display settings to produce a graphical display that are not representation mappings. These include color maps, lighting and shading parameters.

Memory Set Data contains the retrieved data from a query. In addition, it contains a unique identifier, and attributes that describe its total size, number of elements, a listing of the individual data items and their ranges, a reference to the query and / or sequence of operations (queries plus additional data processing) that created it, a representation data reference, a visualization setting reference, and indications of embedded structures of interest to the user. An underlying access table is provided to map data requests to their physical location.

Session Data contains a history of user interactions. This history is a sequence of events or higher-level constructs (operations and tasks), or even multiple resolutions of interactions. Statistical information on the prevalent interactions and sequences of interactions can be determined from this construct.

3.5 Software Architecture Overview

A three-layered software architecture is proposed to support the data types and user requirements of the preceding section (Figure 2). The central layer consists of the visualization-database interface, the core of the ExBase architecture. This layer provides the mappings between the visual domain of the data exploration and the database storage domain of the underlying representations. It also performs all of the major data processing activity within the system, and possesses a well-defined system interface to the user interface and support systems. The highest layer is the data visualization layer, which serves as the user interface to the mapping and rendering functions, and the DBMS. This layer provides the interaction metaphors to the user. The lowest layer contains the database management system, as well as any other additional system services that support the application, such as sound generators, statistical packages, knowledge discovery tools, and computation engines.

Figure 2 shows the primary system components that address the interactions specified in Figure 1. The user interacts with data through the Database User Interface, Representation Manager, and Visualization Manager modules. These modules require a graphical user interface toolkit to be available.

Data specification is decoupled from representations and settings by the database system interface of the High Level Statement Processor and the Memory Set Manager modules. The High Level Statement Processor preprocesses action specifications over the data objects in the system and communicates modified actions to the Memory Set Manager. The Memory Set Manager stores and manages application level query and operation results, and communicates directly with external persistent data stores and processing modules. It also stores local copies of any metadata required by the system. The extracted Memory Sets determine input data possibilities for representation mappings and ultimately visualizations.

Any user action is eventually stored within the User Modeler module. Queries and operations are supplied by the High Level Statement Processor. Memory Set results are supplied by the Memory Set Manager. Any representation or visualization is supplied by the respective manager module as well. Our intent is to store every system action and result for future analysis.

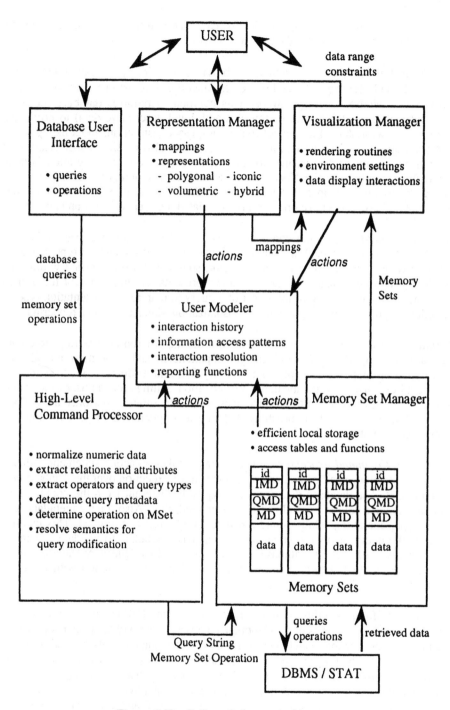

Figure 2 The ExBase Software Architecture.

There are seven main system components, each performing a specific function and sharing metadata generated by the user and system.

Database User Interface - this component provides an action specification interface to the DBMS and Memory Sets, and possesses functions to assist in the construction of queries and Memory Set operations. This component requires database metadata (database system catalog information plus additional descriptive data) to produce a listing of the available tables and attributes for query construction, and a listing of the available queries for the user to load or store. It can also receive a specification of bounds on a region of the visualization display for use in a query or operation from an interaction supplied by the Visualization Manager. It supplies either a query text string or Memory Set operation text string to the High Level Statement Processor. Regardless of how a query or operation is formulated the user can view and alter it.

Representation Manager - this component maps data fields of interest (specified by the SELECT clause of a query) to visualization parameters of the current representation on display. Representations (geometry, color, sound) are also specified within this module. It requires a listing of the available representation mappings for the user to load and store and a listing of the target of a query to map to a representation type. It supplies a representation mapping to the Visualization Manager for data rendering.

Visualization Manager - this component controls the environment settings to create the data rendering. Settings include the global parameters and color maps. It requires a representation mapping to apply to a Memory Set, and a Memory Set to render. It also requires a listing of the available Visualization Settings for the user to load and store. It supplies a function to produce displays and facilities to perform interactions over visualizations, such as brushing, probing and specifying display regions for subsequent operations.

High-Level Command Processor - this component takes an action statement, either a query or operation specification, and repackages it for execution over the database or a Memory Set. The database data format is typically different from the domain data format; numeric data is normalized for faster rendering. Also, query metadata (the query type, operators, relations and attributes used, etc.) is extracted. This module requires the query or operation, as well as database metadata to validate statement components with actual database entities. It supplies Query Metadata and a reconfigured textual statement to the system. It also logs any action with the User Modeler.

Memory Set Manager - this component interfaces to the DBMS, and may contain a number of retrieved subsets of data from the database, along with metadata concerning the memory sets, database, and queries. It may also contain data sets derived from the data, or computed by the application. In the future, facilities can exist here for caching schemes between the DBMS and Memory Sets, retrieval strategies, query optimizations, etc., to closely couple the DBMS to the application. In addition to the various metadata, connections exist to external statistical and knowledge discovery tools. Such tools automatically extract structures of interest to the end user from the data. It requires a query or operation textual string, and Query Metadata from the

HLSP. It supplies all of the data types within the system, as retrieved from the DBMS.

User Modeler - this component maintains the history of interactions between user and data, through an integrated system interface, as a type of knowledge base. Every interaction with the system is logged here. Information access patterns are determined, and tasks are constructed from lower-level interface events for subsequent analysis. Metadata on the session as well as the user is stored here while the system is running. It supplies routines to log any interaction within the system and possess a timestamping mechanism to maintain temporal information on the system actions.

Database - this component is the Orion DBMS (and in the future, the Aurora Dataserver), which possesses a C language client interface, that is callable from C++. It supplies a persistent data store and provides semantic access to all data, either in a load/store fashion or a relational query fashion.

4. Implementation Issues (what we hope to learn)

ExBase is meant to be a development testbed for continued research into the many aspects of data exploration system design. We are taking an object-oriented approach because we want to exploit encapsulation and parameterized types, inheritance and extensibility, as well as the strict compilation checking afforded by C++. We eventually want to create guidelines that will be useful for the development of future data exploration systems. Having visualization, database access, and statistical functions available in a single environment presents many research opportunities into data exploration processing. We summarize here some important areas that we would like to address.

User and Interaction Models

Retaining and analyzing the actions within the system will help in developing a user model of the data explorer. How a user explores data requires not only the actions the user executes, but also the results of those interactions, as they become transition points for further explorations. The sequence of processes from goals to interactions to tasks in specific domains must be better understood. This requires interaction analyses in the HCI fashion in addition to the retention of interactions at the system level. The domain tasks need to be developed in each domain under investigation, which will fall out from the interaction retention.

Visualization is typically perceived as an output technology, but it is also an input technology because it is the visualization that compels the researcher to proceed. Thus, there is both an input and output model for data exploration that must be developed, with visualization as the "glue" that binds them together. There must be methods to specify visualizations as inputs for queries and other data manipulation operations. This will reduce the burden from the user in having to accommodate multiple data models. By making visualizations more like "first class objects" in the programming language sense, such functionality can be realized. The use of object-oriented methodology will assist in creating visualization objects that can have meaningful operations specified over them. Effective methods for data exploration input and output need to be developed that transcend descriptions of new hardware devices and software interfaces. The roles of the input and output models and how they are coupled will help determine the effective methods.

Systems Models

In order to support the user and interaction models, a realizable system model must be developed. The types and functions of the relevant data objects to support data interactions are also needed, as well as the main system components and their interrelations. The degrees of coupling and division of labor between the system components have yet to be reconciled; there are many opportunities for exploiting user access patterns by performing query optimizations and caching schemes. Adequate approaches may be domain or data organization dependent. Such performance gains require a user and interaction model to be developed before great progress can be made. The introduction of intelligent assistants for data exploration requires the interaction histories to be available. Finally, the interoperability of the approach will enable the evaluation of new technologies. The concept of a "software bus" that will allow any other visualization, database, or analysis system to be integrated into this environment is very appealing, and will affect the overall design.

5. Conclusion

We have discussed the important interactions that a data exploration environment should support and introduced the ExBase architecture as a prototypical example. By this implementation, we hope to determine how a user would actually use such a system, and develop a practical interaction model. The recording and analysis of the interaction histories in specific domains will provide the focal points for future systems research, because they will highlight the major objects referenced and tasks undertaken by the user. We anticipate this implementation to shed light on how a database system should be coupled with a visualization system, in terms of the system and user interfaces.

Acknowledgments

The Exvis system was developed over a number of years by many people. The latest version, upon which this design is based, was implemented by David Gonthier, Robert Erbacher and Lisa Masterman at UMass Lowell. David Pinkney assisted with early prototyping of system components. Dr. Georges Grinstein provided many fruitful discussions and critiques.

6 References

[Bergeron89]   Bergeron, R.D., G. Grinstein, "A Reference Model for the Visualization of Multidimensional Data", *Proceedings of Eurographics'89*, 1989.

[Browne90]   Browne, D., M. Norman, E. Adhani, "Methods for Building Adaptive Systems", in Adaptive User Interfaces, D. Browne, P. Totterdell, M. Norman (Eds.), Academic Press, London, 1990, pages 85-130.

[Canter85]   Canter, D., R. Rivers, G. Storrs, "Characterizing User Navigation Through Complex Data Structures", *Behaviour and Information Technology*, v4, n2, 1985, pages 93-102.

[Crawford90]   Crawford, S.L., T.C. Fall, "Projection Pursuit Techniques for Visualizing High-Dimensional Data Sets", Visualization in Scientific Computing, G. Nielson, B. Shriver, L. Rosenblum (Eds.), 1990, 94-101.

[Felger92]   Felger, W., F. Schroder, "The Visualization Input Pipeline - Enabling Semantic Interaction in Scientific Data Visualization", *Proceedings of Eurographics'92*, v11, n3, Cambridge England, 1992, pages 139-151.

[Grinstein89] Grinstein, G.G., R.M. Pickett, M.S. Williams, "Exvis, An Exploratory Visualization Environment", *Proceedings of Graphics Interface'89*, London Ontario, 1989, pages 254-259.

[Grinstein92] Grinstein, G.G., J. Seig, S. Smith, M. Wiliams, "Visualization for Knowledge Discovery", *International Journal of Intelligent Systems*, v7, n7, September 1992, pages 637-648.

[Hachem93]   Hachem, N., M. Gennert, M. Ward, "A DBMS Architecture for Global Change Research", *Proceedings International Workshop on Global GIS*, International Society of Photogrammetry and Remote Sensing WG IV/6, Tokyo Japan, August 1993, pages 85-93.

[Hachem94]   Hachem, N., N. Serraro, M. Gennert, K. Qiu, "GaeaPN: A Petri Net Model for the Management of Data and Metadata Derivations in Scientific Experiments", *Worcester Polytechnic Institute Computer Science Department Technical Report WPI-CS-TR-94-01*, March 1994.

[Kao94]   Kao, D., Bergeron, R.D., "A Conceptual Schema Model for Scientific Data", *Database Issues for Data Visualization*, in this volume, Springer Verlag, 1994.

[Khoshafian85] Khoshafian, S.N., D.M. Bates, D.J. DeWitt, "Efficient Support of Statistical Operations", *IEEE Transactions on Software Engineering*, v11, n10, October 1985, pages 1058-1070.

[Korth91]   Korth, H., A. Silberschatz, Database System Concepts, Second Edition, McGraw-Hill, New York, 1991.

[Lamb91]   Lamb, C., G. Landis, J. Orenstein, D. Weinrib, "The ObjectStore Database System", *Communications of the ACM*, v34, n10, October 1991.

[Larson86]   Larson, J., "A Visual Approach to Browsing in a Database Environment", *IEEE Computer,* May 1986, pages 62-71.

[Lucas92]   Lucas, B., G. Abram, N. Collins, D. Epstein, D. Gresh, K. McAuliffe, "An Architecture for a Scientific Visualization System", *Proceedings of Visualization'92*, Boston, 1992, pages 107-114.

[Norman86]   Norman, D., "Cognitive Engineering", in <u>User Centered System Design</u>, D. Norman and S. Draper (Eds.), Lawrence Earlbaum Associates, Hillsdale NJ, 1986, pages 31-62.

[O'Day93]   O'Day, V.L., R. Jeffries, "Orienteering in an Information Space: How Information Seekers Get From Here to There", *Proceedings of INTERCHI'93*, Amsterdam, 1993, pages 438-445.

[Owen86]   Owen, D., "Answers First, Then Questions", in <u>User Centered System Design</u>, D. Norman and S. Draper (Eds.), Lawrence Earlbaum Associates, Hillsdale NJ, 1986, pages 361-376.

[Paulin90]   Paulin, J., "Task-Aware User Interfaces", *SIGCHI Bulletin*, v22, n1, July 1990, pages 55-60.

[Piatesky-Shapiro91] Piatesky-Shapiro, G., W. Frawley (Eds.), <u>Knowledge Discovery in Databases</u>, MIT / AAAI Press, Cambridge MA, 1991.

[Shneiderman83] Shneiderman, B., "Direct Manipulation: A Step Beyond Programming Languages", *IEEE Computer*, v16, n8, August 1983, pages 57-69.

[Shneiderman93] Shneiderman, B., "Dynamic Queries: A Step Beyond Database Languages", *University of Maryland Technical Report CS-TR-3022*, 1993.

[Seetharaman93] Seetharaman, K., G. Grinstein, H. Levkowitz, R.D. Bergeron, "A Conceptual Model for Interaction in Multiple Representation Spaces", *Proceedings of International Conference on Computer Graphics*, Bombay India, 1993, pages 121-128.

[Shoshani84]   Shoshani, A., F. Olken, H.K.T. Wong, "Characteristics of Scientific Databases", *Proceedings of 10th International Conference on Very Large Databases*, Singapore, August 1984, pages 147-160.

[Shoshani85]   Shoshani, A., H.K.T. Wong, "Statistical and Scientific Database Issues", *IEEE Transactions on Software Engineering*, v11, n10, October 1985, pages 1040-1046.

[Sparr91]   Sparr, T., R.D. Bergeron, L. Meeker, N. Kinner, P. Mayewski, M. Person, "Integrating Data Management, Analysis, and Visualization for Collaborative Scientific Research", *University of New Hampshire Durham Computer Science Department Technical Report TR91-10*, May 1991.

[Speray90]   Speray, D., S. Kennon, "Volume Probes: Interactive Data Exploration on Arbitrary Grids", *Computer Graphics Special Issue on the San Diego Workshop on Volume Visualization*, v24, n5, Nov. 1990, pages 69-76.

[Springmeyer92]   Springmeyer, R., M.M. Blattner, N.L. Max, "A Characterization of the Scientific Data Analysis Process", *Proceedings of Visualization'92*, Boston MA, 1992, pages 235-242.

[Stonebraker90]   Stonebraker, M. , M.L. Rowe, M. Hirohama, "The Implementation of Postgres", *IEEE Transactions on Knowledge and Data Engineering*, v2, n1, March 1990, pages 125-141.

[Stonebraker92]   Stonebraker, M., J. Frew, "The Sequoia 2000 Architecture and Implementation Strategy", *Sequoia 2000 Technical Report 93/23*, University of California Berkley, 1993.

[Stonebraker93]   Stonebraker, M., J. Chen, N. Nathan, C. Paxton, A. Su, J. Wu, "Tioga: A Database-Oriented Visualization Tool", *Proceedings of Visualization'93*, San Jose, 1993, pages 86-93.

[Treinish90]   Treinish, L., "SIGGRAPH'90 Workshop on Data Structures and Access Software for Scientific Data Visualization", *Computer Graphics*, v25, n2, 1991, pages 104-118.

[Treinish92]   Treinish, L. "Unifying Principles of Data Management for Scientific Visualization", *Proceedings of the British Computer Society Conference on Animation and Scientific Visualization*, Winchester UK, December 1992.

[Tukey77]   Tukey, J., <u>Exploratory Data Analysis</u>, Adison-Wesley, Reading MA, 1977.

[Upson89]   Upson, C., T. Faulhauber, D. Kamins, D. Laidlaw, D. Schlegel, J. Vroom, R. Gurwitz, A. vanDam, "The Application Visualization System: A Computational Environment for Scientific Visualization", *IEEE Computer Graphics and Applications*, v9, n4, July 1989, pages 30-42.

[Wickens93]   Wickens, C.D., "Cognitive Task Analysis in Visualization Display Design", *panel statement, Proceedings of Visualization'93*, San Jose CA, October 1993.

[Xidak93]   Xidak, Inc., <u>Overview of Orion</u>, November 1993, Palo Alto CA.

[Xidak94]   Xidak, Inc., <u>Aurora Dataserver Product Preview</u>, August 1993, Palo Alto CA.

Database Requirements
for Supporting
End-User Visualizations

Venu Vasudevan
Satellite Communications Division,
Motorola Inc., Chandler,, AZ.
email: Venu_Vasudevan@email.mot.com

Abstract

Databases have traditionally been architected with large, data-crunching batch applications in mind. This is especially evident to user interface researchers who are trying to tightly couple visualization front-ends to state-of-the-art database backends. This paper discusses the areas of impedance mismatch between databases and user interfaces. It proposes mechanisms that need to be incorporated into databases to reduce the systems integration problems involved in integrating visualization applications to databases. Motivating examples have been drawn from the VLSI domain.

1   Introduction

Constructing an environment for visualizing high-volume data presents challenging problems in both modelling and computation. A database substrate for a visualization environment needs to support a semantic data model to represent complex relationships. It also has to provide mechanisms for the efficient manipulation of data.

This paper reports experiences relating to the *Magritte* project [Vasu93], whose goal is to support end-user visualizations of VLSI design data. Specifically, its focus is on structural meta-data relating to circuit connectivity. While most of the examples given here pertain to VLSI design, a great many of these problems transcend VLSI. For example, the problem of visualizing highly-connected data has been shown to apply to program visualizations [Cons92], transportation networks [Cons92], and to visualizing geographical data [Borr92].

Current literature shows a convergence on the requirements of an object-oriented database management system[Atki92]. There is also a growing understanding that the application model for design applications differs from traditional business applications due to its creative, interactive nature [Barg91]. This paper takes the OODB manifesto [Atki92] and design transactions [Barg91] as starting points for further explorations into the specialized needs of visualization environments.

Database requirements for visualization are analyzed according to the traditional functional subsystems of a DBMS, namely: the *application model*, *data model*, *query subsystem*, *concurrency control* (transactions) and *distribution*.

2 Application Model

2.1 Inter-Client communication model

Traditionally, databases have been geared to support clients that are query-intensive batch jobs. Consequently, databases have aimed to *isolate* concurrently running clients by means of concurrency control mechanisms such as transactions. More recently, design databases in VLSI, CASE and other domains have motivated the notion that applications accessing the database may *communicate* with each other. Different proposals differ in the patterns of inter-client communication that they support, by means of a customized concurrency control model [Pu88, Skar89, Vasu90].

While most of these proposals support specialized, domain-specific forms of inter-client communication, visualization requires support for ad hoc communication patterns between client applications. Inter-client communication in visualization is ad hoc because it is driven by the end-user using *drag-and-drop* operations. A user may choose to drag-and-drop objects from any scene A on his screen to any other scene B on the screen (where A and B are hitherto separate transactions). Any concurrency control scheme that restricts the nature of A and B would place an artificial restriction on the end-user. A visualization database needs to support opportunistic communication between concurrent database applications while also providing many traditional concurrency control mechanisms. Some proposals for such *database clipboards* are discussed in Section 5 on page 7.

Example

Figure 1 shows a *hierarchy window* on the left, displaying a VLSI block hierarchy. The selected objects (in darker shade) are those for which the user wishes to see *flow* information (i.e. understand the objects from which these objects were derived). The *flow window* on the right of Figure 1 is a separate application (i.e. a separate transaction).

The windows in Figure 1 do not (cannot) communicate in a traditional database because they are running as separate transactions. However, the transactions need to communicate for the user interface to support drag-and-drop operations between the windows. In particular, the user might like to drag-and-drop the selected objects from the hierarchy window to the flow window so that flow information about these objects is displayed. In Figure 1, the user has pasted the selected object from the hierarchy window onto the flow window. The notion of a database clipboard can allow limited out-of-band transmissions between transactions without allowing them to interleave completely. In this example, information about the selected object (N3) needs to be an out-of-band data exchange between the hierarchy and flow windows.

2.2 Communication between clients and the database

Traditional databases support the *call/return* model of communication between a client application and the database. In other words, they support synchronous querying whereby the query result is immediately returned to the client application.

Visualization requires *asynchronous communication* between the client application and the database in order to support *dynamic views* [Morg83]. A dynamic view of the database is one that is automatically updated when new information of interest to the view is added to the database. Such a view is *dynamic* because the view is updated without the client having to periodically query the database.

Several object-oriented user interface toolkits such as SmallTalk [Gold89]and UniDraw [Vlis89]support dynamic views by embedding a subject/view protocol into all application objects in the inheritance hierarchy. The *subject/view* protocol distinguishes between subjects (data objects) and view objects (presentations of the data objects). Whenever a subject changes, the subject/view protocol automatically notifies all its views. If visualization databases support display objects, then a variant of this protocol can be used for persistent objects in the database.

Example

Figure 1 presents elements of a VLSI circuit and their relationships. Each node represents a block in the circuit. Links represent hierarchical/derivation relationships between blocks. While user A is viewing this scene, user B may check-in a new version of the block labelled "N2". If the underlying database supports dynamic views, the client controlling the scene could be asynchronously notified of the existence of a new version of N2 by means of application-specific visual cues.

Example

Figure 2 shows the hysteresis(aging) exhibited by three successive releases of a test VLSI design. Nodes that are dark indicate VLSI blocks that have *aged* (i.e. for which more recent versions have been checked-in to the database). Light nodes represent up-to-date

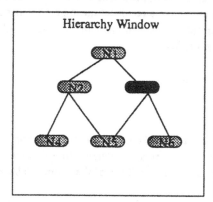 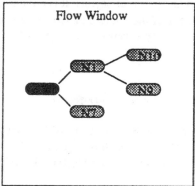

Figure 1: Multi-dimensional information display

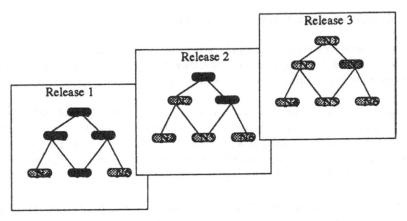

Figure 2: Visualizing multiple related releases

blocks. The leftmost release is the oldest one, and therefore contains more objects that have aged. The newest release (on the right) has no out-of-date objects.

Dynamic views would allow the asynchronous update of hysteresis information. In the absence of dynamic views, a more clumsy "polling" approach would have to be taken in updating hysteresis information.This could get cumbersome as the number of scenes on the user's screen grows.

2.3 Computational assumptions about clients

Visualization applications tend to be compute-intensive as well as large in number. In an end-user visualization environment, each window is potentially a separate transaction. Databases that support the *high availability* that visualization applications require must have a fairly small transaction overhead.

Many of the more compute-intensive visualizations involve *reconnaissance*, i.e. a read-only activity where the end-user surveys a large chunk of the database, rather than modifying a small group of objects. It is not unusual to have a result set during reconnaissance that is 5% of the entire database. Some currently proposed mechanisms such as object locking are too expensive for large read-only queries.

Example(large read-only query)

The project leader of a VLSI design might want to view the data relationships amongst the blocks of the entire design. This could very easily mean a visualization that contains 5,000-10,000 objects and 50,000 links which in turn is about 5% of the entire database.

3 Data Model

The features mentioned in the OODB manifesto provide a pretty fair coverage of the data modelling needs of visualization applications. Two areas in which the OODB manifesto does not mandate adequate requirements are in the handling of *object annotation* and *relationship modelling*.

3.1 Object Annotation

The OODB manifesto mandates that objects will support not only the scalar attributes that relational databases allow, but also structured attributes containing sets, lists, tuples and the like. However, the manifesto does not mandate sufficiently powerful query language features to take complete advantage of structured attributes.

Example

VLSI objects may contain a *list-of-strings* attribute containing all the users who are readers of the object. The database should directly support queries of the form:

Give me all the objects which contain John in their reader list (i.e. objects whose reader property contains John as one of the elements).

The example above is a fairly trivial query on structured attributes. An advanced query language should support queries that use regular expressions to match attribute values for structured attributes.

3.2 Link Modelling

Current object model(s) support complex objects using the notion of *subobjects* rather than *links*. Thus links are not first-class objects in most current OO models. While this is not a crippling feature in modelling, it makes querying a great deal more difficult (see Section 4 on page 6). Modelling and querying links which have attributes becomes very difficult.

For the purposes of visualization both Oids and links need to be treated uniformly because the end-user sees them both as presentation objects. Supporting efficient link queries requires the database to support indexing on links.

4 Query Subsystem

Visualization is a query-intensive process since it involves discovering patterns in high-volume data. In VLSI and several others domains, recursive queries over DAGs (directed acyclic graphs) of Oids and Links is a dominant form of querying.

Current databases do not provide an appropriate framework for querying hierarchical data for two reasons. Firstly, as mentioned in Section 3 on page 5, most current OODBs model relationships only implicitly using the *object-subobject* model. In this model, an object A is related to B by including A as an attribute of B. This makes it difficult to treat links as objects, which is required to support link attribution. More importantly, query languages for object-subobject data models are *set-based* (a la SQL) [Kim89, Fish89, Banc92] as opposed to being *graph-based*. This makes the specification of recursive queries very difficult because it does not support recursive query processing paradigms such as *traversal recursion* [Rose86]. Rudimentary aspects of recursive traversal such as not revisiting a node multiple times in a DAG, are hard, if not impossible to model in set-based query languages. Some current proposals for graph-based query languages such as *G+/GraphLog* [Cons90] and the DAMOCLES Query Language [Vasu92] propose a more appropriate query interface for recursive query processing.

Current standards efforts such as ODMG-93[Catt93] are moving towards adding navigational support to object query languages. However, these features are a long way from supporting traversal-intensive applications such as those cited above.

Example

Below is a simple, but prevalent recursive query expressed in the DAMOCLES query language. The query language syntax is explained only to the extent necessary to clarify the example. More information on the query language is available in [Vasu92].

traverse root_schematic_rel_1 *along* hierarchy | derivation *in direction* CHILD *upto* MAXLEVELS

The above query starts from an Oid (root_schematic_rel_1), and traverse both hierarchical and derivation links as far as they go. It returns a graph containing the entire schematic hierarchy rooted at root_schematic_rel_1, and also all objects (ex: netlists) derived from each schematic in the tree. Aspects of this query that are hard to model in set-based query languages are:

- The above query operates on a graph and returns a graph (Oids and Links), not just an Oid set. So, it is possible to nest recursive queries since the return result is itself hierarchically structured.

- It allows a declarative specification of the type of links to be traversed, and the precedence ordering.

- Depth and direction of traversal can be specified.

The above query is the recursive equivalent of a simple select operation in SQL. Complex recursive queries will takes hundreds of lines of code to duplicate in set-oriented query languages.

5   Transactions

The traditional transaction mechanism has been attractive because it provides atomic behavior for individual applications while allowing concurrency in database access. Much of the current work in design transactions points out that the classical notion of atomicity is too restrictive, and does not permit sufficient concurrency. The next two subsections deal with these two issues separately.

5.1   Atomicity

Transactions have traditionally been atomic operations. Data appears in the database only when a transaction commits. At that point the data is persistent, cannot be rolled back, and is visible to every other database application.

Savepoint proposals [Skar86] make a case for data to be made persistent without being visible to other applications. Savepoints allow long interactive transactions to be broken up into smaller parts, protecting them from catastrophic information loss. To the application, savepoints are themselves like classical transactions because they can revert only to the previous savepoint, not to another intermediate stage. However, savepointed data is private in that it is not visible to other applications until it is committed by the enclosing transaction.

Some proposals have enhanced transactions by allowing the domain of atomicity to include multiple applications. Sessions [Kim89] allow a multi-window workstation screen to behave as a single application. Only one window is allowed to be active at a time. Transaction groups [Skar89] allow a group of applications to interleave operations on shared data. However, the semantics of interleaving has to be defined up front.

None of these proposals seems completely compatible with the drag-and-drop paradigm that visualization applications use. Drag-and-drop creates communication channels between applications dynamically, and the constraint of a single active transaction that sessions place is too restrictive. The interleaving semantics of transactions in a transaction group need to be specified statically. This is incompatible with the dynamic communication patterns caused by drag-and-drop.

Visualization databases need a database concurrency control mechanism that does not conflict with the user-interface communication model. Since clipboards are an accepted paradigm of on-screen, inter-application communication, databases need to circumvent the strict atomicity of classical transactions the same way that clipboards do for an application's private data. These *persistent clipboards* would allow applications to dynamically set up communication without having to share persistent information with everyone else.

5.2   Concurrency

Visualization applications need greater database availability. This can be attained by loosening traditional concurrency control mechanisms.

Databases offering hypothetical transactions [Kim89] assume that database users run many experiments where they modify data without requiring it to persist. For such users, the hypothetical transaction allows a user to modify the database while allowing concurrent writes. The premise is that the data modified in a hypothetical transaction will be written to a shadow database, and eventually deleted.

Other proposals circumvent pure atomicity to allow more concurrency, and therefore greater data availability. The split transaction mechanisms [Pu88] and transaction groups [Skar86] allow applications to make data available to a selected set of other applications. Unfortunately, many of these proposals are not directly applicable to the interactive visualization domains. Visualization applications interact dynamically making static cooperation schemes such as transaction groups less applicable. But the basic idea of selected circumvention of atomicity is quite applicable to visualization.

Visualization requires user-driven communication between transactions. Since non-persistent data is communicated via clipboards in interactive applications, it would be uniform if persistent data followed the same model.

6   Distribution

Databases use the client-server approach as an architecture for decentralized computing. It has been pointed out that the precise division of work between server(s) and client(s) is a design trade-off that has to be decided on the basis of the application domain and its computational nature (the reader should consult [DeWi92] for the gory details).

Current choices of workstation-server architecture fall into two categories: *object-servers* and *page-servers*. Implementations of page servers can be further categorized as *page-to-page* systems and *page-to-object* systems. An example of a commercial object-server architecture is the Versant system [Vers93]. ObjectStore [Lamb91] uses the page-to-page flavor of page-servers, and O2 [Banc92] uses the page-to-object approach. [Chu93] compares alternative client-server database architectures from both performance and non-performance aspects. This section attempts to filter out the issues that might be of greatest relevance to a visualization audience.

In the object-server architecture, both the client and the server understand objects. From a visualization point of view, the following advantages of object-servers are relevant: *support for server-side queries, fine-grained concurrency* and *no limits to client-side buffer size*. Server-side queries are important for visualization applications in which a client needs to run a number of filter queries before finding the object set that he actually visualizes. Without the server-side query facility, the client may have to transport a much larger number of pages to the client (2-3 orders of magnitude larger) than what he actually has to visualize. The network traffic penalty here could be large. *Magritte* exhibits a great need for server-side queries for this reason. Object-servers offer object-level locking, as opposed to a coarser granularity of locking such as page-locks or segment-locks. This is important for visualization applications where there is a great deal of contention on objects. Object-servers provide client-side database buffer management. This allows the client to bring over an unlimited number of objects into the client space. This feature is important for large visualizations that involve in the order of 2^x objects on an x-bit machine. The reason why there are buffer-size limitations on page-servers is explained in [Chu93].

Page-servers offer efficiency for client-dominated computations. Page-server saved network band-width by moving pages of clustered objects across the network. They support coarser granularity locks, which requires less locking overhead. The "warm-start" performance of such databases rivals main-memory access. In other words, if objects are already present in the client-cache, they can be accessed almost as quickly as a main-memory object. Page servers present a greater performance hazard as far as client-crashes are concerned. Clients that core-dump could damage not only objects that they accessed, but also unrelated objects that happen to reside on the same page. Page-servers are probably an optimal choice for visualization applications that bring in a workings set of objects into the application and then perform compute-intensive visualization operations on them.

Conclusion

Visualization applications represent the next grand challenge to databases. They require databases to provide unprecedented bandwidth and computational capabilities. Queries are inherently graph-oriented, requiring recursive query processing capabilities. There is a mismatch between the database model of clients, and the end-user model of a visualization environment. Distribution is one of the most critical problems in a database substrate for visualization because of the number of applications that a single user might start up. Current research in client-server architectures does not provide accurate indicators about how to satisfy the needs of visualization. Furthermore, technological developments such as high-speed networks [Rooh94] and hardware support for database operations [Chan88] promise to cloud the issue further.

References

[Atki92] Atkinson,M., et al., "The Object-Oriented Database System Manifesto", in *Proceedings of the First International DOOD Conference.*

[Banc92] Bancilhon, F., Cluet, S., and Delobel, C., "A query Language for O$_2$", in *Building an object-Oriented System, The Story of O2*, Bancilhon, F. Delobel, C. and Kanellakis, P. (eds), Morgan Kaufmann, 1992, pp.234-255.

[Barg91] Barghouti, N. and Kaiser, G., "Concurrency Control in Advanced Database Applications", *ACM Computing Surveys*, Vol 23, No. 3, Sept. 1991, pp. 269-317.

[Catt93] Cattell,R.(ed), "The Object Database Standard ODMG-93", Forthcoming from Morgan Kaufman, San Mateo, California, 1993.

[Chan88] Chang, A., Mergen, M., "801 Storage: Architecture and Programming", *ACM TOCS*, Vol.6, #1.

[Chu93] Chu,I. and Winslett,M.S., "Choices in Database Workstation-Server Architecture", in *Proceedings of COMPSAC'93*, pp.298-305, 1993.

[Cons90] Consens, M. et al., "Visualizing Queries and Querying Visualizations", *ACM SIGMOD Record*, March 1992, pp. 39-46.

[Cruz87] Cruz, I.B, Mendelzon, A.O., Wood, P.T., "A Graphical Query Language Supporting Recursion", *ACM SIGMOD Record*, Vol. 16, #3, 1987, pp.323-330.

[DeWi92]DeWitt, D. et al., "Three Alternative Workstations-Server Architectures", in *Building an Object-Oriented System, The Story of O2*, Bancilhon, F. Delobel, C. and Kanellakis, P. (eds), Morgan Kaufmann, 1992, pp.411-446.

[Douc92] Doucet, A. and Pfeffer, P., "Using a Database System to Implement a Debugger", in *Building an Object-Oriented System, The Story of O2*, Bancilhon, F. Delobel, C. and Kanellakis, P. (eds), Morgan Kaufmann, 1992, pp.523-540.

[Fish89] Fishman, D. et al., "Overview of the IRIS DBMS", in *Object-Oriented Concepts, Databases and Applications*, Kim, W. and Lochovsky, F.H. (eds), ACM Press, pp.219-250.

[Gold89] Goldberg, A. and Robson, D., "Smalltalk-80: The Language", Addison-Wesley, 1989.

[Kim89] Kim, W. et al., "Features of the ORION Object-Oriented Database System", in *Object-Oriented Concepts, Databases and Applications*, Kim, W. and Lochovsky, F.H. (eds), ACM Press, pp.251-282.

[Lamb91] C.Lamb, G.Landis, J.Orenstein, M.Roth, "The ObjectStore Database System", *CACM*, Vol. 34, #10, 1991.

[Morg83] Morgenstern, M.," Active Databases as a Paradigm for Enhanced Computing Environments", in *Proc. of the 9th International Conference on VLDB*, 1983.

[Pu88] Pu,C., Kaiser, G. and Hutchinson, N., "Split Transactions for Open-Ended Activities", in *Proceedings of the 14th International Conference on Very Large Databases*, 1988, pp.26-37.

[Rose86] Rosenthal, A. et al., "Traversal Recursion: A Practical Approach to Supporting Recursive Applications", in Proceedings of the ACM SIGMOD Conference on the Management of Data, 1986, pp. 166-176.

[Rooh94] Rooholamin, R., Cherkassky, V., and Garver, M., "Finding the Right ATM Switch for the Market", *IEEE Computer*, pp.16-28, April 1994.

[Skar86] Skarra, A. et al., "An Object Server for an Object-Oriented Database System", in *1986 International Workshop on Object-Oriented Database Systems*, pp.196-205.

[Skar89] Skarra,A. and Zdonik, S., "Concurrency Control and Object-Oriented Databases", in *Object-Oriented Concepts, Databases and Applications*, Kim, W. and Lochovsky, F.H. (eds), ACM Press, pp.395-421.

[Vasu90] Vasudevan, V., "Cotools: A Tool Composition Mechanism for Object-Based Environments", in the ACM Eighteenth Annual Computer Science Conference, 1990, pp.326-332.

[Vasu92] Vasudevan, V. et al., "DAMOCLES: An Observer-Based Approach to Design Tracking", in ICCAD 1993, pp.546-552.

[Vasu93] Vasudevan, V., "Comprehending Large-Scale Connectivity in Object-Oriented Databases", submitted to The International Conference on Data Engineering, 1993.

[Vers93] Versant Technical Overview, Versant Technologies Inc.

[Vlis89] Vlissides, J. and Linton, M., "UniDraw: A Framework for building Domain-Specific Graphical Editors", in *ACM SIGGRAPH/SIGCHI User Interface Software and Technologies '89 Conference*, November 1989.

A System Architecture for Data-oriented Visualization

A. Wierse[*], U. Lang[†], R. Rühle[†]

[*]Institute for Computer Applications II
[†]Computer Centre University of Stuttgart (RUS)

Abstract: In this paper we present a system architecture which will allow several users to perform cooperative scientific visualization in a heterogeneous high-performance envi-ronment. In contrast to most available visualization systems this architecture tries to find a balanced relationship between the algorithms and the data. Comparable to the Controller which controls the execution flow storage managers are introduced which control the data flow between modules which might reside on different computers. An overview of the system architecture will be given and an inspection of the potential of this approach will be performed.

1 Introduction

Most visualization systems currently available focus on the visual programming paradigm in an algorithm oriented way. Data itself cannot be accessed by the user directly, but exists only internally. Means are provided to connect modules to networks which perform certain visualization tasks, but the access to the underlying data mostly is limited to typing a filename in the input-module.

There is no explicit control of data by users within most of the current dataflow based visualization systems. Thus either data produced by intermediate steps is kept, even if it is not needed any more, or this caching mechanism can be switched off globally. As data does not exist as directly accessible data objects a selective handling is not possible. On the other hand a user who wants to examine a certain interval in time repeatedly would be delayed by the application creating the same temporary objects over and over again instead of creating the sequence once and then display just out of „cache".

The supercomputers that are available today are able to solve numerical problems that result in amounts of data to be measured in Gigabytes. Solutions of time-dependent problems in fluid dynamics can easily consist of several hundred timesteps, each several Megabytes in size. The efficient visualization of these solutions puts significant weight on the organization of compute resources as well as storage resources.

Think for example about a massively parallel computer system with 1000 nodes, each with 32MBytes of memory, which is used to solve a timedependent fluid dynamical problem via domain decomposition. The transfer of the final solution to a workstation would be very inefficient if possible at all, even if high-performance networks were available. One could try instead to do as much of the visualization work on the parallel system and then transfer the least possible amount of data to the workstation.

Since the position in the visualization pipeline where the least amount will occur can vary, a flexible architecture is desirable.

An architecture should make it possible to decide which data will be processed where to get the maximum throughput for a given visualization algorithm. This involves the need for a flexible handling of the modules available on the participating computers but also the handling and the transfer of data between the different modules must be optimized. Means must be provided to assure an optimal transfer of data between computers under different conditions.

Since database management systems (DBMS) come to mind when data, its organization or distribution are of interest, it is clear that DBMS experience can help a lot when dealing with these problems. Starting from a visualization system we will show in this paper how we integrate the database management and how the whole application benefits from the orientation towards a DBMS. Since the work is performed as a part of an ongoing project not every feature described in this paper is already implemented, but the potential of this approach can be seen none the less.

The architecture as described in this paper is used in the RACE-project R2031 PAGEIN (Pilot Applications in a Gigabit European Integrated Network) sponsored by the European Community. It serves as a base for experiments that are performed to examine the possibilities of visualization in a cooperative working environment.

2 The System Architecture

The following ideas are used within the project to design a distributed software system in cooperation with other partners. Based on experience with own developments and the usage of available packages a system architecture has been designed, which fits all the needs of a high performance distributed visualization application. These are

- distribution
- cooperative working
- supercomputer usage (parallel or vectorizing)
- time dependent simulation
- efficient memory handling
- efficient use of the high speed network
- good overall performance

None of the currently available visualization packages supports all of these features.

2.1 Overview

As has been stated already in the introduction a modular approach is the one that allows the most flexibility in distributing certain parts of the visualization application on specific computers. The need for excellent high speed network utilization makes it necessary to put emphasis on the management of the network connections in dependence of the type of data transferred. This can be combined with the need for a storage manager which evolves out of the requirements the database approach puts onto the system architecture.

Figure 1 shows an overview of the proposed system architecture. The main processes are the user interface (UI), the overall controller, the storage manager (SM) and the application modules (A, B, C, D, E).

The controller is the central part of this architecture. It has the overall view of the whole application. This central controller supervises the distribution of modules across the involved computers as well as the management of the execution of the application.

FIGURE 1: The proposed System Architecture

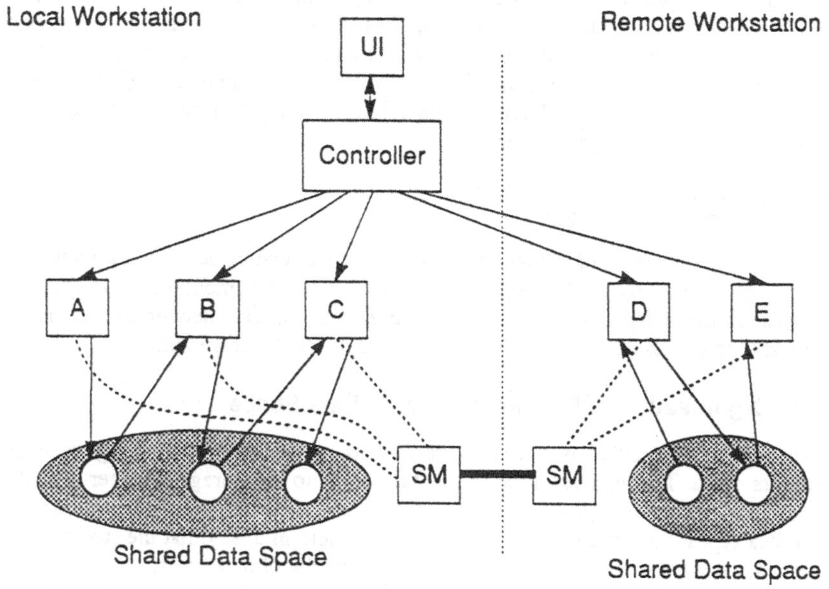

On each machine a shared data space (SDS) exists, which normally would consist of shared memory. All data that has to be exchanged between application modules will be stored in this SDS. The sending of data from one module to another thus means that the „sending" module writes its output data into the SDS and the „receiving" module reads it from the same location. In fact no data will be sent directly from one module to the next.

The storage manager administers the use of this SDS in a database-like fashion. If a module wants to write data, it asks the storage manager for the space in the SDS under a certain name. The storage manager provides the module with an address in the SDS. A module that wants to access this data has been given the name from the controller and queries the storage manager to provide the address for this object. Although the query currently only works by name, other ways of getting access to data objects can be implemented easily.

If modules are running on different computers in a distributed environment, it is possible that the storage manager cannot provide the address of this object. It will then contact the storage manager on the machine, where the data object lies in the SDS and ask for the transfer of the object. Once the object has been copied, the now available address of this object in the SDS can be given to the application module which then can access the data.

As can be seen from the previous paragraphs, an application module only needs connections to the controller and the storage manager. The controller supplies the application module with the information that is necessary to guarantee the proper execution of the overall application. The data that will be exchanged between subsequent application modules is stored in the SDS under the control of the storage manager. This allows a very simple structuring of an application module.

The implementation of this system architecture for the visualization workpackage of the PAGEIN project is currently done using C++. Due to the fact that the project partners are distributed all over Europe the basic communication functionality has been provided to the partners as a library. The controller, the user interface and the storage manager are developed by different people at RUS, while the visualization algorithms are written by other project partners.

2.2 The Storage Manager

The data management of the whole application is handled by dedicated storage managers. Once started by the controller on each participating computer the storage managers run rather independent from the execution of the module network. Each module that wants to access data in the SDS is connected its local storage manager.

2.2.1 Organisation of Data in the Shared Data Space

An item or object that is stored in the SDS is registered by the storage manager under its name. The representation of the data object to the storage manager is held in basic types, such as *int, float, char*, and arrays of these. If the user wants to introduce own data types, the structure of this data must be held in a way that the storage manager can also deal with. This leads to a simple hierarchy of data types:

1. On the lowest level we find the basic data types with the names: CHARSHM, SHORTSHM, INTSHM, LONGSHM, FLOATSHM and DOUBLESHM. An element of these types stored in the SDS needs the space necessary for one element plus the type information.

2. The next higher level are arrays of the basic types: CHARSHMARRAY, SHORTSHMARRAY, INTSHMARRAY, LONGSHMARRAY, FLOATSH-MARRAY and DOUBLESHMARRAY. Additionally to the type information and the space needed for the data a „number of elements" information is stored.

3. Pointers are introduced in the next level: they consist of a shared memory identifier (if we have several shared memory segments on the same machine) and an offset into this segment. Therefore such a pointer needs the space for its own type and for the segment number plus the offset.

4. The highest level can be used to group elements of the lower levels. The main structure of such an object is similar to a CHARSHMARRAY, i.e. a type identifier, a length information and finally the data part. To distinguish it from a character array the type identifier is unique to the real data type. In the data part items of all three lower levels are packed. A pointer of level three can point to an object of level four again.

This organization demands a unique type identifier, but on the other hand absolutely no information about the structure of a new data type other than its basic components are needed. Thus every data type which can be build upon the basic data types can be handled by the data manager. The structuring of the data also supports the handling of persistent objects since it allows a rather simple mapping from the SDS-representation to a file-representation.

2.2.2 Data Transfer to a remote Host

In a distributed environment the storage managers on the different machines are connected if data has to be transferred between them. Upon the request of a module for the address of a data object the storage manager first searches in its own object list. If the required name is found, it sends the address that belongs to this object back to the module. In a future version the access-data for the local objects might be stored in the shared data space, so that for local read accesses no messages have to be sent to the storage manager.

If the data object is not stored in the SDS, the storage manager asks its neighbour storage managers about the object. Since the controller knows about the connectivity of the module network, it can provide the storage manager with some helpful information about where it can find data that is not (yet) available locally. The storage manager which has the data object in its local data space now packs this data object into a message and sends this message back to the asking storage manager.

High speed networks have different characteristics than Ethernet. Ultra-Net for example reaches its high throughput by using rather large packets (up to 32KB). This makes Ultra-Net quite inefficient for the use in an environment where lots of small messages will be sent; instead it is tuned for the fast transfer of large chunks of data. In the case of the availability of Ultra-Net, it should be used to transfer the data objects, but for the exchange of the ordinary messages Ethernet or ATM are suited better. When dedicated storage managers are used, this can be achieved easily, since the application modules don't care about the transport of objects between computers.

Another aspect of the transfer of objects between different computers is the data conversion. In the workstation domain the IEEE standard is established quite well, but in the supercomputer world Cray for example uses different data formats which have to be converted. The xdr-routines are a tool to convert data easily between different formats, but with low performance. Arrays of values of the same type are converted one after another; on a Cray the vectorizing features could be of great use, but special versions of the xdr-routines for this purpose do not exist. In the dedicated storage manager module on a Cray however the necessary routines for conversions between IEEE and Cray format are coded in the most efficient way. So the special hardware features of the supercomputer can be used to speed up the transfer of data.

2.2.3 Consistency Management

With the existence of several copies of a data object the need for a consistency management arises. Since we are in a well known environment, some simple assumptions can be made:

- A data object will only have one module that has write access to it.
- An object will always be updated as a whole (if not, subobjects should be used).

- The controller has the overview of all modules that will access a certain object and can give this information to the storage manager .

- Only the controller can delete an object.

This simplifies the data management to a certain degree. We can assume that if an object is not locally available, we only have to check each of our neighbour storage managers to find it. The update of objects that have been changed always appears in the same direction.

Once an object has been changed, there are two possible ways to update the copies: on the one hand one could bring all copies to the new state immediately; this is very efficient, if the necessary network bandwidth is available. On the other hand „update-on-demand" could be used, which would bring a certain waiting time for the asking module, but would avoid the transfer of unused objects. Due to the rules used in the whole application, the first case seems to be the more useful one: once it has been necessary to copy an object the probability that it will be used again in the next step is high. Thus after a write access has been finished, the copies of this object should be updated as soon as possible.

Again the assumptions above allow us to restrict to a one level depth in the copy-structure: if there is a storage manager which has a copy of the local object, then there is a direct connection to it.

2.3 The Application Module

In the notion of a client/server DBMS the application module is the client which sends requests to the server (the storagae manager). The storage manager then provides the information where the application module finds the data it needs.

When an application module starts, it establishes the infra-structure necessary to communicate to the controller and the storage manager. This includes the attachment to the shared data space. The module is informed by the controller about the names of its input and output objects. In the case of an input object only read-access is necessary; in the case of an output object create- or write-access must be possible.

2.3.1 Read Access to a Data Object

To use a data object which resides in the SDS its address is needed. A message which contains the name of the desired object is sent to the storage manager to get this address. The storage manager now takes care to make this data object available in the local SDS and sends the address back to the module. This address consists of a shared memory segment number to identify several different shared memory segments and an offset into this segment.

The module normally knows what type the data object it wants to read has. The consistency can be checked easily by comparing the type identifier which is derived from the type name. If it is not clearly determined what type the object will have, a kind of virtual constructor is used, which creates an object of the correct type and returns it to the caller.

FIGURE 2: Data Access

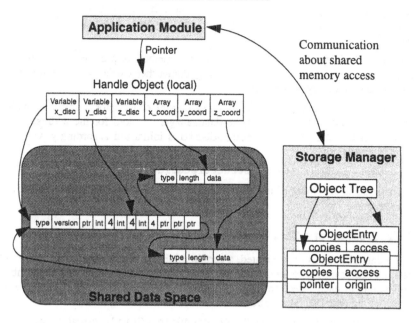

Once the type of the data object in the SDS is confirmed, an object in the modules local memory space is created, which provides the access to the data in the SDS. For example the data object that holds data for a structured grid has the following form:

```
class DO_StructuredGrid {
  IntShm x_disc;          // number of points in x-direction (X)
  IntShm y_disc;          // number of points in y-direction (Y)
  IntShm z_disc;          // number of points in z-direction (Z)
  FloatShmArray x_coord;  // x-coordinates (length X * Y * Z)
  FloatShmArray y_coord;  // y-coordinates (length X * Y * Z)
  FloatShmArray z_coord;  // z-coordinates (length X * Y * Z)
}
```

IntShm and FloatShmArray are the types that have been introduced to access an integer and an array of floating point values in the SDS. Upon the creation of an instance of the class DO_StructuredGrid, these elements are initialized to point to the related data in the SDS.

After the type of the data object has been confirmed, we know exactly what to expect while examining the data part of the character-array which represents the data object. First we will find three integer values and then three pointers to arrays of floating point values (arrays are not included in the character array to make it easier to resize them later). So the first IntShm-element x_disc is initialized to the address of the first integer value, the second to the second and the third to the third. Then the character array has an element of type ShmPtr which holds an address in the SDS. This address is now used to initialize the FloatShmArray-element x_coord which then points with its data pointer to the first value in the floating point array. The array operator [] of the class FloatShmArray is overloaded, so that a direct access of the form x_co-ord[n] is possible; during this access the index is checked against the array boundaries.

To allow a faster but more unsafe access a method is provided that returns the addresses of all the arrays directly. The programmer then carries the full responsibility for checking the array boundaries.

All this initialization is done simply by calling the constructor of this class with the name of the object as argument: the datamanager is asked for the address and the instance of the class DO_StructuredGrid is initialized accordingly without the users intervention:

```
struct_grid = new DO_StructuredGrid(„Grid", appmod);
```

appmod is an object of the class that provides the access to the communications infrastructure.

2.3.2 Creation of a Data Object

If a data object has to be created, a certain minimum knowledge is required to allocate the necessary space. In the case of a structured grid this means that the number of grid points in each direction must be known. So a constructor which creates a new object of the type DO_StructuredGrid has the following form:

```
struct_grid = new DO_StructuredGrid(„Grid", appmod, x, y, z);
```

The x, y and z hold the size of the arrays that will hold the coordinates. The constructor of this class now sends a message to the storage manager in which it requests the space necessary to hold the data for the floating point arrays and the character-array that will hold the data object information. Then the character-array is filled with the type data, the length information, a version number, a pointer to the name of the object, the three integer values and the three pointers to the (empty) floating point arrays. Now the object is ready to be filled. The creation of an object implicitly allows write access for this object.

If the data that will be filled into the floating point arrays is already known, it can be handed to a similar constructor which then takes care of the initialization of the floating point arrays with these values. A null-pointer will be returned if the desired object already exists .

After the writing has been finished, the storage manager should be informed about this, so that it can take care of the copying of the object. This is an asynchronous message which need not wait for a reply. An asynchronous message should also suffice if a module wants to read again from an already attached object for which it has returned the access-rights. In this case the comparison of the version entry in the SDS with the local copy allows to check, whether the data object has changed in the mean time. If so, an update of the instance in the local memory has to be performed. This should be no more than rereading the directly stored values and readjusting the pointers to the arrays.

2.3.3 Write Access to a Data Object

Since there will be at most one module at the same time which writes to the object the only problem that could arise is, that a module wants to write to an object while another one is still reading. So the request for write access cannot be asynchronous. To avoid that a module simply starts reading a data object while it is being written, a flag that shows that the data is currently invalid could be used. This would be set by the writing process after it has got the write permission. The version number of the modified data object will be incremented, so that reading processes can check easily, whether the data object has changed since their last access.

The fact that the visualization environment puts some restrictions on the way objects are accessed has some benefits here too. Due to the execution control by the controller it can be assumed that in an application no read accesses are pending when the writing module wants to change the data: the controller will invoke the reading modules not before the writing module has stated that it is finished with its output object. Thus the handling of simultaneous read and write accesses can be held simple.

In the case of a change in the size of arrays in the object an update mechanism could be used, which simply allocates new arrays of the desired size and frees the old ones. Then the addresses of the new arrays have to replace the ones of the old arrays in the character-array which holds the data objects structure information. All the allocation and deallocation can be handled in one message, so that the network traffic can be held low at this point.

3 Further Advantages of the Database-Approach

In the following chapter the advantages of a system architecture which is based upon a data base oriented approach with respect to its data handling will be explained shortly for several aspects.

3.1 Partitioned Objects

Visualization packages available today only allow the handling of data in one piece. In the case of a non-distributed application on a single processor workstation this is no problem. But if we think of a multi-processor workstation or a distributed application the following bottleneck appears: as long as one module is working, its successors will wait. Even if the output data of the first module is organized linearly, the second module waits until the data object is written completely, although it already could start working on the part of the data object that is already written. Through the availability of an additional processor for the second module the start of this module would not affect the speed of the first module, i.e. they could work in parallel without performance penalty.

So what would be desirable is a kind of pipelining the execution as it can be found in modern RISC CPUs today. While the first module is writing the second part of a data object its successor can already read the first part which has been written already. This can lead to a significant speed-up in the overall performance of the visualization pipeline.

This can work only if the data is organized in a linear way, i.e. an object will be written one part after the other as the computation of the module proceeds. An example for this would be the computation of a clipping surface for a structured grid: the grid would be checked layerwise against the clipping function and the output would be produced in slices. A subsequent mapping module could map velocity vectors on each of these slices separately and thus work one step behind the clipping module. This would also work for an isosurface module on structured grids. In the case of unstructured grids it is much less probable that the organization of the data is in a linear way but under certain circumstances a speedup can still be seen.

Once an object is partitioned it can easily be used in a real parallel environment (MIMD): Each processor would work on a different part of the input object and would produce a different part of the output object. In the case of the integration of visualization and simulation on massively parallel computers this is tightly coupled to data organization (e.g. domain decomposition).

The usage of such techniques could be simplified by the data base approach taken here: The access to the part of an object is achieved by just asking the local object for the next piece. If necessary the underlying communication with the storage manager will be performed invisible and the actual part will be returned after the current object is available.

3.2 Persistent Data Objects

The data base approach as chosen here allows an easy handling of persistent objects. In nearly the same way as an object is transferred from one storage manager to another, it could be transferred from the SDS to the disk. This could also be used to add something like „swapping data to the disk", if the SDS gets too small to hold all the data.

The identity of objects makes it possible for the user to select the objects that shall be held persistent. Saving an intermediate state is not limited to the connectivity and the modules but includes the data as well. By extensive use of persistence a huge amount of data could be held in relatively slow but very easy access by just keeping the object in the environment, but swap it out to disk.

3.3 Special Multi-Media Objects

In a cooperative environment the usage of video or audio communication is obvious. Another application where the use of video can be useful is the comparison between experiment and numerical simulation. Often a video sequence showing the actual experiment can be created without too much effort. The comparison of the simulation results and the experiment would be the most easiest if these two sequences could be overlaid and played simultaneously.

To achieve this it is necessary to have something like a continuous stream of frames. This could be implemented using data objects which have a buffer-like behaviour: they provide storage for some frames, and these frames are updated in a circular fashion with the most recent video frame. The module that displays the sequence would always try to read the frame which has just been written. If the information about the creation of a new frame would have to be exchanged via the storage manager this would cause a certain load for the storage management. So for modules residing on the same machine the communication should be done by using some flags in the shared memory (semaphore like).

If however the video sequence has to be distributed between computers, the storage manager could spawn a process which takes care that each frame that has been written completely is transferred to the copies of this data object as soon as possible. This would allow for a fast transfer without interference with the other tasks of the storage manager.

3.4 Time-dependent Data

The ability to handle time-dependent data in the first place puts responsibility onto the controller. It has to take care of the timing of the visualization pipeline in addition to its mere sequentiality. But the huge amount of data that normally comes with time-dependent data sets also makes efficient storage management an even more important issue.

If a scientist wants to examine a certain phenomenon closer he normally doesn't display it only once, but instead views a sequence around the interesting point in time over and over again. Here the possibility to keep data objects longer than just for the moment of sending will improve the behaviour of the application enormously. During the first execution of the visualization pipeline for each time step the behaviour is the same as with other visualization packages. But the final result of each computation (directly before the rendering stage) can be kept after its display automatically. If the user now decides to see the scene again for the second time or to see it in reverse order all the necessary time steps exist in an immediately displayable form. The whole computation overhead can be avoided now (imagine the computation of an isosurface for each time step).

This speed-up can of course only be achieved if a certain amount of memory is available to hold the necessary data objects. On the other hand the application modules need not care about remembering objects; this is totally transparent to the module programmer. This behaviour can even be given for user written modules which use data types that are not known when the system environment is compiled.

4 Conclusion

The proposed system architecture differs from the currently available packages in many aspects. The main difference is the handling of data by a data base-like storage management. This approach allows a very flexible and efficient handling of data, even in the case of time dependent data which usually involves huge amounts of data. Extensibility is one of the key-features which has been considered while designing the system. The programmer can derive or introduce own special data types and they will be handled by the system in the same efficient manner as the provided data types are.

The existence of a storage manager separates the administration of data clearly from the modules: the interfaces are held simple, but the fastest access possible in a shared memory region is provided. The features that come together with the usage of such a data base approach bring nearly no cost with them (persistent objects, optimal transfer using high speed links, speed-up by keeping objects in the SDS, managing time-dependent data sets, etc.).

In the chosen approach we integrate the visualization and the database as close as possible. By using data base methods even for the internal data management of the visualization system the data base management becomes a core part of the visualization itself. We think that the user will benefit from this integrated view and have a much better understanding about the organization of his data than current visualization systems can offer.

Until now the development is mainly focussed on the usage of the data base kernel for the visualization internal data management (e.g. querying is only supported by the name of an object, which must be unique). Of course in the progress of the project more data base oriented functionality will be introduced, to allow the user a more powerfull data management for the whole application.

Since this is ongoing work which right now comes into the phase where early evaluations and measurements are possible, no final results are available yet. But first measurements support our impression that this system architecture can be an ef ficient environment for several different application areas. The system has been demonstrated at the HPCN '94 in Munich, using a 2 MBit/s connection to Stuttgart. A collaborative working session with participants in Stuttgart and Munich has been shown, utilizing the Cray Y-MP at RUS for a time dependent fluid flow simulation on-line.

This work has partially been sponsored by the Commission of the European Community within RACE Project R2031: PAGEIN Pilot Applications in a Gigabit European Integrated Network.

5 Bibliography

[1] AVS, Technical Overview, Advanced Visual Systems, Oct. 1992, Waltham, MA

[2] User Guide, AIX/Visualization Data Explorer/6000, IBM Corporation, Yorktown Heights, 1992

[3] IRIS Explorer 2.0, Technical Report, Silicon Graphics Computer Systems, Mountain View 1992

[4] W.J.Schroeder, W.E.Lorensen, G.D.Montanaro and C.R.Volpe, VISAGE: An Object-Oriented Scientific Visualization System, Proceedings of the Visualization '92, Boston, MA

[5] Al Globus, Perspectives on the IRIS Explorer Visualization Environment, Computer Sciences Corporation Report RNR-91-021, 1992

[6] Lloyd A. Treinish, The role of data management in discipline-independent data visualization, „Extracting Meaning from Complex Data: Processing, Display, Interaction", Edward. J. Farrell Editor, Proc. SPIE 1259, 261-271 (1990)

[7] U. Lang, R. Rühle, Scientific Application Environments; Positional Paper, SIGGRAPH 90 Workshop on Data Structures and Access Software for Scientific Visualization, August 1990

[8] J. Gray, A. Reuter, Transaction Processing: Concepts and Techniques, Morgan Kaufmann Publishers, San Mateo, 1993

[9] A. Wierse, U. Lang, R. Rühle, Architectures of Distributed Visualization Systems and their Enhancements, Workshop Papers of the Fourth Eurographics Workshop on Visualization in Scientific Computing, Abingdon, UK April 1993

A Hyperspectral Image Data Exploration Workbench for Environmental Science Applications

Mark A. Woyna
David G. Zawada
Kathy Lee Simunich
John H. Christiansen

Advanced Computer Applications Center
Argonne National Laboratory
9700 S. Cass Ave., Argonne, IL 60439
{woyna, zawada, simunich, jhc}@athens.dis.anl.gov
(708) 252-3291

Abstract

The Hyperspectral Image Data Exploration Workbench (HIDEW) software system has been developed by Argonne National Laboratory to enable analysts at Unix workstations to conveniently access and manipulate high-resolution imagery data for analysis, mapping purposes, and input to environmental modeling applications. HIDEW is fully object-oriented, including the underlying database.

1 Introduction

A significant challenge to the information sciences is to provide more powerful and accessible means to exploit the enormous wealth of data available from high-resolution imaging spectrometry ("hyperspectral" imagery) for analysis, for mapping purposes, and for input to environmental modeling applications. As an initial response to this challenge, Argonne's Advanced Computer Applications Center has developed a workstation-based, prototype software workbench which employs AI techniques and other advanced approaches to deduce surface characteristics and extract features from hyperspectral images. Among its current capabilities, the prototype system can classify pixels according to surface type. The classification process employs neural network analysis of inputs which include pixel spectra and a variety of processed image metrics, including image "texture spectra" derived from fractal signatures computed for subimage tiles at each wavelength.

The prototype software system is object-based, written in the C++ language. It employs a readily comprehended graphical user interface for data navigation and visualization, and a flexible data interchange scheme to allow the system to function independently of the source of hyperspectral data. In order to explore the options for optimal access to external image and related data, we have developed and are evaluating two software system prototype variants, one interfacing with external

The submitted manuscript has been authored by a contractor of the U.S. Government under contract No. W-31-109-ENG-38. Accordingly, the U.S. Government retains a nonexclusive, royalty-free license to publish or reproduce the published form of this contribution, or allow others to do so, for U.S. Government purposes.

image files in the University Corporation for Atmospheric Research's (UCAR's) netCDF standard format, and one tightly integrated with an object database management system.

HIDEW prototype is being tested in several land-use classification and feature extraction tasks as an aid to U.S. Department of Energy (DOE) site characterization work, as well as in other application areas in global change research, in proof-of-principle exercises, and pilot studies using actual hyperspectral image data from the Jet Propulsion Laboratory's (JPL) Airborne Visible / Infrared Imaging Spectrometer (AVIRIS) sensor system.

2 The Workbench

HIDEW prototype is being developed both as a software engineering demonstration and as an analysis tool to directly support studies. It is intended that the prototype will provide a general, easily expandable framework for hyperspectral and multispectral image analysis, allowing new tools and approaches for data visualization and analysis, and existing tools from diverse sources, to be brought to bear on the problem of exploitation of hyperspectral and multispectral data. In addition, it is planned that the prototype will be used, with application-specific enhancements, to support studies of interest to the DOE, as outlined in Section 4 of this paper.

2.1 Software System Structure

HIDEW makes full use of the features and capabilities of the object-oriented software development paradigm. The prototype implements a C++ object-based common data representation for data transfer, manipulation, analysis, and archiving, based on the concept of an "Image Data Packet" (IDP). All image-related data manipulated by the system and displayed by its user interface are in the form of IDPs. Scores of different object methods (functions) belonging to the IDP object class have been developed to access, manipulate, and restructure IDP data. IDPs are cataloged into hierarchies of Library objects. Applications of all kinds are encapsulated within Process objects, which interact with IDPs in a consistent fashion. This object-based implementation will greatly facilitate future upgrades to the system. Figure 1 depicts the basic structure of the IDP and Process object classes.

2.2 Database

Portability and expandability were critical design factors. As a software engineering experiment, we are currently comparing two versions of the workbench prototype: one using UCAR's netCDF file representation [Rew90] and the other using the Versant Object Database Management System [Versant92a].

UCAR's netCDF data access library organizes scientific data into a self-describing and network-transparent format. In general, hyperspectral image cubes (originals and manipulated versions) reside in disk files rather than in memory, due to their very large

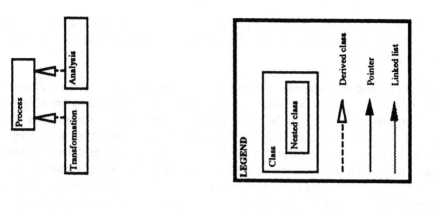

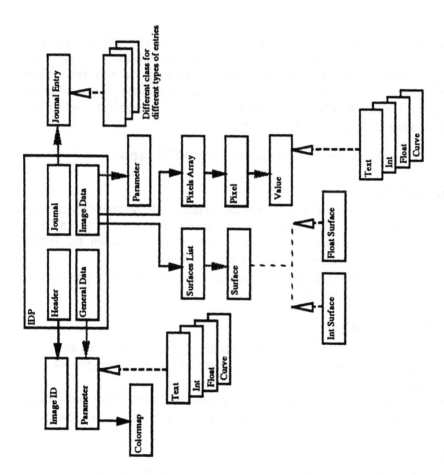

Fig. 1. Structure of the IDP and Process object classes.

size (approximately 140 MBytes). By using the netCDF library, image cubes and processed portions of image cubes may be shared among applications and across many computer platforms.

Operations dealing with whole image cubes (e.g., in applying atmospheric corrections, taking differences between two image cubes, etc.) must be carried out by breaking up very large datasets so they can be manipulated in memory, and reconstituting the results of the manipulation on disk. In order to minimize disk access time where possible, we have implemented an "Image Memory" object which regulates the cache of image data which may be in memory at any given time. This memory management process is transparent to the user. However, this process is very computer resource-intensive, prone to synchronization problems between the inline and database representations of the same data, and represents a potential bottleneck in the image exploitation process.

Using the netCDF library with our object-based in-line data representation has helped to meet our goals of system portability and expandability, but has required a great deal of code simply to accommodate data transfers between the radically different representations of the same information in the netCDF files and in the in-line data objects. It has also introduced the need for our system to include its own memory management and file synchronization code.

We have identified the following limitations of the netCDF approach:

Schema Support:

- The netCDF schema language was the not same as the programming language, requiring that the C++ classes be normalized to produce a set of netCDF file creation subroutine calls. This required that someone on the HIDEW development team be proficient in netCDF file design.
- Complex structures had to be converted to an artificially "flattened" array representation in the netCDF system.

Additional Input/Output Code:

- The need to maintain two representations of data (database and application) was burdensome. Extensive code was needed to keep both representations of the object in agreement.
- Input/output code was needed to translate data from the files to the internal representation. This code was a significant fraction of the overall system code.

Performance:

- Reconstituting complex, normalized objects required joining many files, a relatively expensive operation.
- The need to write a memory manager was burdensome, and provided little flexibility for performance tuning.

- The need to maintain two netCDF representations of the data to obtain reasonable performance for some operations doubles storage requirements.

Since the prototype is an object-based system, it is well suited for use with an object database management system (ODBMS). While most currently available ODBMSs are proprietary, the gains received from not having to write extra reformatting, memory management, and synchronization code may greatly outweigh the expense of the system.

The Versant ODBMS has its own caching mechanism which is transparent to the programmer of the system, as well as to the user. Objects, which contain all the data that the system needs, are referenced within the code as if they were in memory at all times. These same objects are "saved" as persistent objects within the ODBMS, thus encapsulating the data with the object with no need to reformat the data to and from a flat file representation.

The use of an object database management system has provided the following benefits:

Schema Support

- The database schema "language" is the same as the programming language (C++), and the schema is automatically captured from the application code.
- Object structures do NOT have to be "flattened" into another representation.
- No need for additional Input / Output or synchronization code. Objects are referenced as if they are in memory at all times.

Performance

- Client-side object caching makes accessing the objects efficient (most recently referenced objects remain within the cache).
- Tuning parameters allow for fine-tuning of different operations (image loading, surface retrieval).

Unique Features

- Support for design transactions allows transactions which can span multiple database sessions which can last several days with full commit or rollback capability.
- Support for versioning of objects.

Porting to Versant required approximately 10 person-days of effort to convert the approximately 20,000 lines of C++ code. The conversion process required the following steps [Versant92b]:

- Derive all persistent classes from the Versant PObject class to inherit persistent behavior.

- Convert standard C pointers to Versant Links, the persistent database equivalent of a transient pointer.
- Add the Versant dirty() method to all methods that update a persistent object. The dirty() method obtains exclusive locks on the object and mark the object as updated.
- Convert our transient version of a linked list to the persistent Versant VIList linked list class.
- Remove the methods which implemented persistence in the persistent classes which were no longer needed.

2.3 Graphical User Interface

User interaction with HIDEW is facilitated by a sophisticated, yet intuitive, windowing interface. The user may navigate through the system and access the majority of its functions via mouse actions (e.g., pointing and clicking, dragging and dropping of icons). Most of the prototype's abstract concepts are represented visually as icons, with consistent appearance and behavior. The interface was designed to promote work sessions as positive, visual experiences; minimizing procedural details to maximize the user's potential for insight into the data.

2.4 Prototype Image Analysis Tool Suite

The first major capability which was implemented in the prototype workbench was classification of image pixels according to surface types, using a neural network classifier. This analysis was performed on image data captured by JPL's AVIRIS sensor system. The sensor possesses 244 contiguous spectral channels, each having a nominal width of 10 nm, and covers the electromagnetic spectrum roughly from 400 nm to 2500 nm. A single image covers an area of approximately 10 x 11 km, with each pixel representing an approximate 20 x 20 m area on the ground. Pixel classification was accomplished using NASA's NETS backpropagation neural network simulator code [Baffes89], incorporated into the prototype as a Process object.

The next major capability to be built into the system was computation of local fractal signatures for subtiles of an image. The fractal signature module employs algorithms described by Peleg, et al. [Peleg84] and Pentland [Pentland84] to produce curves of fractal dimensions of the image surface (represented as grayscale values) as a function of image distance scale (pixel separation). We expect that these measures of local image texture at various wavelength channels will provide valuable additional context for the determination of surface type for image pixels, when the fractal signature surfaces produced by this module are submitted to surface type classifiers along with the image spectra.

A major aim of our development effort is to add and test new, AI-based tools for image analysis. In addition, we expect to add "standard" image manipulation functions as they are needed to support pilot studies. Many of these functions are readily available due to the remote sensing community's many years experience in multispectral image analysis. Examples of such functions include filtering, altering spatial and/or spectral resolution, converting images from radiance to reflectance units, etc. HIDEW will allow the user to interactively apply atmospheric corrections to images, via the LOWTRAN 7 [Kneizys88] and ARP [CSES92] approaches, among others.

3 Prototype Tests and Pilot Studies

Our initial development work has dealt with hyperspectral images from the AVIRIS sensor system. AVIRIS image cube data were radiometrically corrected by JPL to produce image radiance values (in microwatts / cm^2 / nm / sterradian), and were then normalized for further analysis within the ranges defined by the extreme values for each spectral band. Initial testing has been based on AVIRIS images for the Jasper Ridge Biological Preserve and Moffett Field, both located near Stanford University in Palo Alto, California.

Based on aerial photographs, topographic maps, and limited site reconnaissance of the Jasper Ridge area, we selected a coarse set of abstract surface types: water, meadow, lawn, paved, forest, etc. We then selected a few (typically seven to ten) examples of each type from the image, and trained the net to classify all pixels in an image or subimage section.

For purposes of classifying pixels by surface type, we have employed both three-layer and four-layer backpropagation neural networks. Initially, the network has been configured with an input layer which simply had one input node for each wavelength channel (minus the channels dominated by water vapor absorption), an output layer with an output node for each defined surface class, and one or two hidden layers.

Using this configuration, we have had good success in producing high-resolution land use mappings with very little time and effort expended in "ground truthing" the site or developing complex metrics based on domain knowledge to differentiate surface types. A neural network classifier trained on the Jasper Ridge data also had good success in classifying pixels in the Moffett Field image, indicating that this relatively simple approach is at least somewhat robust.

We are presently assessing the value of local image texture spectra derived from fractal analysis as an aid to surface classification. Although the "naive" approach to surface classification with little aid from domain knowledge has worked surprisingly well in testing, extensive use of domain knowledge to aid in image exploitation is planned for future work, as outlined below in Section 4.

4 Work Planned or in Progress

There are at present several major areas of DOE work planned or in progress in which the Argonne Hyperspectral Image Data Exploration Workbench plays a significant role. These include global environmental change assessment, and high-resolution surface characterization, both for DOE site environmental management purposes and to support improvements in General Circulation Models for climatic change prediction.

4.1 Global Environmental Change Assessment

Argonne's Decision and Information Sciences Division has an ongoing effort to identify, evaluate, and test methods of quantifying environmental change, in order to develop a capability to utilize remote sensing data for research problems on vegetation and land surface changes due to human activity and/or climate change. Both multispectral (Landsat Multi-Spectral Scanner) and hyperspectral data are being utilized in this study.

To support this effort, the prototype workbench will be enhanced to compute fractal-based measures of biodiversity from classified images. Pixel classification will be based on spectral data, derived local fractal texture data, and domain knowledge. The initial prototype neural net-based surface classification schemes are fully general in that they do not depend upon *a priori* knowledge of the contents of the image. However, they are somewhat limited in that they do not take advantage of well-understood physical laws, ecosystem and landform interrelationships, etc. as aids to proper surface characterization. We, therefore, have begun to add a knowledge-based system (KBS) component which will provide a real-world context to aid the image exploitation software in its tasks. The knowledge base for this KBS, covering relevant interrelationships among surface types, will be articulated in a rules-based expert system component capable of aiding in surface identifications for individual image pixels. The classification accuracy for individual image pixels should be substantially improved by access to such domain knowledge. For example, if a single 20 m pixel is identified spectrally as "rain forest", it is highly unlikely that adjacent pixels will represent "desert".

In addition, the KBS can be used to assist in examining an image at a higher level of abstraction, to identify and characterize features extending across several pixels, and to detect more abstract features such as biomes. This process will produce an object-based interpretation of the image in terms of spatially distributed objects representing overlapping and interacting regions with distinct characteristics. This data abstraction process will feed, and be fed by, the pixel classification process, resulting in both a detailed characterization of the surface and the extraction of key features.

4.2 Surface Characterization Studies

In developing or reviewing environmental assessments or impact analyses for remediation plans or other site projects, there is a strong need for accurate, high-resolution data characterizing the site. Until recently, such data have been prohibitively expensive to acquire, and very difficult to analyze effectively, even when available. Exploitation of hyperspectral imagery makes possible the acquisition of such high-resolution databases at relatively low cost. We are planning to try a variant of our neural network surface classifier as a front end processor to feed high-resolution surface characterization data, based on automated hyperspectral image exploitation, to an object terrain database. The database supported would be an intelligent terrain database based on a prototype currently under development at Argonne and George Mason University, in which characteristics and dynamic behavior of pixels are specified via embedded models and knowledge bases, implemented over a true object database.

Another key application area for high-resolution surface characterization via hyperspectral imagery exploitation is the Atmospheric Radiation Monitoring (ARM) Program [DOE90]. A cornerstone of the ARM program is an extensive field study to provide better characterizations of surface energy and momentum exchange for general circulation models (GCM's) used to make global climate predictions. One of the general measurement strategies of the ARM program involves measurements to support the "single column" GCM - that is, measurements made to improve the parameterization of sub-grid scale processes within a GCM. A key element in this strategy is an investigation of the appropriate scale of surface feature characterization which is necessary to adequately describe atmosphere-surface interactions. Acquisition and exploitation of hyperspectral imagery could allow us to map the entire 300 x 280 km Southern Great Plains ARM site at 20 m resolution, for relatively low cost. Aggregations of surface characteristics from the 20 m scale on upwards can then be constructed and tested in the surface exchange models used in the single cell grid characterization.

5 Summary

The work which has been done to date on the Hyperspectral Image Analysis Workbench prototype has demonstrated the feasibility of hyperspectral image exploitation using an object-oriented data model, software design, and implementation paradigm coupled with state of the art analysis and visualization techniques. By designing the prototype system to be easily expandable, we have made it possible for the system to support a wide range of image analysis applications. We have also demonstrated the feasibility of utilizing an object database management system in the support of large, complex, scientific data sets.

6 Acknowledgments

The work discussed in this paper was supported by the U. S. Department of Energy under contract W-31-109-Eng-38.

7 References

[Baffes89] Baffes, P.T., 1989: NETS User's Guide, Version 2.0, Software Technology Branch, Lyndon B. Johnson Space Center, Publ. JSC-23366, September 1989.

[Gao92] Gao, B.-C., K.B. Heidebrecht, and A.F.H. Goetz, 1992: Atmospheric Removal Program (ARP) User's Guide, Version 1.0, Center for the Study of Earth From Space (CSES), Cooperative Institute for Research in Environmental Sciences (CIRES), University of Colorado, Boulder, May 1992.

[Kneizys88] Kneizys, F. X., E.P. Shettle, L.W. Abreu, J.H. Chetwynd, G.P. Anderson, W.O. Gallery, J.E.A. Selby, and S.A. Clough, 1988: User's Guide to LOWTRAN 7, Optical/Infrared Technology Division, Air Force Geophysics Laboratory, Hanscom AFB, Publ. AFGL-TR-88-0177, 16 August 1988.

[Peleg84] Peleg, S., J. Naor, R. Hartley, and D. Avnir, 1984: Multiple Resolution Texture Analysis and Classification, IEEE Computer Society Transactions on Pattern Analysis and Machine Intelligence, Vol. PAMI-6, No. 4, July 1984, pp. 518-523.

[Pentland84] Pentland, Alex P., 1984: Fractal-Based Description of Natural Scenes, IEEE Computer Society Transactions on Pattern Analysis and Machine Intelligence, Vol. PAMI-6, No. 6, November 1984, pp. 661-674.

[Rew90] Rew, R.K., and G.P. Davis, 1990: The UNIDATA netCDF: Software for Scientific Data Access, Preprints of Sixth International Conference on Interactive Information and Processing Systems for Meteorology, Oceanography, and Hydrology, Anaheim, CA, February 1990, pp. 33-40.

[DOE90] U.S. Department of Energy, 1990: Atmospheric Radiation Measurement Program Plan, Office of Energy Research, Office of Health and Environmental Research, Atmospheric and Climate Research Division, Publ. DOE/ER-0441, February 1990.

[Versant92a] Versant Object Technology, Inc. Versant DBMS, 1992.

[Versant92b] Versant Object Technology Corporation, 1992: Versant System Reference Manual, Release 1.7, Menlo Park, CA, January 1992.

Papers: Interaction, User Interfaces and Presentation

Design of a 3D User Interface to a Database

John Boyle[1,2], John E. Fothergill[1], and Peter M.D. Gray[2]

[1] Dept. of Molecular and Cell Biology, Marishal College, Aberdeen University
[2] Dept. of Computing Science, King's College, Aberdeen University

Abstract. One of the strangest paradoxes of the silicon era is the dichotomy between 'enjoyable' recreational computer activities and 'mundane' work-based computer operations. How can an activity as pointless as a computer game have so much appeal? The answer to this lies in the user interface, and not the functionality, of the program. Computer games rely heavily on an interface which is natural and enjoyable to use. We believe that an interface should appeal to the user, and to do so must capture the user's interest and imagination. To this end, we have been using high performance graphics to generate meaningful three dimensional representations for our graphical user interface. We propose new metaphors for both query construction and result representation.

1 Introduction

The design of interfaces to databases lags behind other areas of human computer interaction. As the amount of data and the requirement for information technology increases so too does the need for easy to use interface systems. Graphical user interfaces aid the novice user to work with an information system [16]. Interfaces to databases are equally important: most of the existing ones are to relational databases [20, 27, 14, 11]. Interfaces to semantic data model databases are mainly concentrated on interfaces to the E-R model ([2, 25, 26, 5, 12, 3, 9], however there are interfaces to other semantic data models [6, 1, 10, 13].

The use of high performance graphics in interface design has recently become more important [18, 23]. The use of 3D graphics for interfaces to databases is limited. Their use has been suggested [22], and there is a limited implementation, to a DBS based on the binary relational model [17]. Three dimensional graphics offer opportunities not available in flat WIMP GUIs. We believe, that for information systems, the concept behind the desktop metaphor needs to be extended. Some novel metaphors for database interfaces have been designed and implemented [19]. We have tried to extend the desktop metaphor in directions that will keep the usability and familiarity of WIMP system, but allow for integration of new ideas based upon the use of high performance graphics. For this we have designed new 'hyper-real' graphical descriptions for both query construction and result representation. We show the query as being made up of subqueries. Central to the query construction is a 'flying' schema representation (**Figure 1**).

The subqueries are each represented by a box attached to its entity class. Such a system should be both engaging to use and should also allow the user to see

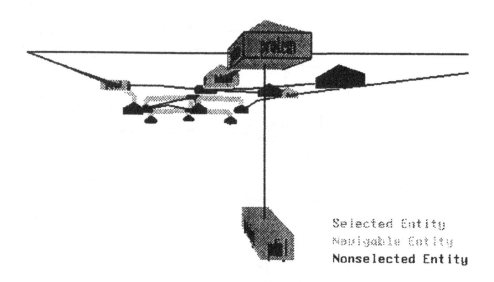

Selected Entity
Navigable Entity
Nonselected Entity

Fig. 1. Three dimensional representation of the schema and query construction

how their query is constructed. Also such a representation gives the user a visual feel for the querying, giving it some physical form and shape. We also introduce the idea of a result maze. With the concept of the user being able to interact with results to a query, where each result is represented as an object in the 3D space. Boxes of the same class are grouped by colour, and the interrelationships between results are also shown. The user can visualise n-relationships by the use of a 'turning the corner' display.

2 Background

Our graphical interface to P/FDM uses a client-server model. The client processes reside on an SGI Indigo. The graphical interface process, which is implemented in C, uses the X11 windowing system, with the OSF/Motif toolkit. Extensive use is also made of the API to the gl 3D graphics routines. The server processes reside on a SUN 4 workstation, and network communication is managed by the use of RPC calls. The database, an object oriented implementation of the functional data model [24] has been developed, using the Prolog language [7]. This DBMS, P/FDM, could originally be queried by either the use of a set of prolog primitives or by the use of the Daplex query language [24]. This OODBMS was used to help model the complex scientific data needed to describe protein structure [8](**Figure 2**) . A graphical interface was designed and implemented to the database [13]. This interface is similar to QBE [27], and involves the same use of 'constraints'. Further improvements are still being made.

Protein chemists generally have little or no experience with database query languages. So there is a need for a powerful and easy to use graphical interface.

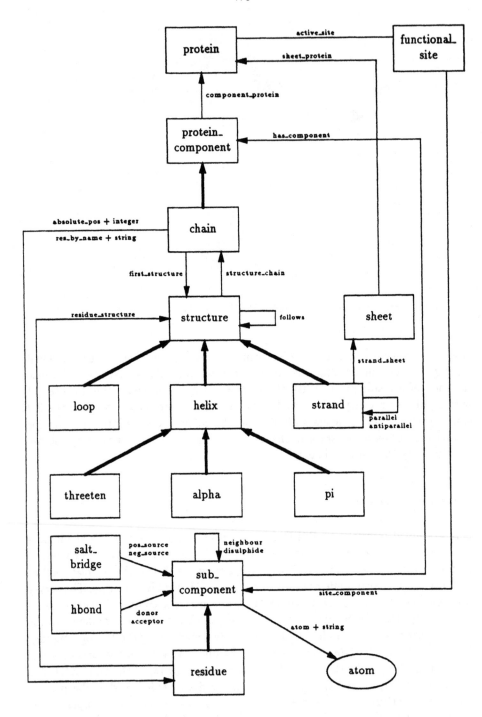

Fig. 2. Diagrammatic representation of the Protein Database schema

These users have some experience with high performance graphics. The use of powerful graphics machines and three dimensional molecular display and mechanics software is becoming more important in molecular biology. As our users already have some familiarity with three dimensional manipulations, our design of the interface had to be consistent with their idea of how 3D representations of objects can be managed. It was decided that the basis of the interface must follow the same basic arrangement as a molecular modelling package (**Figure 3**).

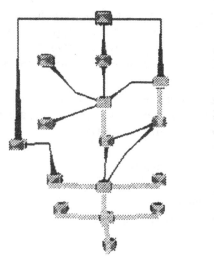 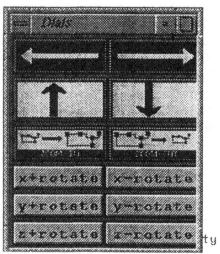

Fig. 3. Showing schema window with navigational 'dials' window

For other users the method of three dimensional navigation may have to be altered to something they are more familiar with. A combination of 3D representations within a standard WIMP framework would hopefully allow the interface to make use of the best parts of the desktop metaphor system, while allowing for the enhancements that can be offered by using the extra expressive visual power available with high performance graphics.

3 Schema Representations

There have been various attempts to define visual languages for database design and querying. Such languages should provide an easy concept which the end user can understand. Most graphical user interfaces to databases are either form based, typically QBE [27] style (for review [21], or representations of the schema are used [25]. As all models are a method of abstraction used to explain the underlying framework of the database these play an important part in the user's understanding. As such these are often used for the basis of interface design. As stated, an approach often used when designing a graphical interface to a database, is to present the user(s) with a schema depiction. This is often used with entity relationship based models. This type of interface allows the user to visualize the data so that he/she can perform complex navigational queries easily. This approach can be adopted for the functional data model.

If the schema is presented to the user, then this presumes that the user has a basic understanding of entity classes and relations between them. The user selects the desired entity class and is then given a method for entering queries upon that class (as in QBE constants). The user can then navigate to other classes directly and so form more complex queries. The schema gives the user a reference to how the data is stored and so less burdening on the user's memory occurs.

We have used this idea of using the schema as the centre of query construction and taken it a step further. A third dimension has been added to our schema interface to enhance its expressive power in a number of ways:

1. allows for multi orientated viewing of the schema.
2. hierarchical entities can be shown.
3. queries can be shown as groups of subqueries.
4. clearer depiction of large/complex schemas(wires and meshes).
5. naturalness of three-dimensions.
6. colour used to indicate possible navigations.

Central to query construction is a three dimensional visualisation of the database schema. A query is made up from partial queries. The user performs partial queries by navigating around the schema and attaching constraints to the appropriate entity class. Linking these partial queries allows depiction of the whole query.

The schema is initially presented in such an orientation that the user is looking down at the schema. This top-down positioning of the users viewpoint means that the schema can be thought of as being in two dimensions only. The advantage of initially presenting the schema in this manner means that the novice user can perform simple queries as if the schema was visualised in 2D only. Simple translations would allow the user to zoom in and out of parts of the schema. As the user grows in confidence and familiarity with the interface, and wishes to construct more complex queries, experimentation in the third dimension can easily be performed.

The basic level of detail of schema shows the entity classes as cubes with their relationships to other entities draw as simple lines. Hierarchical classes are linked by thicker lines, subclasses are also visualised by being in a lower plane to their superclass. More complete visual descriptions of the schema would be required for the user to perform more complex queries. At present two levels of detail are available. The basic level shows labelled entity classes, while the second level shows and labels all relations.

Queries are performed by use of a dialogue box, which pops up when an entity class is selected (**Figure 4**). The dialogue box can then be used by the user to select value attributes and choose the relevant constants that are to be used to form the basis of the query. In the present implementation only logical and comparison operators are supported. Once the user has finished with the window, a box representing the sub-query is shown linked to its entity class. This enables the user to visualise the complete complex query as being made up of separate sub-queries.

A colour scheme is used to help the user perform navigational queries more easily. The currently selected entity class is shown in one colour, entity classes it has direct relations with in a second colour, all other entity classes are shown in a third colour.

The functional data model supports inheritance. And so functions are inherited from an entity class from its superclass. And so when a user selects a subclass, all classes related to its superclass must also be shown as being directly navigational. While FDM also supports nested relations, this feature has not been used in the current version of the interface. Nested relations are shown on the second more detailed schema description, and so the user would have to be familiar with this feature to be able to perform a query using such a relation.

The basic schema description only shows one relation between different entity classes. As there can be more than one relation between two distinct entity classes a system of default relations is used. If the user wishes to change the default this can be done by using the more detailed schema description. The metadata querying facility [4] is used to obtain the entity classes and their functions.

4   Result Visualisation

The results from a query are also shown in three dimensions. This allows the user to see the size of the data set and its interrelationships(**Figure 5**). The user can then browse through the data space and upon request will be shown the relevant attribute information. As the user moves through the data only closely related information is shown: this allows for multi-dimensional representation in the three dimensional space available.

The user is presented with a window which can be navigated around by using the normal navigation tool provided. Each result from the query is shown as a cube. If the user has used relationships in the querying then the set of results returned from this relationship are shown as being connected to the relevant instance.

The user is presented with a maze of results with each entity class shown in a different colour, and each instance shown as a discrete cube. The user can interactively query any instance, this current instance is then highlighted. If the user has performed a query which uses more then three navigations, then all the instances cannot be shown in the three dimensions available. The interface uses a system of only showing a subset of results. When the user moves forward in the maze the entity class that they move from is faded out and the next related entity class is faded in. This is equivalent to turning a corner in the maze. When the user moves backwards in the maze, the most extreme entity class is faded out. At any one time the user can only see ahead a limited distance in the maze.

It would be desirable for the user , from inside the maze space, to interactively extend the result maze in any direction he/she finds desirable. This is discussed further below. Use of the result maze means that the user can browse complex navigational query results relatively easy: this is also aided by a common metaphor for displaying result instances and their relationships to sets of other instances of different entity classes.

5 Browser

A tool has also been constructed to aid browsing in the result maze. The browser tool allows the user to choose in what manner the data is to be displayed. The user is presented with a menu bar with a selection of customisable display actions on them.

While the query construction and result maze are generic, the browser tool can be specialised for specific users. The basic display action outputs all attribute data, whether a derived attribute(method) or or a value attribute. Our interface has been customised specifically for protein chemists by designing a three dimensional molecule displayer (**Figure 6**). The different types of display read in the required information from a file. An action must be defined by the user which will, given an object identifier, return the desired information in the correct format. The display actions are defined in the database query language, daplex, and are stored in the database.

The user also has the ability to move through the data by using the four basic browsing buttons provided. The buttons < *next* > and < *previous* > allow the user to move back and forth in the current entity class instance set. Linked views are supported so, any movement using these entity class browsing buttons is echoed in the result maze window. There are also buttons which allow the user to examine different sets of instances from a related entity class. The < *nextrelation* > button moves the user to a related entity class, this is echoed in the maze by a fading out of the old entity class and a fading in of a new related set of instances. The < *previousrelation* > allows the user to move back from the current position.

6 Further Work

The interface is still under development. There are two main areas where the work is being focused, its querying capacity and its result representation. The querying power of the interface is going to be greatly increased by the inclusion of aggregate operators and hierarchal query formation. The present query structure allows a logical AND between sub-queries of the same entity class: this must be extended to allow for both the NOT operator and the OR operator.

e.g.

this would allow the user to find all the proteins with molecular weight between 4000 and 2000, where the sources are either human or mouse, and if the source is mouse than the resolution must be less than 2.0.

In Daplex:

```
for each p in protein
  such that molecular_weight(p)>2000
  and molecular_weight(p)<4000
  and ((source(p)="human")
    or
    (source(p)="mouse"
    and resolution(p)<2.1));
```

A more complex problem is that of aggregate operators, aggregation by example (Klug 81) solves this by allowing for a hierarchical query where sub-queries can be used to output the results from aggregate operators, so they can be included in other subqueries. Such a method could be used in the present interface. An output/input option could be used to allow for the construction of an aggregate query. Once the user has constructed an aggregate query, the result would have to be selected for output. The result from such an aggregate operation could then be used in another subquery.

e.g.

this would allow the user to find all protein with a molecular weight greater than the average.

In Daplex:

```
for each p1 in protein
  such that molecular_weight(p1)
    > average
    (over p2 in protein of molecular_weight(p2));
```

Different levels of detail have also been implemented in the interface. These will be available to support other improvements to the querying system. Mainly this will enable the user to use nested relations and to perform more complex queries.

e.g.

this would allow the user to find all the proteins with two adjacent secondry structure elements with a lenght greater than 10.

In Daplex:

```
for each p in protein
  for each c in component_protein_inv(p)
    for each s in structure
      such that lenght(s)>10
      and lenght(follows(s)) >10;
```

the user would also be able to find all the proteins that have two or more beta-sheets.

In Daplex:

```
for each p in protein
    such that count (sheet_protein(p)) >1;
```

Interactive extensions to the maze of results would mean the user can move in any direction he/she wishes. The user should also be able to combine querying with such extended navigation. A mechanism to allow users to mark instances of interest should be supplied, to interactively allow the user to reduce the result set and this should be extended further so that the user can perform operations upon such a set. Both the browser and the maze support linked views to a certain extent. When we navigate from one instance, via a multi-valued relation, to another, new information about the new instance is obtained. In most such cases the user would still like to retain the original information as well. This should be supported. This is more important in a graphical display action, such as the 3D molecule displayer. If the user navigated from protein to chain then it would desirable for the instance chain region on the protein to be highlighted, and not displayed separately. Such a system would allow the user to choose subsequent chains from either the result maze or the 3d displayer interactively, with the views being completely linked. The use of a versioning window, to support both user defined macros and query construction, will be made available. The choice between flat or 3D graphics has yet to be made. However with multiple queries, two dimensions could suffer from overcrowding.

7 Discussion

The use of high performance graphics does offer the interface designer opportunities not ordinarily available in the normal flat windowing systems. The system has the advantage of being introduced to users who already should have some familiarity with three dimensional manipulations, and the navigation system has been tailored towards their concept of moving in computer-generated three dimensional worlds. When evaluation studies are being done the new aspects of the interface will be introduced slowly. The schema can be viewed as a flat two dimensional representation, similar to other systems, and as the users become comfortable with the system they can then use the three dimensions, when they desire, by rotating the schema plane to what ever angle they wish. For viewing the results the browsing tool can be used on its own. So the three dimensional abstractions can be used by the user when desired, and are not essential to basic querying. The system was designed this way, due to the novelty of some aspects of its visualizations. This does not force the user to use concepts that are unfamiliar to them, but should encourage the user to experiment with them. As the interface can be customised for other users, by changing the display metaphors, this interface could be adapted for use by other groups of people. The use of three dimensional graphics is not meant to break away completely from the two dimensional WIMP system. The high performance graphics allow the interface designer to enhance the power of the 'normal' 2D interface, while still keeping the familiarity of the desktop metaphor. This should hopefully result in an interface which has better expressive power, has a natural feel to it, and is entertaining to use. The human mind and computers both have exceptional model building capabilities. The challenge to the graphical user interface designer lies in enhancing this ability. The naturalness of the interface, and the enjoyment of using it, are important if the user is to be able to perform the desired tasks successfully. This interface offers a novel approach in attempting to fulfill these requirements.

References

1. Bryce D., Hull R.: *SNAP: A Graphics-based Schema Manager.* IEEE Conf. on Data Engineering (1986) 151–164
2. Cattell R.: *An Entity-based Database User Interface.* ACM-SIGMOD Conf. on Management of Data (1980)
3. Czejido B., Elmasri R., Rusinkiewicz M.: *A Graphical Data Manipulation Language for an Extended Entity Relationship Model.* IEEE Computer (1990).
4. Embury S.M., Jiao Z., Gray P.M.D.: *Using Prolog to Provide Access to Metadata in an Object-Oriented Database.* Proc. 1st Int'l Conf. on Practical Applications of Prolog, Applied Workstations Ltd 2 (1992)
5. Fogg D.: *Lessons from Living in a Database.* ACM-SIGMOD Conf. on Management of Data (1984) 100–106
6. Goldman K., Goldman S., Kanellakis P.C, Zdonik S.B.: *ISIS: Interface for a Semantic Information System.* ACM-SIGMOD Conf. on Management of Data (1985) 328–342
7. Gray P.M.D.: *Expert Systems and Object-oriented Databases: Evolving a New Software Architecture.* Development in Expert Systems V,Cambridge University Press (1989) 203–214
8. Gray P.M.D., Paton N., Kemp G., Fothergill J.E.: *An Object-Oriented Database for Protein Structure Analysis.* Protein Engineering. 3 (1990) 235–243
9. Gulla B.: *A Browser for a Verioned Entity Relationship Database.* Proc 1st Int'l Workshop on Interfaces to Databases (1992)
10. Gyssens M., Paredaens J., Van Gucht D.: *A Graph-Oriented Object Model for Database End-User Interfaces.* ACM-SIGMOD Conf. on Management of Data (1990) 24–33
11. Herot C.F.: *Spatial Management of Data.* ACM Trans. on Database Systems 5, 4 (1980) 493–514
12. Larson J., Wallick J.: *An Interface for Novice and Infrequent Database Management System Users* Proc. Nat'l Computer Conf. 53 (1985) 523–529
13. Kemp G.J.L., Melvin D.G.: *A Graphical Interfacefor an Object-Oriented Database.* In Brown H.(ed), Hypermedia/Hypertext and Object-Oriented Databases, Chapman and Hall (1991) 307–322
14. Kim H., Korth H., Silberschatz A.: *Picasso: a Graphical Query Language.* Software Pract. and Experience 18, 3 169–203
15. Klug A.: *ABE: a Query Language for Constructing Aggregates by Example.* Proc. 1st Int'l Workshop on Statistical Database Managemnt (1981) 190–205

16. Jones S.:
    Graphical Interfaces for Knowledge Engineering: an Overview of Relevant Literature. The Knowledge Engineering Review (1988) 221–247

17. Mariani J., Lougher R.: *TripleSpace: an Experiment in a 3D Graphical Interface to a Binary Relational Database.* Interacting with Computers 4, 2 147–162

18. Marcus A, Marcus A. and Associates, Van Dam A.: *User Interface Developments for the Ninties.* IEEE Computer (Sep. 1991) 49–56

19. Meyer B.: *Towards New Metaphors for Visual Query Languages for Spatial Information Systems.* Proc 1st Int'l Workshop on Interfaces to Databases (1992)

20. McDonald M., Stonebraker M.: *CUPID: the Friendly Query Language.* ACM-PACIFIC (1975) 127-131

21. Ozsoyoglu G., Wang H.: *Example-Based Graphical Database Query Languages* IEEE Computer (1993) 25-38

22. Reid P.: *Dynamic Interactive Display of Comples Data structures.* Graphics Tools for Software Engineering, BCS Documentation and Display Group (1988)

23. Robertson G., Card S., Mackinlay J.: *Information Visulaization using 3D Interactive Animation.* Communications of the ACM **36**, 4 (1993) 57-71

24. Shipman E.W.: *The Functional Data Model and the Data Language DAPLEX.* ACM Trans. on Database Systems **6** (1981) 140–173

25. Wong H., Kuo I.: *GUIDE: Graphical User Interface for Database Exploration.* VLDB (1982) 22-32

26. Zhang Z., Mendelzon A.: *A Graphical Query Language for Entity Relationship Databases.* Entity Relationship Approach to Software Engineering, Elsevier (1983)

27. Zloof M.: *Query by Example.* National Computer Conference (1975) 431-437

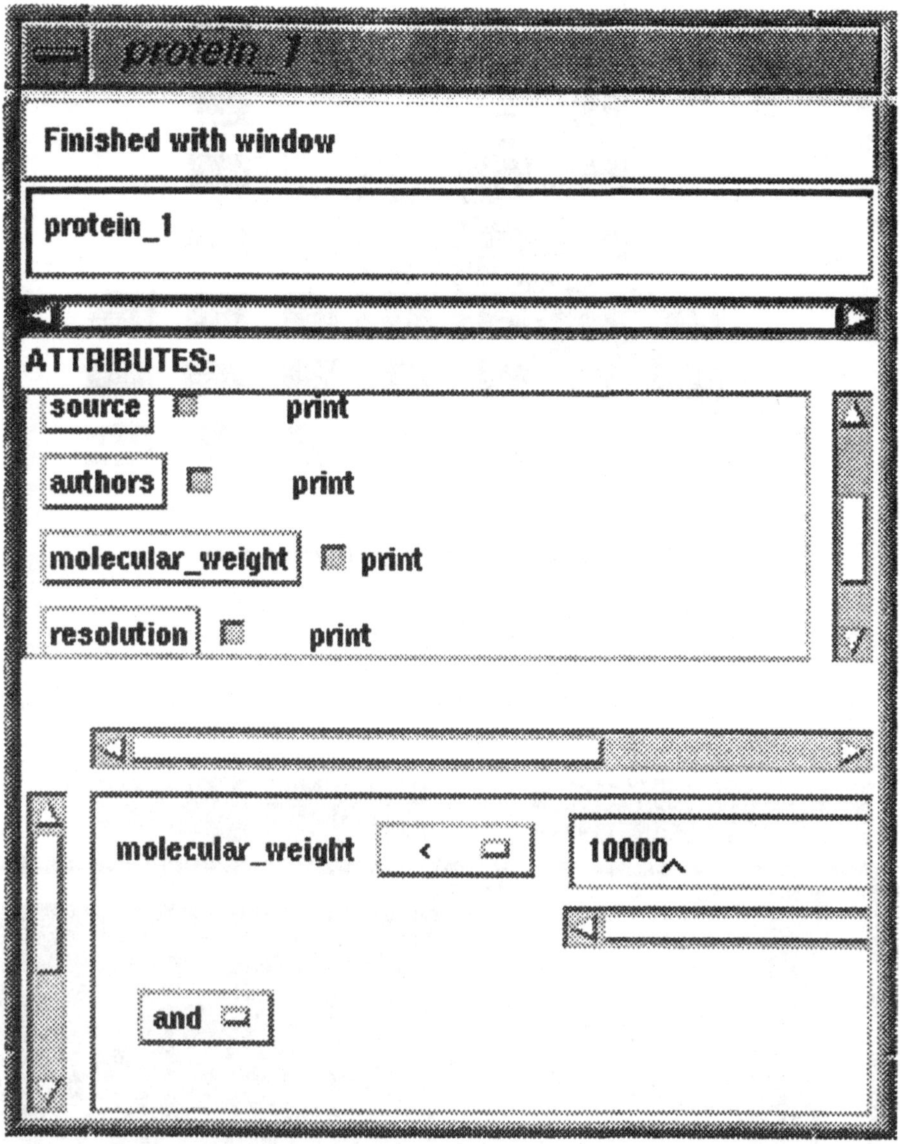

Fig. 4. Basic query box uses comparison and logical operators

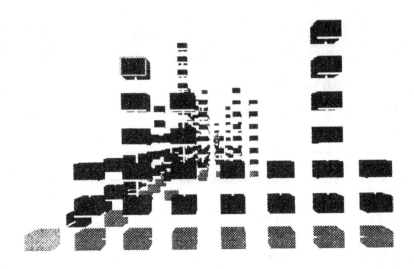

Fig. 5. 3D navigation through the result maze

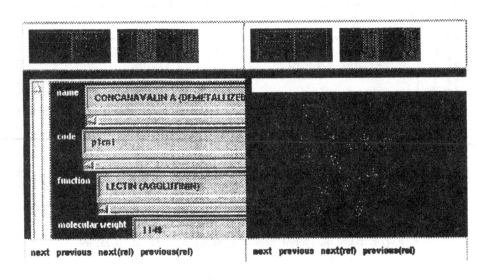

Fig. 6. Showing two different display actions available to the user

Visualizing Reference Databases

Stephen G. Eick, Eric E. Sumner Jr., Graham J. Wills

AT&T Bell Laboratories - Rm 1G-351
1000 East Warrenville Road
Naperville, IL 60565 USA
email: {eick,ees,gwills}@research.att.com

Abstract. This paper describes a graphical method for visualizing reference database searches. The motivation for inventing this technique comes from analyzing the *Current Index of Statistics* reference database. This database contains 128 thousand references to articles from statistical journals, conference proceedings, and books, published during the last 20 years. The paper traces the evolution of the *bootstrap* technique, a statistical research breakthrough, in the statistical literature, shows yearly trends, discovers which journal publish articles on *bootstrapping*, and identifies books on this subject.

1 Introduction

This paper describes a technique for visualizing information in reference databases. These database are becoming increasing available, necessitating the need for better analysis tools. The motivation for developing the methods in this paper comes from studying the 1992 *Current Index of Statistics* (CIS) database [17]. This reference database, available for a nominal[1] charge to members of the Statistical professional societies, contains 128 thousand references to articles from statistical journals, conference proceedings, and books published during the last 20 years. Each entry contains several fields including the article *title*, *authors*, and *key words and phrases*. The database, unfortunately, contains neither citation cross references nor the text of the articles.

Good searching software for key word, author, or title searches is widely (and freely) available [18] and [19]. A user enters a search criterion and the searching software returns a list of *hits*—the references satisfying the search. Searching software is oriented toward finding specific articles. Each search is a slow[2] batch oriented process. Formulating good search strings, unfortunately, is tricky, even for experienced researchers. Often searches result in either thousands of hits or no hits at all.

Salton [14] defines the *precision* of a search as how accurately a search zeros in on a particular article and the *recall* as the ability to find an article. There is a trade-off between precision and recall. As we described before, searches are often too precise, yielding too few hits, or too general yielding too many hits.

---

[1] About $100 for a personal license.

[2] Searches take seconds to minutes, which is fast compared to library searches but much too slow for a real-time response.

Besides finding specific articles, there are other interesting questions about the statistical literature that the CIS database can answer. These questions involve trends in Statistical research, breakthroughs, hot topics, and areas of focus for particular journals. When, for example, did the articles about *bootstrapping* first appear? How quickly did *bootstrapping* spread through the statistical literature? Which journals do *bootstrapping* articles appear in? What books on this subject have appeared? When did the most recent book come out? Meta questions, such as these, about the literature are difficult to answer with traditional software directed at finding specific articles.

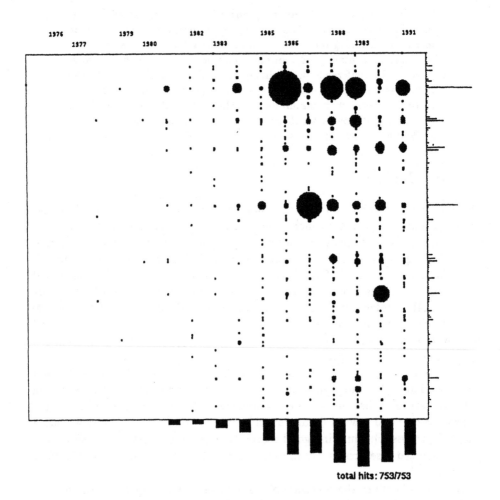

Fig. 1. Articles About *bootstrapping*.

The technique described in this paper visualizes the results of key word and author database searches. The idea is to display the hits on a journal-by-year grid, using size and color to show the number and type of hits for each symbol (see Figure 1). As the user touches a symbol with the mouse, additional information, the journal name and number of hits, are displayed below. If the user clicks on a symbol, the actual references corresponding to the symbol are printed in another scrollable window.

A challenge for information retrieval systems is how to display the information. The standard techniques for multidimensional visualization [11] are not well-suited for this problem. Because of the volume of information and its unstructured nature, it is hard to find a natural 2-dimension layout for the information. A possibility is to use neural networks for positioning related information in a spatial layout [8]. These methods yield interesting results, but the displays are difficult to interpret. The algorithms used in the neural networks are opaque and give little insight into the structure of the information. The visualization technique demonstrated here uses a straight-forward layout: present large volumes of information in a regular grid whose axes represent two independent dimensions of the information. Presenting the information in a grid makes the display easy to interpret, and, with direct manipulation, a user can probe the display for the structure of the information. Showing large volumes of information on a single display gives a perspective that is unavailable when using other methods.

The remainder of this paper describes the visualization technique and system implementing it in more detail. Section 2 illustrates the general technique by tracing *bootstrap* through the statistical literature. Section 3 describes the software, user interaction, and query methods used in the system creating the displays. Finally, Section 4 summarizes and concludes.

2 Reference Database Visualization

This section describes a visualization technique to display hits in a reference database. By visualizing the hits, it is possible to understand overall patterns that would be impossible to detect using a conventional text display. These user interaction techniques in this system are motivated by dynamic graphics [1]. They are similar in approach to methods for the investigation of text line oriented statistics described by Eick [4].

Figure 1 shows the hits for a key word search on *bootstrap*. There are 753 articles and books that have *bootstrap* in the title or the key words–too many for a textual display. The display technique positions the hits on a year by publication grid, with a colored, scaled symbol coding the number of and types or articles in each publication for the year. The scale of the symbol is proportional to the number of hits; the symbol for exactly one hit is a square, with a circle for two or more hits. Figure 1 shows the years, 1975 through 1992 along the x-axis and the publications containing hits down the y-axis. Articles appearing before 1975 are shown in the 1975 column because the coverage in the CIS database is spotty for those years. The biggest symbol represents the twenty-four articles that appeared during 1986 in the *Annals of Statistics*. The second biggest symbol represents the nineteen articles that appeared during 1987 in *JASA*.

The display is interactive. When the mouse touches any symbol, the journal name, year, and number of articles are shown below. If the user clicks on any symbol, the references corresponding to that symbol are displayed in another window.

The first article mentioning the word *bootstrap* in its keywords or titile appeared in 1972 [6]. This article is apparently unrelated to Efron's seminal paper introducing the *bootstrapping* technique in 1979 [2]. Three other papers mentioning *bootstrap* appeared in 1978, before Efron's 1979 *Annals* paper, that are apparently related to Efron's *bootstrap*. It is possible that Efron's paper was delayed in publishing, that these authors had preprints or personal communication with Efron, enabling them to publish first.

The bar plots at the bottom and right-hand side of Figure 1 show the total number of articles by journal and by year. The number of articles increased from a handful per year in the late 70's to over a hundred per year in the late 80's. *Bootstrapping* is an example of a statistical breakthrough: the interest in the technique surged after it was introduced and quickly disseminated throughout the statistical literature. The dissemination time lag for *bootstrapping* was about five years.

What journals publish articles about *bootstrapping*? The bar plots along the right-hand side of the display show the total number of articles by journal. The program permanently displays all of the journal names if there is enough space, and temporarily displays the journal name for a particular row as the mouse touches any symbol in the row. The two longest bars correspond to the *Annals of Statistics* and *JASA*, the two most popular journals for publishing *bootstrap* articles.

In Figure 2 the symbol size shows the number of pages devoted to *bootstrapping* articles. The large square symbols represent books, monographs, or large articles with many pages. The earliest large square represents a 92 page SIAM review article by Efron [3]. Since then there has been one Wiley book in 1989 [12], and Chapman Hall books in 1989 [16] and 1991 [9].

According to the 1992 version of the CIS database, Efron has published 93 articles. Figure 3 shows the results of a search on **Efron**. The two most frequent journals that Efron's papers appear in are *JASA* and the *Annals of Statistics*. Other likely locations are the *American Statistician*, the *Annals of Mathematical Statistics*, and *Biometrica*. The page display (not shown) indicates that he has written one Wiley book in 1980 [10].

One particularly interesting feature of Figure 3 concerns the yearly pattern. Efron, an extraordinarily active author, has exceptional years in 1981 (ten publications) and 1986 (12 publications), according to the database.

3   System Implementation

The reference visualization system runs under Unix, using X11 [13] graphics with the Motif [5] widget set. Figure 4 shows a screen dump of the system's windows. The main window on the left shows the hits. The **Article/Pages** radio button

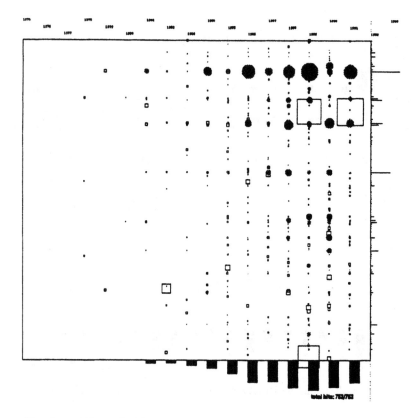

Fig. 2. Number of Pages Published About *bootstrapping*. The three large squares represent books. The smallish square in 1982 represents a 92 page review article.

determines whether the symbol size is tied to the number of articles or pages. The leftmost slider proportionally scales or shrinks all of the symbols. This lets a user solve the symbol overlap problem where the large symbols obscure the smaller ones. The second slider is a threshold for restricting the display to show symbols corresponding to more than a specified number of hits.

The user types key words or author names into choices_popup windows. There are two choices_popup windows in Figure 4, one for *bandits* (currently active) and the other for *bootstrapping*. There are 123 *bandit* hits as indicated by the total hits: 123/123. As the mouse moves around the screen and touches any symbol, the journal and number of articles corresponding to that symbol are shown below. In Figure 4 the mouse is off the screen. If the user clicks the mouse on any symbol, the actual references are printed in the Article_view window on the right. This window is a Motif scrollable window for displaying text.

For fast searching, the system uses an inverted index, several layers of caching, and memory mapped IO [15]. By carefully caching the indices, the system can resolve many keyword or author searches in a fraction of a second when running on a Silicon Graphics Indigo workstation. Memory mapping each of the index files increases speed by saving overhead of *stdio* [7]. Each search is cached after

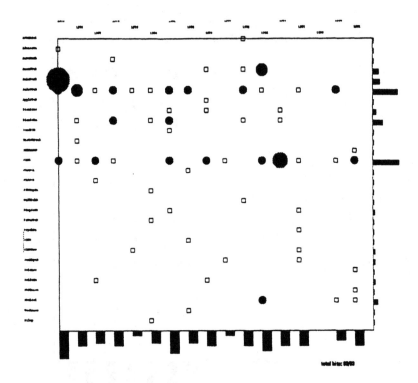

Fig. 3. Publications by Bradly Efron. There is a five year cyclic pattern.

it completes, so that executing it again will be nearly instantaneous. Screen updates are double buffered using off-screen X pixmaps [5].

A useful user interaction technique is to create several choices_popup windows with different searches in each one and click the Do It button in each window sequentially. When this occurs, the display instantly updates showing the hits because of the caching. The technique is useful for comparing different searches.

4 Summary And Conclusions

This paper describes a graphical method for displaying reference database search hits. The technique shows search hits on a journal-by-year grid using a scaled symbol. Touching any symbol with the mouse causes the number of articles and the journal name to display. Bar plots along the axes show the by-year and by-journal totals.

This method is well-suited for understanding temporal publication trends of statistical research topics. The paper gives an example of *bootstrapping*, a statistical breakthrough. It traces the evolution of a new idea in the statistical literature, shows which journals publish articles on *bootstrapping*, and investigates other publications by Efron, the inventor of the *bootstrapping* technique.

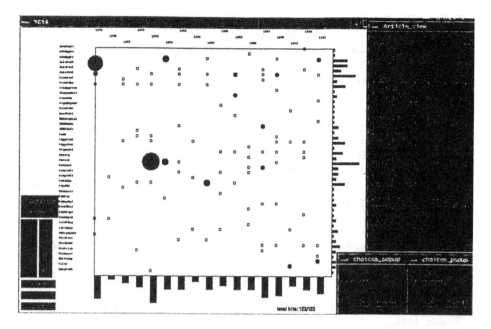

Fig. 4. Hits for a search on *bandits*. The references are shown in the Article_view window and search strings in the choices_popup windows.

Within five years after it was introduced, *bootstrapping* became a widely referenced algorithm.

The technique displays a large volume of information on a single display. This is ideal for gaining insights into the overall patterns in the literature. These insights are difficult to obtain using conventional searching software and textual listings.

References

1. William S. Cleveland and Marylyn E. McGill, editors. *Dynamic Graphics for Statistics*. Wadsworth & Brooks/Cole, Pacific Grove, California, 1988.
2. Bradley Efron. Bootstrap methods: Another look at the jackknife. *Ann. of Statistics*, 7:1–26, 1979.
3. Bradley Efron. *The Jackknife, the Bootstrap and Other Resampling Plans*. SIAM:PA, 1982.
4. Stephen G. Eick. Graphically displaying text. *Journal of Computational and Graphical Statistics*, 1994.
5. Dan Heller. *Motif Programming Manual*. O'Reilly & Associates, Inc., Sebastopol, California 95472, 1990.
6. J. S. Huang. A note on robbins' compound decision procedure. *Ann. of Mathematical Stat.*, 43:348–350, 1972.

7. Brian W. Kernighan and Dennis M. Ritchie. *The C programming language.* Prentice-Hall, Englewood Cliffs, New Jersey 07632, 1978.

8. Xai Lin. Visualization for the document space. *Visualization '92 Conference Proceedings*, pages 274–281, 1992.

9. Bryan F. J. Manly. *Randomization and Monte Carlo methods in biology.* Chapman & Hall, London, 1991.

10. Rupert G. Miller, Bradley Efron, Byron Wm. Brown, and Lincoln E. Moses. *Biostatistics Casebook.* John Wiley & Sons, New York, NY, 1980.

11. Gregory M. Nielson, Thomas A. Foley, Bernd Hamann, and David Lane. Visualizing and modeling scattered multivariate data. *IEEE Computer Graphics And Applications*, 11(3):47–54, 1991.

12. Eric W. Noreen. *Computer-intensive methods for testing hypotheses: An introduction.* John Wiley & Sons, New York, NY, 1989.

13. Adrian Nye. *Xlib Programming Manual.* O'Reilly & Associates, Inc., Sebastopol, California 95472, 1990.

14. Gerard Salton and Michael J. McGill. *Introduction to Modern Information Retrieval.* McGraw-Hill, New York, NY, 1983.

15. Inc. Silicon Graphics. *IRIX User's Reference Manual, Versin 5.2.* Mountain View, California, 1990.

16. Peter Sprent. *Applied nonparametric statistical methods.* Chapman & Hall, London, 1989.

17. Bruce E. Trumbo. *Current Index to Statistics, 1992 Edition.* Hayward, California, 1992.

18. Paul Tukey and Douglas Bates. *CIS Searching Software.* statlib@lib.stat.cmu.edu, Carnegie Mellon University, 1992.

19. Michael J. Wichura. *CIS.* statlib@lib.stat.cmu.edu, Carnegie Mellon University, 1992.

A 3D Based User Interface
for Information Retrieval Systems

Matthias Hemmje
German National Center for Information Technology (GMD)
Integrated Publication and Information Systems Institute (IPSI)
Research Department for Visual Interaction Tools (VISIT)
Dolivostr. 15, D-64293 Darmstadt, FRG
e-mail: hemmje@darmstadt.gmd.de

Abstract.The paper describes how 3D-based visualization and interaction techniques can be used in information retrieval user interfaces. It demonstrates that information retrieval systems based on state of the art retrieval models can be supplied with an intuitive interface functionality by applying the cone-tree metaphor for the visualization of content spaces. The natural ability of humans for spatial perception, orientation and spatial memories is outlined as an advantage in the process of perceiving information spaces by means of spatial metaphors. It is shown how the models, concepts and mechanisms of the retrieval system underlying its user interface can become more transparent and perceptible for the user at the interface level and how some of the cognitive costs of navigations in information spaces can be reduced. This goal is achieved by transforming document-term networks with two levels of abstraction into hierarchical and directed cone trees that use the spatial depth of 3D to achieve an easy perception of their topological structure. Finally the paper presents a 3D-based information system user interface which gives the user intuitive control over content-oriented search paths resulting in a query generation for the underlying automatic retrieval mechanisms. In order to improve the presentation of the query results as well, it is shown that 3D-based graphical metaphors can provide very intuitive ways of perceiving the relevance of the result in accordance to the query.

Keywords: user interface, information retrieval, navigation, 3D, spatial perception

1 Introduction

Graphical user interfaces are nowadays state of the art within modern computer systems. The basic metaphors for such interfaces are in most cases desktop, window or similar metaphors, which are derived from real-world objects and their real-world properties and functionalities. Besides the metaphors derived from real-world objects (e.g. [Pejtersen 1989]) several visualization methods for abstract information structures have been developed (e.g. [Kerner/Thiel1991]). In contrast to the world in which humans live, the design of graphical user interfaces, their visualization methods and metaphors were restricted to plain 2 or 2 1/2D graphics for a long time because the available systems could not cope with the visualization of more than two-dimensional scenes on the graphical side. This situation has changed very significantly now. Computer systems of the most recent past provide the necessary hardware and software performance to visualize static 3D scenes as well as animated sequences in very high quality (e.g. [Seligmann/Feiner 1991]).

The development outlined above has forced the current research activities in the field of information visualization to concentrate on the design of new 3D-based metaphors that take advantage of these high graphics abilities (e.g. [Feiner/ Beshers 1990]). Some of the results are metaphors for the visualization of abstract structured information sets. In this paper we will describe how 3D-based visualization and interaction techniques of this kind can be used in information retrieval applications. We will demonstrate how the probabilistic information retrieval system INQUERY [Callan/Croft/Harding 1992], can be supplied with an intuitive interface functionality by applying architectural models like the one proposed by [Agosti/Gradenigo/Marchetti 1991] in combination with 3D-based presentation components. It will be shown how the models, concepts and mechanisms underlying the system design can become more transparent and perceptible for the user at the interface level and how some of the cognitive costs of navigations in information spaces can be reduced. This goal is achieved by taking advantage of 3D presentation forms similar to those in [Robertson et al. 1991] and [Card et al. 1991] on the one hand and the natural ability of humans for spatial perception, orientation and spatial memories on the other hand.

Finally the paper presents a 3D-based information system prototype which gives users intuitive control over a query generation. It is outlined how 3D presentation forms and intuitive interaction with spatial information structures contribute to transparency of the applied retrieval model for the user. In order to improve the presentation of the query results as well, we show how a 3D-based presentation component can provide an intuitive perception of the relevance of the result in accordance with the query by extending the approach of [Olson et al. 1991]. We will conclude with some indications for the statement that from the user's point of view user interfaces of information systems of the next generation will take advantage of walking–through–db–contents metaphors instead of the traditional query–retrieval–presentation dialog sequences.

2 Retrieving Information from a Document Space

In modern retrieval systems, access to the document set should be given in such a way that the user can get an impression of the database's contents without the necessity of understanding its organizational structure. In other words the user shall be able to explore the document space following content-oriented and not organizational search paths. To show what shall be regarded as *content-oriented search paths* in our approach, we would like to derive and summarize a few thoughts about the document set and the conceptual relations that its elements have from state of the art models and concepts.

2.1 The Content Space of the DB and the Interest Space of the DB Users

The information space containing all documents shall be referred to in the following as the *content space* of the database. In our approach we take this space to be defined by the subjects that the documents contained in the database deal with. These subjects are specified by the choice of words the document's authors use to describe them. So every document is related to a vector of specifying terms, and the total content space can be regarded as the vector space built on a base of all such vectors. We formalize to achieve a description that is more precise and better to understand:

If d may be a document existing in the database at a given time t and W_t may be the set of specifying terms $(w_1, w_2, w_3 ... w_n)$ of the subjects within d, one could define the content of a document in the following way: $content\ (d, t) = (w_1, w_2, w_3 ... w_n) = W_t$

The set of all information needs of users who query the database, shall be referred to in the following as the interest space of the database users. In analogy to the specification of a document's content we shall regard the interest of the users as the subjects that they would like to get information about. These subjects again can be specified by sets of terms which describe the field of interest. If u may be a user and W_t again a set of specifying terms $(w_1,$ $w_2, w_3 ... w_n)$ for the users interest, one could define the information need of u at a given time t as: $interest\ (u, t) = (w_1, w_2, w_3 ... w_n) = W_t$

Given the task that users have to be supported their search for information which satisfies their interest as closely as possible, the obvious link between the content of the database and the information need of the user are sets of terms which specify either parts of the former or of the latter. This link appears to be essential in the information dialog between the user and the system.

Similar models and abstractions similar are introduced by [Croft 1983], [Callan/Croft/ Harding 1992] and [Agosti/Gradenigo/Marchetti 1991] and displayed in the figures 1, 2 and 3. Networks of terms and documents with two levels of abstractions for the content space (document and term level) and therefore with at least document-term relations are defined and integrated with relations of interest , content and others to establish a base for the retrieval task.

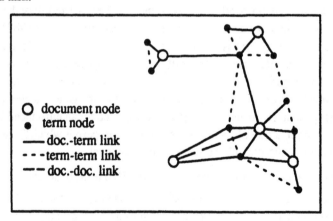

Figure 1: Documents and related terms [Croft 1983]

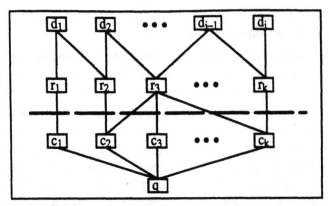

Figure 2: Document retrieval inference network [Callan/Croft/Harding 1992]

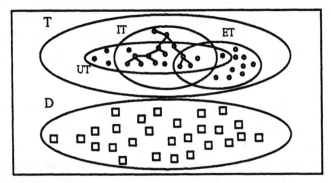

Figure 3: Basic model for two level abstraction [Agosti/Gradenigo/Marchetti 1991]

Besides the mentioned probabilistic approaches, also knowledge-based models that operate on term/document-based networks (e.g. [Thiel/Hammwöhner 1987]) have been introduced to achieve a better base for the document retrieval task. In all these works, the resulting network models were not explicitly visualized by the resulting systems to support the user's perception and understanding of the dialog situation. The original purpose of these approaches was to be the basic concept for the design and development of an automatic retrieval mechanism or the abstract background for an introduced interface architecture. Our approach shall reveal the metaphorical properties which these models can also have, if applied graphically at the user interface level.

2.2 The Traditional Search Dialog in Document Retrieval Systems

The information search dialog between user and system is a sequence of statements of interest by the user and offers of contents by the system. All these statements are directed by the user's information need and the system's database content. In each single dialog step, either the system retrieves information or the user judges its relevance for his need and requests further information. So one step influences the next. One can describe a search dialog sd of a user u in the period (s, e):

$$sd\,(u, s, e) = (\quad interest\,(u, s\quad),\quad retrieval(interest\,(u, s\quad), s+1),$$
$$interest\,(u, s+2),\quad retrieval(interest\,(u, s+2),\quad s+3),$$

$$interest\ (u,\ e{-}1),\quad retrieval(interest\ (u,\ e{-}1),\ e\ )\ )$$

In this case the user's interest is the input for the system's retrieval. The output of the system's retrieval is in the ideal case one document d, but normally a set D_t of several documents $(d_1, d_2 \ldots d_n)$ that match the interest most closely. It is a result of the automatic retrieval mechanism of the system, which can be regarded as processing an inverse content function. One can describe this as:

$$retrieval\ (interest\ (u,\ t)) = retrieval\ (w_1, w_2, \ldots w_m) = content^{-1}\ (w_1, w_2, \ldots w_m)$$
$$= (d_1, d_2 \ldots d_n) = D_t$$

If we now reduce the above described search dialog to the parameters exchanged between user and system, by applying the necessary substitutions, we get the following description of the dialog process: sd $(u, s, e)= (W_s, D_{s+1}, W_{s+2}, D_{s+3}, \ldots W_{e-1}, D_e)$

In our approach such a dialog sequence defines a *content-oriented search path* between the content space of the database and the interest space of the user. Within every dialog step the dimensions of content and interest descriptions change from documents to terms and vice versa. This is the way in which we will interpret the information dialog between human and computer in a document retrieval situation.

Traditional retrieval systems often suffer from some problems concerned with this search dialog, e.g., users can often neither understand how the system's offers are created (i.e. how the inversion of the content relation works), nor can they estimate if their search has any chance to get satisfied by the database's contents (what means if there is a matching set of documents for his interest which can be retrieved via the content relation). Furthermore users are often unable to intuitively judge the relevance of the retrieval result in accordance with their query. These and related problems are outlined in [Korfhage 1991].

3 Deriving Metaphors for the New User Interface

3.1 Motivation and Goals

The overall goal of the work described here is to reduce the above-described problems of the search dialog while setting up a user interface to an already existing probabilistic information retrieval system that enables the user to access the documents of a database containing about 800 abstracts of publications. This data set is part of a larger database converted and transferred ([Gu/Thiel 1993]) from CORDIS data (IR database of the Commission of the European Communities), which was organized as linear free-text, to a relational DBMS. From this, the part dealing with publications was extracted into a format accessible for INQUERY's [Callan/Croft/Harding 1992] indexing and retrieval mechanisms.

To achieve transparency of the retrieval dialog (i.e. controllability of its development within the content space along content-oriented search paths) is a basic constraint for the design of our system. An approach for the solution of this problem is the visualization of the retrieval dialog by visualizing content-oriented search paths in dimensions of terms and documents. Therfore the content space itself has to be visualized. In the following we introduce a way to achieve this goal. We visualize the document term networks which define the content space by using *cone trees* [Card et al 1991] and introducing an appropriate mapping from the network to the tree.

3.2 Visualizing the Content Space

In order to visualize the content space in dimensions of terms and documents as described above, the content of a network of the following form has to be visualized:

$content(d) = (w_1, w_2, w_3 \ldots w_n)$ for all documents d contained in the database

This means that one would have to display a network quite similar to the one in figure 1, but with (in our case) only one kind of links: document-term links (see figure 4), indicating how important a term is in a document (if the problems concerned with this visualization task are solved, the approach could be easily extended to multiple types of links). If one would try to visualize the above-described network directly by mapping it to the 3 dimensions of the Cartesian Space, a complex and probably unsolvable clustering and crossing problem would appear (from the graphical layout's point of view) soon. Furthermore such a complex graph would be difficult to perceive by the user. Therefore it would stand in contrast to the main goals of the visualization metaphors and the corresponding user interface design.

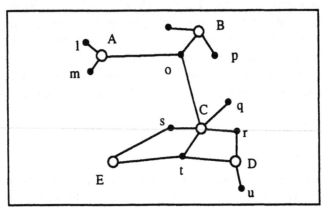

Figure 4: Reduced network from figure 1 (labels added)

We decided to visualize the network indirectly by means of hierarchical cone trees. As [Card et al 1991] outlines, cone trees can be perceived easily by the user, because they are hierarchical and directed. Their *topological structure* is quite similar to that of 2D trees, The main advantage of a 3D cone trees compared to a 2D tree is, that their *geometrical structure* makes use of the third dimension – the spatial depth. Parts of the tree can be positioned behind others by simply rotating subtrees to the front or the back.

The content of every document-term network can be displayed by means of such a tree which reproduces the set of all nodes and links in the network in a topological structure.

Depending on the starting point and the development of the reproduction, some nodes of the original network have to be either duplicated or connected by hidden links which do not belong to the cone-tree structure. We decided do choose the latter opportunity. In figure 5 we display a transformation of the network from figure 4 into a tree as it could have been unfolded, when starting with document A. This tree's topological structure is the same as that of the corresponding cone tree which would have been more difficult to draw in a 2D paper.

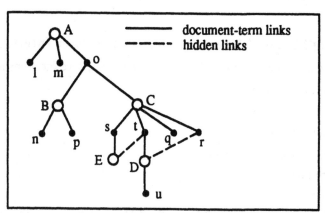

Figure 5: Cone tree reproducing the network in figure 4 starting with document A

The crossing problem is replaced by the optimization problem for the radii of the cone tree's circular node levels. Solutions for this problem can be calculated quite easily.

Every root of a tree is either of the term dimension or the document dimension. The leaves connected to this root node are again either the terms which specify the root-node's document, or they are the documents in which the term, symbolized by the root node, is used. From level to level, the tree can be expanded from each of its leaves, according to the structure of the document-term network. By this means step by step new parts of the content space are declared to be currently of interest and therefore become integrated into the topological structure of the tree. As users explore the database through such content-oriented search paths, they cover more and more relevant parts of its content space. Automatically expanding the maximal tree in the beginning and at once is neither easy, because a content-oriented search path which reproduces the whole networks content has to be calculated, nor does it make sense, because users could not perceive it as easily as the one created by their own interests.

3.3 Perceiving the Content Space via Cone Trees

It is a property of trees that, if their topological structure grows, their geometrical structure forms a spatial object. This means that the user can recognize and remember areas of trees not only by its topology but also by the form, the density, etc., which the spatial object, the corresponding subtree, has. We take advantage of this property to reduce the cognitive load of recognizing the content oriented position for users while they are following content-oriented paths or in other words are navigating in the content space. User will easily recognize that they have visited a certain area before, because the geometry of the tree still looks the same or because the topology requires the same, repeated navigational decisions from the user. The cognitive costs for this are low for the user because the human perceptual system, its visual and spatial memory, is specialized for such tasks [Strong/O'Neil Strong 1991]. Therefore, users can develop a feeling, which areas of content of the database are already covered, without looking at each document. As far as this problem, also mentioned in [Korfhage et al 1991], is concerned, the situation has started to improve.

4 Designing Modes of Interaction for the new User Interface

In this section of the paper we will describe how basic interface functions for

> semantic association,
>
> navigation,
>
> sequential reading,
>
> associative reading,
>
> backtracking and
>
> history

as requested in [Agosti/Gradenigo/Marchetti 1991] can be realized within the proposed visualization metaphor and become more intuitive for the user. We reflect the problem of getting lost in hyperspace according to our interface design.

Furthermore we will outline for which tasks automatic retrieval is still necessary and important and how its results can be presented as intuitively as the content space and the content-oriented search paths.

4.1 Exploring the Content Space via Content-Oriented Search Paths

In the following, we would like to explain the interactive functionality of the cone-tree and other metaphors which are to be used within the user interface's graphical display. We will reflect where and in which way the interface functionalities defined by [Agosti/ Gradignio/Marchetti 1991] are realized and how underlying parts of the retrieval system INQUERY become more transparent. As outlined above, the trees are composed of alternating levels of terms and documents. Within the graphical display the dimension of each level (terms/documents) can be easily recognized by the color of its elements. The starting point of a content-oriented search path can be a document or a term node, which has to be determined by the user. If users are not sure about which starting point to define, they can query the automatic retrieval mechanism of INQUERY for either a set of documents to set up the first level or they could choose one document of the suggested set to define the root node. From this entry point, the user can navigate in dimensions of terms and documents, which means on tree levels of terms and documents. How can the user perform content-oriented search paths creating his search dialog's cone tree?

At all times one level of the tree is the *current level*, the level that is actually visited. The elements of the level have labels which tell the term or the document name. Within this level, one element, depending on the level's type, either a document or a term node, is the *selected item*. This is always the one at the front, closest to the user's point of view. The current level and the selected item can be recognized by their high-lighted appearance in contrast to their neighbors. If the user wants to select a different element of the current tree level, he simply rotates the level including all its subtrees like a merry-go-round until the desired element is at the front and therefore selected. From the selected item of the current level, the user can now request the system to unfold the corresponding new subtree.

If the selected item was a document, the new subtree of which the selected item is then the root node, will consist of all specific terms of the selected document. This set of terms is automatically generated by INQUERY's powerful indexing mechanism. If the selected item was a term, the new subtree will consist of all documents in which the term is used. This set is also derived from INQUERY's indexing results. In the same way as the tree's structure can be expanded, it can also be reduced, if the user decides that a visited subtree is of minor interest. The user is also free to change the current level between existing levels without reducing or expanding the tree. Whenever the cone tree's structure changes, the radii of all tree levels are again optimized to avoid collisions between different levels.

By such interactions, the user expands or reduces the tree's topology, depending on the choice of selected items. The sequence of all selected items from the absolute root node to the current level's selected item defines the current content-oriented search path. The tree is dynamic concerning the display of its geometrical structure, because all subtrees can independently be rotated. However the tree's topological structure between two expansions or reductions is always constant. By this means an intuitive interactive functionality for *navigation* and *semantic association* [Agosti/Gradignio/Marchetti 1991] is realized and the structure of INQUERY's network of index terms and documents becomes transparent to the user.

4.2 Estimating Relevance of Documents

How can the user decide if a document is of interest for his needs? To achieve a base for this decision, users can either expand a document's term subtree to browse the specific terms, or they can *enter* the symbol displaying the document label by changing his position *into* it, to read its full content. If this happens, the user leaves the tree world and enters the document as an information room (see figure at the end of the paper), where the document content is displayed. Currently the documents text is projected to one of the walls of the room, but one could also imagine to display documents of other media types like video, sound etc. if the database contains them. Users can leave this room either to neighboring rooms to read the documents next on the current cone-tree level, or they can leave the rooms alltogether and return to the tree world. By this means an intuitive interactive functionality for *sequential reading* [Agosti/Gradignio/Marchetti 1991] is achieved and the level of abstraction between the document and its content becomes transparent at the interface level. The mode of *associative reading* [Agosti/Gradignio/Marchetti 1991] is achieved by combinations of the above-described tree navigations and sequential reading.

Interface functionalities like *backtracking* and *history* [Agosti/Gradignio/Marchetti 1991] can intuitively be performed by the user himself, because the tree structure itself is the metaphoric memory for the search dialogs development, because every level of every subtree is a former step in the past dialog history.

4.3 How About *Getting lost in ...*

During all these navigational tasks on network structures, one has expect that the user will experience the traditional problem of *getting lost in hyper space*. We reduced this risk by taking several actions. At first we state that a tree can have multiple occurrences of the same document or term item, whether represented by a root or a leaf node, but furthermore the tree must not have duplicate subtrees. This means, as soon as a leaf is selected to be the root of a newly created subtree, it will be checked whether this item already exists as a root node of a subtree. If this is true, a cone symbol instead of another subtree is created. If the user follows on this symbol, his position will change to the root of the detected fist occurrence of the subtree. This implementation of hidden links guarantees, that the user will always reach the same area in the tree when he reaches the same area in the content space.

Another action that can be taken is directly related to the 3D-graphical character of the displayed situation. The user can at all times zoom in or out and change the position and direction of view to get a better impression of where his current position in the search tree is and what the tree's topological structure as a whole looks like at the moment.

If the user should however and despite the above described actions experience a situation of disorientation, he can at all times consider to query the automatic retrieval mechanism for a new entry point, or an additional explicit history mechanism can bring him back to an earlier position on his navigational path if he feels unsure about doing it himself.

4.4 The Importance of Automatic Retrieval

Besides the above introduced interactive functions of the user interface, access to a traditional retrieval interface supplied with a powerful automatic retrieval mechanism, is still necessary within the user interface for more than the simple delivering of the next subtree's leaf elements.

As already mentioned users have to find an appropriate entry point for their search dialog, a starting point for his content oriented search path. The user has to be supported in this task, especially in large document collections. An intuitive graphical solution to achieve this goal has not been found, but the traditional automatic retrieval system in the background enables the user to find such a point in an area of the content space that is close to a point of the user's interest space by querying the user interface with natural language text input. In other words, the root node term or document for the whole search tree has to be determined, whether it is by the user alone or with the help of an automatic retrieval mechanism, in our case INQUERY's retrieval mechanism and basic user interface.

Another type of interaction which has not been mentioned yet, is the entering of a term item. The interface interprets this user action as a request to *summarize all results of the search dialog*, represented by the content-oriented search path. This means that users can take advantage of their search dialog's content-oriented search path to formulate a query which then has a relevant result, because the user query are more contentbased. In this case the automatic retrieval mechanism can be applied under a summarizing aspect to the current search path. This means that at a certain point users will be satisfied with their browsing activities and they want to summarize the results of the session, according to their interest which they expressed by navigations. From the system's point of view it is very easy to extract the necessary key words for a hidden query from the content-oriented path that the user was *navigating* on and use them as input for a traditional and now more complex query to the automatic retrieval mechanism. This is the case if the user enters a term item in the tree world – a summary of the dialog's history with a special focus on the terms that remained relevant while the user's creation of the path takes place.

4.5 Presentation of the Result

The query as a summary of a content-oriented search path, requires an appropriate presentation form to enable the user to take advantage of the retrieval mechanism's relevance measurement features. To achieve this, 3D-based presentation forms offer an appropriate medium too. It is necessary for the user to understand that the query result has some relevance to the search path. This can easily be achieved and the search process itself becomes more transparent if the current path becomes high-lighted at query time. As the retrieval mechanism of INQUERY delivers also probabilistic relevance-measure values for each result member in relation to the query's parts, the presentation should reflect this too. We decided to extent the presentation form used in the VIBE system ([Olsen et al. 1991]) from the 2D circle to a 3D sphere (see figure at the end of the paper) with the properties described in the following.

When users enter a term item on the current tree level, they leave the tree world and the slightly transparent sphere is displayed. Users can now rotate and enter this sphere from any point on the surface that seems most interesting for them and will find the most relevant results close to their point of view (in either sense). The position of the entry point on the sphere's surface can be interactively determined by the user by examining the query's key words (the term elements of his content-oriented path in the tree world). Their items are equally distributed positioned on the surface of the sphere. These key word items are *attracting* the query's result members (documents from the content space the user was browsing through while navigating the path), depicted by their graphical symbols within the sphere from the center towards the surface. Their positions in the sphere are calculated according to the relevance measure values that INQUERY delivered for the query result. Therefore the user will experience those documents closest to his entry point into the sphere, which have the greatest probabilistic relevance to the keywords in the neighborhood of his entry point.

5 Architecture

This section of the paper gives a short overview over the proposed interface's prototypical architecture (displayed in figure 6). We will not explain the INQUERY retrieval system's architecture (therefore see [Callan/Croft/Harding 1992]).

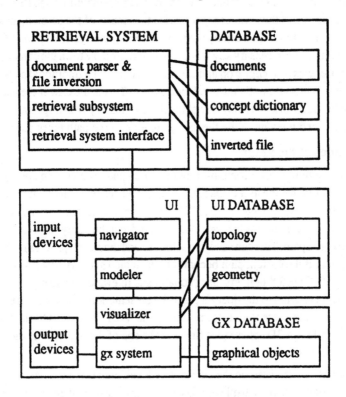

Figure 6: System architecture

The *navigator* module handles the user's input messages. When transmitted as input signals from the input devices, they have to be interpreted by the navigator into navigational, reading or querying requests. Besides the keyboard for textual input, the user controls the whole scene via a force input device [Spaceball]. This device gives him an intuitive control appropriate to the 3D character of the application [Felger 1992]. By that means, users are in control of their own point of view (position and orientation) and over all parts of the displayed scene.

In case of a navigational request, the navigator performs the access operations on the retrieval system which are necessary to achieve information about the content structure of the database, mostly so called *transitions* (see [Callan/Croft/Harding 1992]). If a reading or querying request is received by the navigator module (i.e. if a term or document item is entered), it queries the retrieval system for the necessary results too. These informations are transmitted to the *modeler* module. It transforms the received transitions into the topological data which compose the cone tree's representation in the user interface database.

In case of a query the modeler calculates the positions of items in the sphere and on the surface.

At the end of the visualizing pipeline, the *visualizer* module is requested to layout the geometry of the scene (in case of a navigation according to the topological information). Furthermore, it performs the necessary visualizing requests and operations on the *graphics system* and its database of graphical objects. This design enables to stay independent from the choice of a specific graphics system. In our case the graphical services are provided by Silicon Graphics Iris Inventor, an object-oriented 3D toolkit integrated with X Windows and described in [Strauss/Carey 1992]. The output device is a stereo-driven high-resolution CRT or a headmounted display. Hard-copies of all introduced visualization metaphors are included at the end of the paper.

6 Conclusions and Outlook

We have introduced a first example for a new kind of human-computer interface based on 3D graphical metaphors which demonstrates that information retrieval applications can benefit in the same way from the performance boom in the field of graphics hardware as, e.g., CAD applications already do. We state that this interface supports only one kind of retrieval model and user interface design. Despite this, we expect that other models like, e.g., knowledge-based ones can be supplied with a more intuitive interface in the same way, because their inventors already had graphical metaphors in mind when they developed their models.

The next steps in the prototype's progress will be the evaluation of its current state and expanding its functionality also to other retrieval models. Therefore other types of metaphors and the corresponding navigators and modelers are necessary. We will also try to integrate a model for information seeking strategies and make these transparent at the interface level.

It seems to be a promising work to reveal the metaphorical properties of existing models and concepts to find appropriate ways to visualize abstract information sets with complex structures. By means of walk-through or fly-through metaphors that substitute the traditional query-retrieval-presentation sequences and make underlying models and concepts transparent, the user can achieve a deeper level of understanding for the systems functionality. Furthermore the user has a better base to estimate the system's properties and limits.

Nevertheless intelligent automatic assistance by the system is still required (especially when dealing with very large information sets), as outlined for the automatic retrieval mechanism integrated in our system.

References

Agosti, M., Gradegnio, G., Marchetti, P.G. (1991) Architecture and Functions for a Conceptual Interface to very large Online Bibliographic Collections. Intelligent Text and Image Handling, RIAO 91, Barcelona, Spain, April 1991.

Card, S.K., Robertson, G.G., Mackinlay, J.D. The Information Visualizer, an Information Workspace, In: Proc. CHI '91, New Orleans, April 1991, ACM Press, p.181

Croft, W.B., Wolf, R., Thompson, R. (1983) A Network Organization used for Document Retrieval. Proc. of the 6th Annual Int. ACM SIGIR Conf., SIGIR Forum, Vol. 17, No. 4, 1983

Feiner, S. & C. Beshers (1990) Visualizing n–Dimensional Virtual Worlds with n–Vision. In: Proc. ACM SIGGRAPH '90, ACM Press p. 37

Felger, W. (1992)How interactive visualization can benefit from multidimensional input devices. In: Alexander, J.R. (ed.): Visual Data Interpretation, Proc. SPIE 1668, 1992

Gu, J. & Thiel, U. (1993) Automatically Converting Linear Text to Hypertext: A Case Study. To appear in: Proc. Hypermedia '93, Zurich, Switzerland, Berlin et al.: Springer 1993

Kerner, A. & Thiel, U. (1991). Graphical Support for Users Inferences within Retrieval Dialogues. In: Proc. 1991 IEEE Workshop on Visual Languages, Kobe/Japan, October 1991. Washington: IEEE Computer Society Press, 1991, pp. 211-216

Korfhage, R.R. (1991) To see or not to see – Is that the Query?, In: Proc. of the 14th Annual Int. Conference on Research and Development in Information Retrieval (SIGIR '91), Chicago, 1991, p. 134

Olson, K.A., Korfhage, R.R., Sochats, K.M., Spring, B.M. and Williams, J.G. (1991) Visualization of a document collection: The VIBE system. Report LIS033/IS91001, School of Library and Information science, University of Pittsburgh, 1991

Pejtersen, A.M. (1989) A Library System for Information Retrieval based on a Cognitive Task Analysis and Supported by an Icon Based Interface. In: Belkin, N.J., van Rijsbergen, C.J. (eds.): Proc. of the 12th Annual Int. Conference on Research and Development in Information Retrieval (SIGIR '89), Cambridge, Mass. 1989

Robertson, G.G., Mackinlay, J.D., Card, S.K. (1991) Cone Trees: Animated 3D Visualizations of Hierachical Information, In: Proc. CHI '91, New Orleans, April 1991, ACM Press, p.189

Seligmann, D.D. & S. Feiner (1991) Automated Generation of Intent–Based 3D Illustrations. In: Computer Graphics 25(4), 1991, pp. 123–132

Spaceball, Spaceball Technologies Inc. 1991

Strong, G.W. O'Neil Strong, K.E. (1991) Visual guidance for information navigation: a computer-human interface design principle derived from cognitive neuroscience. In: Interacting with computers: the interdisciplinary Journal of HCI, vol. 3, no. 2, Butterworth-Heinemann,1991, pp. 217–231

Thiel, U. & Hammwöhner, R. (1987) Information Zooming: An Interaction Model for the Graphical Access to Text Knowledge Bases. In: Yu, C.T., van Rijsbergen, C.J. (eds.): Proc. of the 10th Annual Int. Conference on Research and Development in Information Retrieval (SIGIR '87), New Orleans, Louisiana 1987

Strauss, P.S. & Carey, R. (1992) An Object-Oriented 3D Graphics Toolkit, Computer, 26, 2, July 1992 pp. 341-349

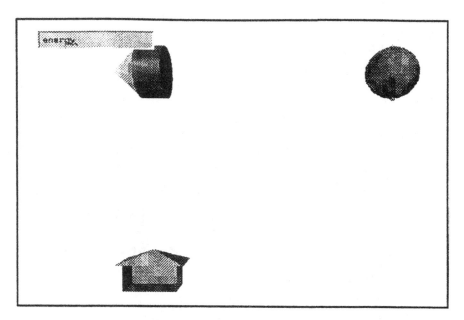

Figure 7: Session start, tools iconified, first keyword entered

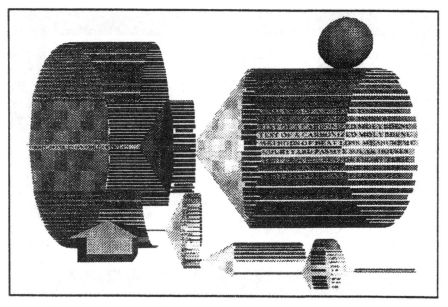

Figure 8: NavigationCones containing a complete search context

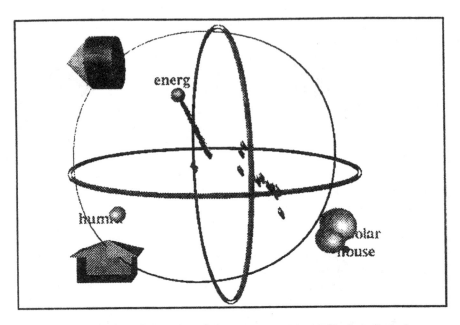

Figure 9: RelevanceSphere containing a context space with document clusters

Figure 10: RelevanceSphere and InformationRoom activated

Using Visualization to Support
Data Mining of Large Existing Databases

Daniel A. Keim, Hans-Peter Kriegel

Institute for Computer Science, University of Munich
Leopoldstr. 11B, D-80802 Munich, Germany
{keim. kriegel}@informatik.uni-muenchen.de

Abstract. In this paper, we present ideas how visualization technology can be used to improve the difficult process of querying very large databases. With our VisDB system, we try to provide visual support not only for the query specification process, but also for evaluating query results and, thereafter, refining the query accordingly. The main idea of our system is to represent as many data items as possible by the pixels of the display device. By arranging and coloring the pixels according to the relevance for the query, the user gets a visual impression of the resulting data set and of its relevance for the query. Using an interactive query interface, the user may change the query dynamically and receives immediate feedback by the visual representation of the resulting data set. By using multiple windows for different parts of the query, the user gets visual feedback for each part of the query and, therefore, may easier understand the overall result. To support complex queries, we introduce the notion of 'approximate joins' which allow the user to find data items that only approximately fulfill join conditions. We also present ideas how our technique may be extended to support the interoperation of heterogeneous databases. Finally, we discuss the performance problems that are caused by interfacing to existing database systems and present ideas to solve these problems by using data structures supporting a multidimensional search of the database.

Keywords: Visualizing Large Data Sets. Visualizing Multidimensional Multivariate Data. Data Mining, Visual Query Systems. Visual Relevance Feedback. Interfaces to Database Systems

1. Introduction

The need for database system support visualization systems has been widely recognized and has been a main focus of two previous workshops which were held in conjunction with the *SIGGRAPH '90* and *Visualization '91* conferences. The main question that has been dealt with is how database technology can adequately support visualization systems. In this context, researchers are working on extending current object-oriented database management systems, designing adequate database schemas and formats that allow storing and accessing the large amounts of data which are needed by visualization systems. The question of database support for visualization, however, is only one side of the coin; the other side is visual support for databases. In this paper, we take up the question, how to visually support database users in accessing, analyzing and understanding the growing amount of data that is stored in the computer.

The progress made in hardware technology allows today's computer systems to store very large amounts of data. The available storage space is easily filled with data that is often automatically recorded via sensors and monitoring systems. Today, even simple transactions of every day life, such as paying by credit card or using the telephone, are typically recorded by using computers. Even larger amounts of data are generated by automated test series in physics, chemistry or medicine and satellite observation systems are expected to collect one terabyte of data every day in the near future [FPM 91]. The data of all areas mentioned so far is collected because people believe that it is a potential source of valuable information providing a competitive advantage (at some point). Querying and analyzing the databases to uncover the valuable information hidden in them, however, is a difficult task. Traditional database query languages such as SQL [ISO 92] allow people to query the databases, but finding the data a person is interested in is often a problem. Even experienced database users may have difficulties to find the interesting hot spots. Since, in general, the user does not exactly know the data and its distribution, many queries may be needed to find the interesting data sets. The result for most queries will contain either less data than expected, sometimes even no answers, so-called 'NULL' results, or more data than the user is able to deal with. With today's database systems and their query tools, it is only possible to view quite small portions of the data. If the data is displayed textually, the amount of data that can be displayed is in the range of some one hundred data items but this is like a drop in the ocean when dealing with millions of data items. Having no possibility to adequately query and view the large amounts of data that have been collected because of their potential usefulness, the data becomes useless and the database becomes a data 'dump'.

The need for supporting the process of querying and analyzing databases has been widely recognized and was even ranked one of the most important topics of database research for the 90s [SSU 90]. The US government, for example, sponsors large projects, such as the Sequoia 2000 project, to develop advanced data analysis techniques for very large databases. Many companies also recognized the potential of analyzing their databases. Banks and retail stores, for example, analyze their transaction records to understand customer habits better and thus, tailor their marketing promotions accordingly. Banks also analyze loan and credit history to improve their loan approval policies. Over the last several years, many tools and algorithms for data analysis have been developed. It seems, however, that advanced techniques for data analysis are not yet mature - at least for the flood of data we are facing today. Since, on the other hand, the technology for generating, collecting and storing data is available, the gap between the amount of data that has to be analyzed and the amount of data that can be analyzed is growing.

Visualization technology seems to provide important potentials to improve the process of querying, analyzing and understanding the data. With visualization techniques, larger amounts of data can be presented at the same time on the screen, colors allow the user to instantly recognize similarities or differences of thousands of data items, the data items may be arranged to express some specific relationships and so on. To our knowledge, up to this point visualization techniques are only used in databases in the rare cases where the data has some inherent two- or three-dimensional semantics. In geographic databases, for example, 2D visualizations are used to adequately support spatial queries and basically all Geographic Information Systems (GIS) provide such visual representations of the data. In most application areas, however, the data does not lend itself to an easy visualization and, therefore, in most cases no visual support for querying the database is provided. We believe that in dealing with very large amounts of data, visual support allowing database users to profit from the progress made in visualization hard- and software, is essential to support the process of exploring the data.

Most of the data collected in the past is stored in relational database management systems. In particular, large (unstructured) data sets are usually stored in relational systems. However, for visualization purposes relational systems are not well suited. and often there is no other way to access the data than to completely extract the whole database. There are many reasons for using relational systems instead of better suited systems such as object-oriented database management systems. One of them is the proliferation of relational systems. Another reason is, as recent studies show, that object-oriented database technology is not yet mature for really large amounts of data. In the context of this paper, we focus on available databases and therefore, we mainly refer to the relational data model. However, most of the ideas that will be presented in this paper also work in conjunction with object-oriented or other database systems.

The rest of the paper is organized as follows: Section 2 elaborates on the tasks that are important to querying large databases. The term 'data mining' is introduced and discussed with respect to related areas of research. Section 3 gives an overview of our ideas to visually support the querying of large databases and describes the query specification and visualization interface of the VisDB system. In section 4, some of the problems in interfacing with (traditional) database systems are described and potential solutions are discussed. Section 5 summarizes our approach and points out some of the open problems for future work.

2. Data Mining

The process of searching and analyzing large amounts of data is also called 'data mining'. The large collections of data are the potential lodes of valuable information but, like in real mining, the search and extraction can be a difficult and exhaustive process. Therefore, for the mining to be successful, adequate and efficient mining tools are essential. In some sense, data mining is like the work of radiologists. It is like scanning the database to identify phenomena that need to be looked at, showing the regular structure of the data but also helping to find anomalies. Before we describe the differences of data mining to related research areas, we will first try to define the term 'data mining'.

2.1 Definition of Data Mining

'Data Mining' can be defined as the (non-trivial) process of searching and analyzing data, in particular to find implicit but potentially useful information. Let $D = \bigcup_{i=1}^{m} D_i$ with $D_i = \{d_1, ..., d_{n_i}\}$ be the data set to be analyzed. Note that the D_i do not need to be stored in the same database management system. The process of data mining can be described as the process of finding a subset D' of D and hypotheses H_U (D', C) about D' that a user U considers *useful* in an application context C. The hypothesis may describe properties of the data set D', it may identify relationships between subsets of D' or it may be a combination of both. Our definition can be further formalized, e.g. by defining a hypothesis description language, a context description formalism and so on. The user and his/her notion of 'usefulness', however, can hardly be formalized since 'usefulness' not only depends on the changing knowledge of the user and the application domain, but it also includes some notion of creativity and users may not be able to define their usefulness criteria. On the other hand, if a data mining tool helps the user to find useful D' and to find and verify hypotheses, then it may not be important to have the hypothesis, the context and so on formally specified. All these aspects are present in the mind of the user who will also be able to express and communicate his/her ideas towards other humans.

2.2 Related Research Areas

Our definition of data mining is a quite broad definition and relates to a wide range of other research areas including statistics (data analysis, cluster analysis), artificial intelligence (knowledge discovery, machine learning), database interfaces (data browsing, cooperative database interfaces) and information retrieval. In the following, we give a brief overview of these areas.

Simple statistical parameters such as average, variance or correlation coefficients only allow special kinds of hypotheses, namely those with D' = D or $D' = D_i$ in the case where D is partitioned into relations $D_1, ..., D_m$. More complex statistical methods such as multidimensional cluster analysis and mathematical taxonomy [DE 82] try to find hypotheses about real subsets of the database ($D' \subset D$ with $|D'| \ll |D|$ and $|D'|$ sufficiently large). An exhaustive cluster analysis of multidimensional data would require checking of relationships between all combinations of dimensions for all subsets of data items which is computationally intractable for large data sets. Therefore, most cluster analysis algorithms use some kind of heuristics to reduce the search space (e.g. [Hub 85, GSSK 87, GPP 90]). Still, for really large databases with millions of data items, cluster analysis is not feasible without human guidance. Additionally, statistical methods are not suited for nominal and structured data and often lead to results that are difficult to interpret. Furthermore, statistical methods do not help to find single exceptional data, so-called hot spots. In our context, we talk about hot spots if $D' \subset D$ and $|D'| = 1$ or sufficiently small when compared to $|D|$.

In artificial intelligence, researchers are working in related fields of knowledge discovery and machine learning which can also be considered to be data mining. Among the AI techniques used in data mining are inverted expert system approaches, probabilistic theories, bayesian statistics, neural networks and genetic algorithms. In contrast to our approach, in knowledge discovery the hypotheses are usually rules or facts which are formally specified in some high-level language [FPM 91]. In some cases, the knowledge is even not made available to the user to support hypothesis finding since it is extracted from samples, either unsupervised or supervised by experts and directly used for decision making in similar cases (well-known examples are [Qui 86, RM 86, HHNT 86]).

Another area related to data mining is database query interfaces. The ability to extract data satisfying a common condition is like data mining in its ability to produce interesting and useful hypotheses. Traditional query interfaces, however, do not help the user in finding interesting data. The usefulness of the results largely depends on the user's a priori knowledge and intuition. In many cases, however, it is like the search of a needle in a haystack. Many approaches have been made to improve the database query interface. One approach is graphical database interfaces that allow the user to browse the data (e.g. FLEX [Mot 90] or BAROQUE [Mot 86]). Another approach is cooperative database interfaces [Kap 82, ABN 92] that try to give 'approximate answers' in cases where the query does not provide a satisfactory answer. Such systems use techniques like query generalization [Cha 90], that is, dropping or relaxing a selection predicate in cases where the original query fails, and statistical approximation or intensional responses instead of full enumeration in the cases of large results (key ideas are already presented in [JKL 77] for the first time).

In the area of information retrieval, a lot of research has been done to improve recall and precision in querying databases of unstructured data such as (full) text. The search is usually supported by some kind of 'descriptor' that may be extracted automatically or assigned by the user. In this context, distance functions for text, strings or descriptors [HD 80], ranking functions [NMK 81, FM 91] and weighted queries [SB 88] have been examined. To improve the effectiveness of information retrieval systems, the notion of relevance feedback (using relevance assessments provided by the user) and approximate matching algorithms have been proposed [Sal 88, FS 91]. Although the work in information retrieval mainly focuses on (full) text databases, we believe that it is an essential prerequisite of our research.

2.3 The Tasks Involved in Data Mining

For querying and analyzing a database, first a query needs to be specified. In most database applications, query specification is restricted to predefined, possibly parameterized queries which have been designed and implemented by the database designer. If the user wants to issue other queries than the predefined ones, usually an interactive interface for ad hoc queries is available. The queries, however, have to be expressed in specific database query languages such as SQL which represents a quasi-standard. The

SQL query language with its linear syntax was developed two decades ago and has not changed substantially since then. Major problems are that queries need to be issued in a one-by-one fashion providing no possibilities to slightly change a query, to express uncertain or vague queries and to intuitively specify complex queries. As we will show in the next section, visualization technology may help to improve the query specification process considerably.

After issuing the query, the user gets the resulting data set fulfilling the given query conditions. However, as already explained in the introduction, in many cases the result does not provide adequate feedback helping the user to find interesting hypotheses or to refine the query. This is true for very large data sets consisting of multiple attributes with a flat structure, e.g. data generated by automated test series (physics), periodical observations (weather) or statistical recordings (credit card payments). For large structured data sets, it is even more difficult to find interesting hypotheses. In the relational data model, for example, related data is usually stored in multiple relations which need to be joined in order to find relationships between the data. In cases, where relations are joined using (foreign) keys which are specially designed for connecting multiple relations. the join can be executed efficiently providing exactly the desired tuple. In data mining, the goal is to find new relationships and, therefore, (foreign) keys do not provide any help. Often, such relationships are vague and thus, possibilities to express vague or approximate joins are needed. Additionally, it would be helpful, if the results of such joins provide feedback on the closeness in fulfilling the approximate join condition, which is also not provided by current database systems. In the next section, we will present our ideas to use visualization technology to provide better feedback for querying large flat (c.f section 3.2) as well as structured data sets (c.f section 3.3).

If the data is stored in multiple independent databases, the task of finding interesting hypotheses about the data is even harder to solve. In addition to the problem of having different data models, query languages. database management systems and so on, the problems of incompatible structures. incompatible instances, inconsistencies, etc. have to be solved. Again, as we will describe in section 3.4, our visualization technique may be helpful to solve some of the problems in dealing with multiple databases.

At this point, we want to draw the reader's attention to a problem arising in performing data mining on large existing databases, namely the poor support by existing database management systems which are used to store the data. This problem is especially relevant when trying to visualize large amounts of multidimensional data. Current database management systems support neither incrementally changing nor uncertain queries. Furthermore, they do not adequately support range conditions on multiple attributes which require a fast multidimensional search of the database. We believe that existing database systems need to be extended to better support the requirements of data mining and visualization systems. In section 4, we will describe the mentioned problems in more detail and discuss potential solutions.

2.4 Key Characteristics of Data Mining Tools for Large Databases

Before we describe our ideas to support data mining, in this subsection we briefly mention the characteristics of data mining tools that we consider to be the most important ones: interactiveness and efficiency.

For data mining of really large databases to be successful in the near future, we believe that it is essential to make the human being part of the data analysis process. It will be important to combine the best features of humans and computers. The unmatchable intelligence, creativity and perceptual abilities of humans need to be supported by computers, which are best suited to do searching and number crunching. A major research challenge is to find human-oriented forms of representing large amounts of information. In today's systems, the perceptual abilities of humans are only used to a very limited extent. Only a few systems use vision and sound to help the user in data analysis (see [SBG 90] for an example). In the future, data mining tools need to be built in a human-centered way supporting an effective interaction between the user and the system.

A second important characteristic of data mining tools is efficiency. Efficiency is important for the algorithms to scale up well enough when dealing with very large data volumes. Although there is no universally agreed definition of 'efficient', it has been stated that algorithms whose computational requirements are of the same order as sorting [$O(n \log n)$] or better can be considered efficient [FPM 91]. Given that hardware improvements will continue at the same rate as in the past, it is unlikely that algorithms with a complexity that is substantially higher than $O(n \log n)$ will be useful in dealing with data volumes in the range of terabytes.

3. Visual Support in Querying Databases

The basic idea of our query and visualization interface is to present as many data items as possible at the same time on the screen with the number of data items being only limited by the number of pixels of the display. Our goal is to visualize the data in a way that the user gets visual feedback on the query and thus can easily explore the database, understand the influence of various query components and find out why slightly different queries have completely different results. In the following, we will give a brief overview of our VisDB system: query specification component (subsection 3.1), visualization of large flat data (subsection 3.2), visualization of complex data (subsection 3.3) and ideas for extending the system to partially solve the problems that arise in dealing with multiple independent databases (subsection 3.4).

3.1 Query Specification

In exploring very large databases, an easy-to-use query interface for 'ad hoc' queries is important. Most of the currently available 'ad hoc' query interfaces, such as SQL, are not user friendly and, in particular, not suitable for data mining. Most of them only provide line-driven, textual interfaces allowing queries to be issued in a one-by-one fashion only. Furthermore, they do not allow interactively modifying queries nor do they adequately support the specification of complex queries. Our idea to solve these problems is to visually support the query specification process allowing even inexperienced users to retrieve data from the database without knowing a specific query language. In contrast to most of today's database management systems where the user is forced to think in terms of the data model and the query language, with our system the user can interactively construct the query and, using the visual representation of the query provided by the system, the user can understand and modify the query more easily.

The main ideas of our visual database query interface have been presented in [KL 92]. Although the visual query interface has been developed in the context of a multimedia database management system, it is generally useful for specifying SQL-like queries. Note, that the query specification interface is largely independent from the rest of the VisDB system. For the purpose of query specification. the user may also use traditional query languages such as SQL or other graphical user interfaces such as QBE [Zlo 77], Visual SQL [TC 90] or Iconic Query [PC 93] instead of our visual query specification interface. However, as we will see in subsection 3.3, our query specification interface is especially useful in conjunction with our technique for visualizing complex query results since it allows direct access to all parts of complex queries.

To briefly explain the query specification process, let us go through an example that will be used in subsection 3.3 to demonstrate the visual feedback in case of complex queries. Assume a user of an environmental database with local weather parameters (temperature, humidity, direction and speed of the wind, solar radiation. precipitation, etc.) and air pollution values (CO, SO_2, NO_2, ozone, etc.) wants to find a correlation between temperature, solar radiation and humidity on one hand and the ozone level on the other hand. According to his/her assumption that there is a correlation between the parameters with a time delay of two hours. the user may specify the following query:

> *'Select the temperature, solar radiation, humidity and ozone level if*
> *at the same location the temperature is higher than 15°C or the solar*
> *radiation is higher than 600 watt/m^2 or the humidity is lower than*
> *60% and between recording temperature and ozone there is a time*
> *difference of two hours.'*

In specifying this query, the user starts by selecting the tables needed for the query from the *Tables* window, namely *Weather* and *Air-Pollution*. As a result, all attributes of the *Weather* and the *Air-Pollution* table are displayed in separate windows. To specify the projection, the user may then move the attributes *Temperature, Solar-Radiation, Humidity* and *Ozone* into the *Result List* window. The next step is to specify the condition. Assume, the user wants to start with the *at-same-location* part. By clicking to *Cond* in the *Tool Box*, s/he gets an empty condition box in the *Query Representation* window and by clicking to the connection *'Air-Pollution at-same-location Weather'* the desired join condition may be specified. 'Connections' are joins which are defined and named by the database designer (or the user) prior to their actual use. Next, the user may want to specify the 'OR'-part of the condition. For each of the three attributes *Temperature*, *Solar-Radiation* and *Humidity*, the user selects *Cond* from the *Tool Box*, the attribute from the *Weather* table, the desired comparison operator and finally, s/he types in the corresponding value of the limit. Then, all three parts are selected and by clicking to 'OR' in the *Tool Box*, the boxes get 'OR'-connected. The last part that needs to be specified is the time related join condition. Since a join with the intended meaning is already predefined, the join may easily be specified by selecting *Cond* from *Tool Box*, *'Air-Pollution with-time-diff(min) Weather'* from the *Connections* window and typing in the desired time value of 120 minutes. The last step is to combine the conditions into the final result. This is done by selecting all separate parts and by clicking to the logical operator 'AND' from the *Tool Box*. The final result of the query specification is shown in figure 1. The details of the query specification interface are beyond the scope of this paper and are given in [KL 92].

3.2 Visual Feedback in Querying Large Flat Data Sets

As indicated by our definition, we view data mining as an interactive hypotheses-generation process. Our goal is to get the data to ask questions, rather than asking questions to the data. In contrast to most other approaches to data mining (c.f. section 2.2), our idea is to use the phenomenal abilities of the human vision system which is able to analyze compact to midsize amounts of data very efficiently and immediately recognizes patterns in images which would be very difficult (in some cases even impossible) and at least very time-consuming if done by the computer. The research challenge is to find adequate ways of visually presenting multidimensional data to support the user in analyzing and interpreting the data.

Visualization of data which have some inherent two- or three-dimensional semantics has been done even before computers could be used for visualization, and since computers have been used for this purpose, a lot of interesting and efficient visualization techniques have been developed by researchers working in the graphics field. Visualization of large amounts of arbitrary multidimensional data, however, is a relatively new research area. Researchers in the graphics/visualization area are currently exploring techniques in different application domains [Bed 90, FB 90, ID 90, LWW 90, MGTS 90, MZ 92]. In most of the approaches proposed so far, the number of data items that can be visualized on the screen at the same time is quite limited (in the range of 100 to 1,000 data items), but it is a declared goal of the visualization community to push this limit [Tre 92]. In dealing with databases consisting of tens of thousands to millions of data items, our goal is to visualize as many data items as possible at the same time to give the user some kind of feedback on the query. The obvious limit for any kind of visualization is the resolution of current displays which is in the order of one to three million pixels, e.g. in case of our 19 inch displays with a resolution of 1,024 x 1,280 pixels it is about 1.3 million pixels. Our idea is to use each pixel of the screen to give the user a visual feedback on the query allowing him/her to easily focus on the desired data, understand the influence of various query components and find out why slightly different queries have completely different results.

The basic idea of our visualization technique for large flat data sets is described in [KKS 93]. In our approach, as a result for a query the user does not only get the data items fulfilling the query but also a number of data items that approximately fulfill the query. The approximate results are determined using distance functions for each of the selection predicates which are combined into the relevance factor. The distance functions are datatype- and application-dependent and must be provided by the application. Examples of distance functions are numerical difference (for metric types), distance matrices (for ordinal and nominal types), lexicographical, character-wise, substring or phonetic difference (for strings) and so on. Having calculated the distances for each of the selection predicates, the distances are combined into the relevance factor. Important aspects such as normalizing and weighting the different selection predicates, the formulas we use to calculate the relevance factors and the heuristics used to reduce the number of data items that are displayed are described in [KKS 93]. The relevance factors are then sorted resulting in a one-dimensional distribution ranking the approximate responses according to their relevance. The basic idea for visualizing the relevance factors is to map them to colors and represent each data item by several pixels colored according to the relevance of the data item. The colored relevance factors are displayed on the screen with the highest relevance factors (yellow) centered in the middle of the window and the approximate answers with colors ranging from green over blue and red to almost black rectangular spiral-shaped around this region (c.f. figures 2-5). To relate the visualization of the overall result to visualizations of the different selection predicates, we generate a separate window for each selection predicate of the query. In these separate windows, we place the pixels for each data item at the same relative position as the overall result for the data item in the overall result window. The separate windows for each of the selection predicates provide important additional feedback to the user, e.g. on the restrictiveness of each of the selection predicates and also on single exceptional data items. After having the visual feedback, the user may interactively change the query according to the impression from the visualized results. Using highlighting of corresponding pixels in different windows or a projection of the visual representation to specific color ranges, the user may further explore the data helping him/her to relate the relevance factors in the different windows. By being able to get the attribute values corresponding to some specific color, the user may better understand and interpret the visualizations. According to the discoveries made during this process, the user may then incrementally change the query using sliders provided for each of the selection attributes (c.f. figures 2-3).

As already indicated in the previous section, our approach to data mining largely differs from the techniques used in statistics, artificial intelligence, database interfaces and information retrieval. The most obvious difference is that we are using visualization and coloration to support the data mining process. In our approach, we try to adequately support the excellent vision capabilities of humans whom we believe to be the most important factor in data mining. Additionally, our technique is fast enough to be used in very large databases. For simple queries and standard distance functions the complexity is O(n logn) with n being the number of data items. Obviously, query processing time is dominated by the time needed for sorting. Furthermore, our technique is completely application-independent. and. in contrast to most other approaches to data mining, with our approach it is possible to find single exceptional values which are difficult, maybe even impossible, to find with traditional cluster analysis or knowledge discovery methods.

3.3 Visual Support in Querying Large Structured Data Sets

Up to this point, we have only considered the simplest types of queries, namely queries on flat data sets with all selection predicates being connected by the same Boolean operator. In this subsection, we briefly describe how complex queries, i.e. queries with the selection predicates being arbitrarily connected (nested 'AND's and 'OR's), multiple table queries and some types of nested queries may be supported visually in our system.

In dealing with complex conditions that consist of arbitrary Boolean expressions of selection predicates, in the first step the user gets only the visualization of the top level of selection predicates. In terms of the graphical representation of the query in the query representation window, it is the leftmost logical operator with the corresponding selection predicates. If one of the selection predicates itself consists of a Boolean expression, then the user may not understand how the visualization of that part is generated since only one visualization with the overall result for that part is displayed. To be able to explore the impact of any query part, in the VisDB system the user may get visualization and query modification windows for arbitrary subparts at any level of the Boolean expression by simply double clicking the corresponding Boolean operator in the query representation window. The query representation window is available to the user during the whole process of data mining to provide an overview of the actual query, reflecting all changes made by direct modifications and to allow access to all parts of the query. In general, the arrangement of data items in the upper left part of the visualization representing the overall result of the corresponding query part is the same arrangement as for the overall result of the whole query. However, the user may also examine the query part independently and use an option to get the data items arranged according to the relevance factors calculated for the query part only. In our example query (c.f. subsection 3.1), in the first step the visualization consists of four parts: one for the overall result of the query and three for the three parts connected by 'AND' (see figure 2). If the user wants to see visualizations for each of the selection predicates connected by 'OR', s/he might double click on the 'OR'-box in the query representation window and, as a result, s/he will get another query visualization and modification window for this subpart (see figure 3).

Another type of complex queries are multi-table queries which, in general, involve some kind of join. The totality of data items that need to be considered in this case is the cross product of all tables involved. Our idea for visually supporting multi-table queries is to consider all data items of the cross product that approximately fulfill the join condition. As for all other selection predicates. the user gets a separate window with the data items of the cross product that fulfill the join condition being yellow and the others being colored according to their distance. In some cases, e.g. if the tables are connected by foreign keys which are designed to connect related data items, this may not be helpful since the distances on foreign keys may not have any semantics. In such cases, only those data items that fulfill the join condition should be considered and no visualization for the join condition needs to be generated. In most other cases, however, it is quite helpful to consider data items that approximately fulfill join conditions. In our example from environmental science, for example, we have a time- and a location-related join condition both of which may well be considered as vague ones. Such approximative joins may even be crucial to find the desired results if, for example, the time interval for measuring the weather and air pollution parameters is different or if the weather and the air pollution measurement station are not at the same but at close-by locations. In these cases, join conditions requiring time or location equality would provide only very few or even no results though they would be quite helpful. Again, the distance functions used to determine the distance of the join tuples are user and application dependent (c.f. section 3.2). For joins on numerical attributes, for example, the numerical difference between the considered data items from the two relations might be used as an approximation of the join condition to be fulfilled. In a similar way, the distance functions for non-equijoins ($a1 < a2$) or parametrized (non-equi)joins ($a1 - a2 < c$) may be determined. Special joins, e.g. to relate geographical locations (c.f. example query), require more complex distance functions. In a different context, other distance functions may be helpful, e.g. if the user is only interested in one relation and in the number of join partners that each data item of this relation has with another relation, the user might use the inverse of that number as the distance.

In the last part of this subsection, we briefly describe how our visualization technique may support the user in dealing with nested queries. As an example, we describe the case of nested queries where the subquery is connected by using 'exists' or 'in'. In dealing with such types of queries, the user may choose the outer relation(s) to be the basis for displaying the relevance factors of the results. Again, the user will get a separate visualization part for each of the (top level) selection predicates. In the visualization part corresponding to the overall result of the subquery, the user gets yellow in case the subquery condition is fulfilled and otherwise the color corresponding to the distance of the data item most closely fulfilling the subquery condition. The data item most closely fulfilling the subquery condition can be determined by the minimum distance in performing an approximate join of the inner and the outer relation(s). Using this single value to be displayed for the whole subquery, the user gets no feedback on the distribution of distances for the approximative join and on the other selection predicates that may be involved in the subquery. For this reason, we provide the possibility to select one single data item in the visualization window and to get the complete subquery with all its selection predicates including the join of inner and outer relation(s) presented in a separate visualization and modification window. This way, the user is viewing the impact of the subquery in the context of a single data item from the outer relation(s). If the user is more interested in the connections between inner and outer relation(s), s/he might use the cross product of inner and outer relation(s) as a basis for displaying the relevance factors. In this case, the user gets a better feedback on the amount and distribution of distances for data items that only approximately fulfill the join of inner and outer relation(s). However, since we are dealing with the cross product, the totality of data items that are considered is much larger and the percentage that can be displayed is correspondingly lower.

Note, that in most cases where negations are used (negated conditions, NOT IN, NOT EXISTS etc.), no distance values may be obtained and hence no coloring is possible. Exceptions are negated comparison operators [*not (a1 op a2)* with $op \in \{>, <, \geq, \leq\}$] where the comparison operator may be inverted. The problem of not having distinguishable values in case of negations is similar to the problem of negations in logic programming.

3.4 Visual Support for Interoperating Multiple Independent Databases

In this section, we will give a brief overview of some ideas to use our visualization technique to perform data mining on data that is stored in multiple independent databases. Many of the problems arising in this context are related to schema enrichment, transformation and resolution as well as query decomposition, translation and optimization. In our papers [KKM 93a-b, KKM 94], we propose algorithms to solve part of these problems for relational and object-oriented databases. Our algorithms and most other algorithms proposed in this context only use techniques that work at the schema or query level but do not consider the data instances. Many problems, however, such as finding corresponding or conflicting data items, can only be solved by comparing the data instances of the different databases and we believe that our visualization technique may be helpful to solve such problems. In addition to using our visualization technique for joining relations from multiple independent databases which can be performed in the same way as multiple table joins within one database (c.f. section 3.3), our technique may be used to identify similar or related data, to discover relationships between tables from multiple databases, to find relations representing the same data items, to find conflicting or incorrect data (typing errors, wrong data entries, lost updates) and so on. Similar patterns in the visualizations, for example, which may easily be identified provide hints for relating sets of data items or even whole relations. Special distance functions may be defined to find related data items in multiple databases (e.g. by mapping the keys of different databases). Approximate joins between relations from different databases may help to find out whether the relations contain similar or related data. Specific differences in the visualizations of two relations may provide hints for conflicting data, and single exceptional data items may help to find incorrect data instances. Up to this point, we did not have a change to extend the VisDB system to be able to evaluate the mentioned ideas but we believe that visualization technology in general and our visualization technique in particular will be of great help in querying, analyzing and comparing large amounts of data as it is required in interoperating multiple independent databases.

4. Extending Existing Database Systems

Our query and visualization interface is designed to work on top of commercially available relational database systems. We are focusing on the relational data model since it is widely used especially to handle large amounts of flat data. A similar query interface, however, may be built to query databases with different data models and query languages. In the following, we describe the problems in interfacing with relational database systems and present ideas on how to realize an on-line interface that is fast enough to directly work on the data stored in the database system.

4.1 Problems in Interfacing with Relational Database Systems

The most important drawback of currently available relational systems is that they do not provide the performance needed to support a query and visualization interface like ours. Most systems are optimized to support high transaction rates but do not adequately support the retrieval and transfer of large continuous ranges of data items. In particular, queries with range conditions on multiple attributes require a fast multidimensional search which is not adequately supported in current systems. Another problem is the poor support for queries that are changed incrementally by the user. In current systems, each query is processed separately and, for a sequence of similar queries having only minor differences, there is no way to incrementally retrieve the changes of the resulting data. For our query and visualization interface, however, an adequate support of incremental queries is crucial to allow interactive querying of the database guided by visual feedback.

One additional problem in accessing the database with complex queries is that we need an independent result for each selection predicate or subquery. This is necessary to display the separate windows corresponding to the different parts of the query. To get the necessary information, we either have to issue one query for each window or get the necessary information automatically while the database system is processing the query. For performance reasons, the first alternative is out of the question since it requires multiple scans of the data; the second alternative is not supported by today's database systems.

4.2 Improving the Performance in Interfacing with the Database System

Since the performance of retrieving data from relational systems is by far too poor to be useful for our system, the current prototype used to evaluate our ideas does not interface directly to a database system. We think that currently the only way to achieve a dynamic visualization of the results that is fast enough for interactively changing queries is to keep the relevant part of the database or at least their distance values in main memory. Keeping data in main memory without re-querying the database means working with a possibly non-actual version of the database. This however implies that after slightly changing the query, the visualization may not be completely correct because some data items in the database might have changed after retrieving the data from the database. For most applications, this is not a problem since we are dealing with very large databases that are changing only gradually and, since we are not presenting the data items themselves but only their relevance factors, minor changes of the data have almost no impact on the visualization.

Another important restriction of keeping the data in main memory is the limitation of the amount of data that can be handled. This is a serious restriction since we are dealing with very large databases with millions of data items. Even for simple datatypes with only 4 bytes per data item about 5 megabytes of main memory are needed to store the about 1.3 million data items that may be displayed on the screen at one moment. If we think of the database as being at least 100 times the amount of data that is retrieved as the result for a query, we would need about 500 megabytes to keep the data in main memory. For datatypes such as strings that require more bytes per data item, there is no possibility to keep the data in main memory. Therefore, for large databases it will be necessary to directly interface to the secondary storage based database system that additionally guarantees consistency, integrity and recoverability in a multi-user environment.

Our idea to make interactive query modification possible, is to retrieve more data than necessary in the beginning and to get only the additional data needed for the modified query later on. It will be important to find adequate heuristics that determine the superset of the data which is retrieved in the beginning. Since a modification of the different selection predicates as well as the weighting factors may cause major changes of the resulting data set, in general it cannot be avoided that additional data must be retrieved from the database. In this case, our idea is to generate 'delta'-queries that only retrieve the additionally needed data which, in most cases, can be done quickly. Additionally, to support a fast (real time) access to the database, data structures that support range queries on multiple attributes may be used. Multidimensional data structures such as R*-Tree [BKSS 90] or Buddy-Tree [SK 90] are important to find the data fulfilling the query criteria without searching the whole database. With these ideas, we support some limited kind of an incremental query processing strategy with one longer processing time in the beginning and shorter processing times later on (when interactiveness is important), hopefully providing access to the database that is fast enough to allow interactive modifications of the queries.

5. Conclusions

Data mining in very large databases is one of the big challenges that researchers in the database area are currently facing. The task is to efficiently find interesting data sets, i.e. hot spots, clusters of similar data or correlations between different parameters. Our approach to support the data mining process combines traditional database querying and information retrieval techniques with new techniques of visualizing the data. Our 'VisDB' system can visually represent the largest amount of data that can be displayed at one point of time on current display technology, providing valuable feedback in querying the database and allowing the user to find results which, otherwise, would remain hidden in the database. The interactivity of the system supports focusing on interesting data providing a promising way to efficiently explore the database. Our approach is independent from any specific application area and requires no knowledge of the application other than the distance and weighting functions. In contrast to traditional cluster analysis or knowledge discovery algorithms, no complete analysis of the data resulting in facts or rules in a high-level language is done by the system. The user with his/her perceptual capabilities and general knowledge is responsible for doing the analysis and interpretation. As a result, the performance of our approach is better than in most other approaches to data mining, making it fast enough to be used for very large amounts of data.

The visualizations presented in figures 2 - 5 are generated by a prototype of our 'VisDB' system. The prototype has been implemented to evaluate the concepts and design of our query and visualization interface. The implementation of some parts of the interface, especially the interactive modification of queries and the visualization in case of nested queries, is not yet completed. Furthermore, we are working on improving the performance in interfacing to traditional database systems. The ideas presented in section 4 are our starting point, but additional ideas will be necessary to allow the VisDB system to work fast enough even for midsize to large amounts of data.

In this paper, we have shown that for exploring large data sets the principle of *incremental query refinement guided by visual feedback* can be very helpful for the user to discover interesting data sets and to derive and verify hypotheses about them. Our VisDB system, being built around this principle, provides a simple and elegant but remarkably powerful way of supporting data mining in very large databases.

References

[ABN 92]   Anwar T. M., Beck H. W., Navathe S. B.: 'Knowledge Mining by Imprecise Querying: A Classification-Based Approach', Proc. 8th Int. Conf. on Data Engineering, Tempe, AZ, 1992, pp. 622-630.

[Bed 90]   Beddow J.: 'Shape Coding of Multidimensional Data on a Mircocomputer Display', Visualization '90, San Francisco, CA. 1990, pp. 238-246.

[BKSS 90] Beckmann N., Kriegel H.-P., Schneider R., Seeger B.: 'The R*-Tree: An Efficient and Robust Access Method for Points and Rectangles', Proc. ACM SIGMOD Int. Conf. on Management of Data, Atlantic City, NJ, 1990, pp. 322-331.

[Cha 90]   Chaudhuri S.: 'Generalization and a Framework for Query Modification', Proc. 6th Int. Conf. on Data Engineering, Los Angeles, CA. 1990, pp. 138-145.

[DE 82]   Dunn G., Everitt B.: 'An Introduction to Mathematical Taxonomy', Cambridge University Press, Cambridge. MA, 1982.

[FB 90]   Feiner S., Beshers C.: 'Visualizing n-Dimensional Virtual Worlds with n-Vision', Computer Graphics, Vol. 24, No. 2. 1990. pp. 37-38.

[FM 91] Frei H. P., Meienberg S.: *'Evaluating Weighted Search Terms as Boolean Queries'*, Proc. GI/GMD-Workshop. Darmstadt 1991. in: Informatik-Fachberichte, Vol. 289, 1991, pp. 11-22.

[FPM 91] Frawley W. J., Piatetsky-Shapiro G., Matheus C. J.: *'Knowledge Discovery in Databases: An Overview'*, in: Knowledge Discovery in Databases, AAAI Press, Menlo Park, CA, 1991.

[FS 91] Frei H. P., Schäuble P.: *'Determining the Effectiveness of Retrieval Algorithms'*, Information Processing & Management, Vol. 27, No. 2, 1991.

[GPP 90] Geiger D., Paz A., Pearl J.: *'Learning Causal Trees from Dependence Information'*, Proc. 8th National Conf. on Artificial Intelligence, 1990. pp. 771-776.

[GSSK 87] Glymour C., Scheines R., Spirtes P., Kelly K.: *'Discovering Causal Structure'*, Academic Press, San Diego, CA. 1987.

[HD 80] Hall P. A., Dowling G. R.: *'Approximate String Matching'*, Proc. 6th Annual Int. SIGIR Conf., in: SIGIR, Vol. 17, No. 4, 1983. pp. 130.

[HHNT 86] Holland J. H., Holyoak K. J., Nisbett R. E., Thagard P. R.: *'Induction: Processes of Inference, Learning, and Discovery'*, MIT Press. Cambridge, MA, 1986.

[Hub 85] Huber P. J.: *'Projection Pursuit'*, The Annals of Statistics, Vol. 13, No. 2. 1985, pp. 435-474.

[ID 90] Inselberg A., Dimsdale B.: *'Parallel Coordinates: A Tool for Visualizing Multi-Dimensional Geometry'*, Visualization'90. San Francisco, CA. 1990, pp. 361-370.

[ISO 92] ISO/IEC: *'Database Language SQL'*, ISO/IEC 9075:1992 (German Standardization: DIN 66315).

[JKL 77] Joshi A. K., Kaplan S. J., Lee R. M.: *'Approximate Responses from a Data Base Query System: Applications of Inferencing in Natural Language'*, Proc. 5th Int. Joint Conf. on Artificial Intelligence (IJCAI). Boston, MA, 1977, pp. 211-212.

[Kap 82] Kaplan S. J.: *'Cooperative Responses from a Portable Natural Language Query System'*, Artificial Intelligence. Vol. 19, 1982. pp. 165-187.

[KKM 93a] Keim D. A., Kriegel H.-P., Miethsam A.: *'Integration of Relational Databases in a Multidatabase System based on Schema Enrichment'*, Proc. 3rd Int. Workshop on Interoperability in Multidatabase Systems (RIDE-IMS), Vienna. Austria, 1993, pp. 96-104.

[KKM 93b] Keim D. A., Kriegel H.-P., Miethsam A.: *'Object-Oriented Querying of Existing Relational Databases'*, Proc. 4th Int. Conf. on Database and Expert Systems Applications (DEXA), Prague. Czech Republic, 1993, in: Lecture Notes in Computer Science, Vol. 720, Springer, 1993, pp. 325-336.

[KKM 94] Keim D. A., Kriegel H.-P., Miethsam A.: *'Query Translation Supporting the Migration of Legacy Databases into Cooperative Information Systems'*, Proc. Int. Conf. on Cooperative Information Systems. Toronto, Canada, 1994.

[KKS 93] Keim D. A., Kriegel H.-P., Seidl T.: *'Visual Feedback in Querying Large Databases'*, Proc. Visualization'93, San Jose, CA, 1993, pp. 158-165.

[KL 92] Keim D. A., Lum V.: *'Visual Query Specification in a Multimedia Database System'*, Proc. Visualization'92, Boston, MA. 1993. pp. 194-201.

[LWW 90]   LeBlanc J., Ward M. O., Wittels N.: 'Exploring N-Dimensional Databases', Visualization'90, San Francisco, CA, 1990, pp. 230-239.

[MGTS 90] Mihalisin T., Gawlinski E., Timlin J., Schwendler J.: 'Visualizing Scalar Field on an N-dimensional Lattice', Visualization'90, San Francisco, CA, 1990, pp. 255-262.

[Mot 86]   Motro A.: 'BAROQUE: A Browser for Relational Databases', ACM Trans. on Office Information Systems, Vol. 4, No. 2, 1983, pp. 164-181.

[Mot 90]   Motro A.: 'FLEX: A Tolerant and Cooperative User Interface to Databases', IEEE Trans. on Knowledge and Data Engineering, Vol. 2, No. 2, 1990, pp. 231-246.

[MZ 92]   Marchak F., Zulager D.: 'The Effectiveness of Dynamic Graphics in Revealing Structure in Multivariate Data', Behavior. Research Methods, Instruments and Computers, Vol. 24, No. 2, 1992, pp. 253-257.

[NMK 81]   Noreault T., McGill M., Koll M. B.: 'A Performance Evaluation of Similarity Measures, Document Term Weighting Schemes and Representations in a Boolean Environment', in: Information Retrieval Research, Butterworths, London, 1981.

[PC 93]   Parsaye K., Chignell M.: 'Intelligent Database Tools & Applications', John Wiley & Sons, New York, 1993.

[Qui 86]   Quinlan J. R.: 'Induction of Decision Trees', in: Machine Learning, Vol. 1, No. 1, 1986, pp. 81-106.

[RM 86]   Rummelhart D. E., McClelland J. L.: 'Parallel Distributed Processing', MIT Press, Cambridge, MA, 1986.

[Sal 88]   Salton G.: 'A Simple Blueprint for Automatic Boolean Query Processing', Information Processing & Management, Vol. 24, No. 3, 1988, pp. 269-280.

[SB 88]   Salton G., Buckley C.: 'Term-Weighting Approaches in Automatic Text Retrieval', Information Processing & Management, Vol. 24, No. 5, 1988, pp. 513-523.

[SBG 90]   Smith S., Bergeron D., Grinstein G.: 'Stereophonic and Surface Sound Generation for Exploratory Data Analysis', Proc. Conf. Special Interest Group in Computer and Human Interaction (SIGCHI), 1990, pp. 125-131.

[SK 90]   Seeger B., Kriegel H.-P.: 'The Buddy Tree: An Efficient and Robust Access Method for Spatial Databases', Proc. 16th Int. Conf. on Very Large Data Bases, Brisbane, Australia, 1990, pp. 590-601.

[SSU 90]   Silberschatz A., Stonebraker M., Ullman J. D.: 'Database Systems: Achievements and Opportunities', Technical Report. No. TR-90-22, Dept. of Computer Sciences, University of Texas at Austin, 1990.

[TC 90]   Trimble J. H., Chappell D.: 'A Visual Introduction to SQL', John Wiley & Sons, New York, 1990.

[Tre 92]   Treinish L. A., Butler D. M., Senay H., Grinstein G. G., Bryson S. T.: 'Grand Challenge Problems in Visualization Software', Proc. Visualization'92, Boston, MA, 1992, pp. 366-371.

[Zlo 77]   Zloof M. M. 'Query-By-Example: A Data Base Language', IBM Systems Journal, Vol. 4, 1977, pp. 324-343.

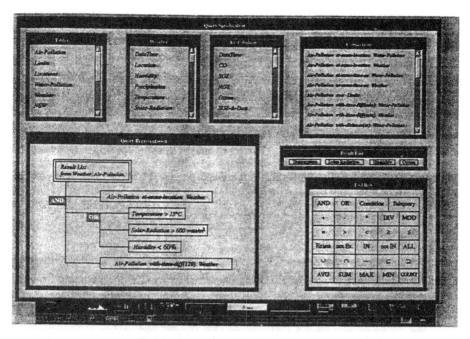

Fig. 1. Query Specification Window

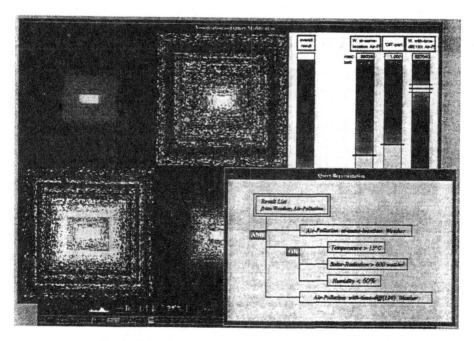

Fig. 2. Query Visualization and Modification Window

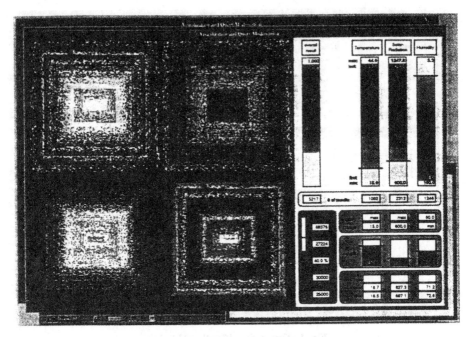

Fig. 3. Visualization of the 'OR'-Part of the Query

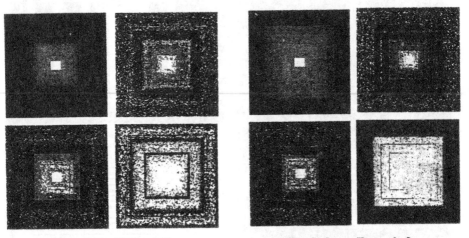

Fig. 4. Query Example 2 **Fig. 5. Query Example 3**

Springer-Verlag
and the Environment

Lecture Notes in Computer Science

For information about Vols. 1–793
please contact your bookseller or Springer-Verlag

Vol. 831: V. Bouchitté, M. Morvan (Eds.), Orders, Algorithms, and Applications. Proceedings, 1994. IX, 204 pages. 1994.

Vol. 832: E. Börger, Y. Gurevich, K. Meinke (Eds.), Computer Science Logic. Proceedings, 1993. VIII, 336 pages. 1994.

Vol. 833: D. Driankov, P. W. Eklund, A. Ralescu (Eds.), Fuzzy Logic and Fuzzy Control. Proceedings, 1991. XII, 157 pages. 1994. (Subseries LNAI).

Vol. 834: D.-Z. Du, X.-S. Zhang (Eds.), Algorithms and Computation. Proceedings, 1994. XIII, 687 pages. 1994.

Vol. 835: W. M. Tepfenhart, J. P. Dick, J. F. Sowa (Eds.), Conceptual Structures: Current Practices. Proceedings, 1994. VIII, 331 pages. 1994. (Subseries LNAI).

Vol. 836: B. Jonsson, J. Parrow (Eds.), CONCUR '94: Concurrency Theory. Proceedings, 1994. IX, 529 pages. 1994.

Vol. 837: S. Wess, K.-D. Althoff, M. M. Richter (Eds.), Topics in Case-Based Reasoning. Proceedings, 1993. IX, 471 pages. 1994. (Subseries LNAI).

Vol. 838: C. MacNish, D. Pearce, L. Moniz Pereira (Eds.), Logics in Artificial Intelligence. Proceedings, 1994. IX, 413 pages. 1994. (Subseries LNAI).

Vol. 839: Y. G. Desmedt (Ed.), Advances in Cryptology - CRYPTO '94. Proceedings, 1994. XII, 439 pages. 1994.

Vol. 840: G. Reinelt, The Traveling Salesman. VIII, 223 pages. 1994.

Vol. 841: I. Prívara, B. Rovan, P. Ružička (Eds.), Mathematical Foundations of Computer Science 1994. Proceedings, 1994. X, 628 pages. 1994.

Vol. 842: T. Kloks, Treewidth. IX, 209 pages. 1994.

Vol. 843: A. Szepietowski, Turing Machines with Sublogarithmic Space. VIII, 115 pages. 1994.

Vol. 844: M. Hermenegildo, J. Penjam (Eds.), Programming Language Implementation and Logic Programming. Proceedings, 1994. XII, 469 pages. 1994.

Vol. 845: J.-P. Jouannaud (Ed.), Constraints in Computational Logics. Proceedings, 1994. VIII, 367 pages. 1994.

Vol. 846: D. Shepherd, G. Blair, G. Coulson, N. Davies, F. Garcia (Eds.), Network and Operating System Support for Digital Audio and Video. Proceedings, 1993. VIII, 269 pages. 1994.

Vol. 847: A. L. Ralescu (Ed.) Fuzzy Logic in Artificial Intelligence. Proceedings, 1993. VII, 128 pages. 1994. (Subseries LNAI).

Vol. 848: A. R. Krommer, C. W. Ueberhuber, Numerical Integration on Advanced Computer Systems. XIII, 341 pages. 1994.

Vol. 849: R. W. Hartenstein, M. Z. Servít (Eds.), Field-Programmable Logic. Proceedings, 1994. XI, 434 pages. 1994.

Vol. 850: G. Levi, M. Rodríguez-Artalejo (Eds.), Algebraic and Logic Programming. Proceedings, 1994. VIII, 304 pages. 1994.

Vol. 851: H.-J. Kugler, A. Mullery, N. Niebert (Eds.), Towards a Pan-European Telecommunication Service Infrastructure. Proceedings, 1994. XIII, 582 pages. 1994.

Vol. 852: K. Echtle, D. Hammer, D. Powell (Eds.), Dependable Computing – EDCC-1. Proceedings, 1994. XVII, 618 pages. 1994.

Vol. 853: K. Bolding, L. Snyder (Eds.), Parallel Computer Routing and Communication. Proceedings, 1994. IX, 317 pages. 1994.

Vol. 854: B. Buchberger, J. Volkert (Eds.), Parallel Processing: CONPAR 94 – VAPP VI. Proceedings, 1994. XVI, 893 pages. 1994.

Vol. 855: J. van Leeuwen (Ed.), Algorithms – ESA '94. Proceedings, 1994. X, 510 pages.1994.

Vol. 856: D. Karagiannis (Ed.), Database and Expert Systems Applications. Proceedings, 1994. XVII, 807 pages. 1994.

Vol. 857: G. Tel, P. Vitányi (Eds.), Distributed Algorithms. Proceedings, 1994. X, 370 pages. 1994.

Vol. 858: E. Bertino, S. Urban (Eds.), Object-Oriented Methodologies and Systems. Proceedings, 1994. X, 386 pages. 1994.

Vol. 859: T. F. Melham, J. Camilleri (Eds.), Higher Order Logic Theorem Proving and Its Applications. Proceedings, 1994. IX, 470 pages. 1994.

Vol. 860: W. L. Zagler, G. Busby, R. R. Wagner (Eds.), Computers for Handicapped Persons. Proceedings, 1994. XX, 625 pages. 1994.

Vol: 861: B. Nebel, L. Dreschler-Fischer (Eds.), KI-94: Advances in Artificial Intelligence. Proceedings, 1994. IX, 401 pages. 1994. (Subseries LNAI).

Vol. 862: R. C. Carrasco, J. Oncina (Eds.), Grammatical Inference and Applications. Proceedings, 1994. VIII, 290 pages. 1994. (Subseries LNAI).

Vol. 863: H. Langmaack, W.-P. de Roever, J. Vytopil (Eds.), Formal Techniques in Real-Time and Fault-Tolerant Systems. Proceedings, 1994. XIV, 787 pages. 1994.

Vol. 864: B. Le Charlier (Ed.), Static Analysis. Proceedings, 1994. XII, 465 pages. 1994.

Vol. 865: T. C. Fogarty (Ed.), Evolutionary Computing. Proceedings, 1994. XII, 332 pages. 1994.

Vol. 866: Y. Davidor, H.-P. Schwefel, R. Männer (Eds.), Parallel Problem Solving from Nature - PPSN III. Proceedings, 1994. XV, 642 pages. 1994.

Vol 867: L. Steels, G. Schreiber, W. Van de Velde (Eds.), A Future for Knowledge Acquisition. Proceedings, 1994. XII, 414 pages. 1994. (Subseries LNAI).

Vol. 868: R. Steinmetz (Ed.), Multimedia: Advanced Teleservices and High-Speed Communication Architectures. Proceedings, 1994. IX, 451 pages. 1994.

Vol. 869: Z. W. Raś, Zemankova (Eds.), Methodologies for Intelligent Systems. Proceedings, 1994. X, 613 pages. 1994. (Subseries LNAI).

Vol. 870: J. S. Greenfield, Distributed Programming Paradigms with Cryptography Applications. XI, 182 pages. 1994.

Vol. 871: J. P. Lee, G. G. Grinstein (Eds.), Database Issues for Data Visualization. Proceedings, 1993. XIV, 229 pages. 1994.